THE LAST GREAT
ADVENTURE
of SIR PETER BLAKE

THE LAST GREAT
ADVENTURE
of SIR PETER BLAKE

With *Seamaster* and blakexpeditions
from Antarctica to the Amazon

Sir Peter Blake's logbooks edited by Alan Sefton

S
SHERIDAN HOUSE

This edition published 2004 in the United States of America by
Sheridan House Inc.
145 Palisade St
Dobbs Ferry, NY 10522
www.sheridanhouse.com

First published 2003 by Viking, the Penguin Group, New Zealand

Library of Congress Cataloging-in-Publication Data

Blake, Peter, 1948-2001.
    The last great adventure of Sir Peter Blake : with Seamaster and Blakexpeditions
from Antarctica to the Amazon : Sir Peter Blake's logbooks / edited by Alan
Sefton.
        p. cm.
"First published 2003 by Viking, the Penguin Group, New Zealand"--T.p. verso.
Includes index.
ISBN 1-57409-190-5 (hardcover : alk. paper)
1. Blake, Peter, 1948-2001. 2. Sailors--New Zealand--Biography. 3. Seamaster
(Yacht) I. Sefton, Alan. II. Title.
GV812.5.B58B58 2004
797.124'092--dc22
                                    2003027652

ISBN 1-57409-190-5

Designed by Nick Turzynski
Printed in China

Contents

From Pippa, Lady Blake

I have often been asked what it was like being married to a man like Peter — a man who single-mindedly pursued his dreams and ambitions with such passion and commitment and who loved a challenge. Sarah-Jane, James and I were immensely proud of Peter's achievements and of the way he followed his star. Life for the family was never dull.

Peter brought passion and commitment to everything he did, not least to his endeavours to generate greater awareness of the needs of the world and wildlife around us. Having spent the best part of his life racing through the oceans of the world, he recognised that all was not well with the environment and, quite typically, he decided that he would do something about it.

Peter formed blakexpeditions to sail to the pulse points of the planet — to monitor the changes taking place in the world around us and, through television and the Internet, to remind people just how beautiful and remarkable the world truly is.

I was fortunate enough to join him aboard *Seamaster* and share with him an amazing month of Rio Negro and River Amazon experiences just before the tragedy of his death.

As *Seamaster* made her way back down the Amazon towards Macapa, I wrote in the ship's daily log:

> *There is an enigma and mystery about the Amazon that I know has made a deep and lasting impression on me. I am a painter and I now feel very excited about returning home with a stream of images to work from. I am hoping that what I have gained will be with me forever and feel that it has been a profound and humbling experience to have been here. I will be sad to leave.*

Some of those images are included in this book and are part of my way of expressing and sharing not only what affected me so deeply but also what, I know, inspired Peter to go there in the first place.

I can think of no better way to celebrate Peter's work in the Antarctic and the Amazon than this collation of his logs and of the beautiful imagery that accompanied them. The end result is a memorable record of his last great adventure.

Pippa
Lady Blake
Emsworth, England
1 June 2003

Foreword

I met Sir Peter Blake on just three occasions. The first was remotely, during a United Nations Environment Programme (UNEP) Governing Council meeting in Kenya in February 2001. Peter spoke by satellite telephone to a group of environment ministers assembled in my office in Nairobi.

Standing on the Antarctic ice at nearly 70 degrees south latitude, he did not dwell on the facts, figures and projections that had been prepared for the Council by the Intergovernmental Panel on Climate Change. He recounted what he had observed as he had journeyed down the Antarctic Peninsula in the blakexpeditions vessel *Seamaster*. He described being at anchor among icebergs created by the break-up of the King George VI ice shelf and the wildlife he had encountered while sailing through channels traditionally impassable to boats but now free of sea ice due to changing climes.

I then met Peter in person in Auckland, New Zealand, in July 2001 when I announced his appointment as a UNEP Special Envoy. The venue was the Royal New Zealand Yacht Squadron, then home to the America's Cup, and we looked out over a city waterfront that Peter had helped transform, through his vision and the public enthusiasm it generated for competing in the world's most prestigious yachting contest.

In appointing him a UNEP Special Envoy, we recognised the potential of combining Peter's explorations with the environmental knowledge of UNEP, to generate compelling television documentaries and website content.

The last time I met Peter was in October 2001, in Rio de Janeiro, Brazil. Environmental ministers from all over Latin America were meeting to discuss issues relevant to the World Summit of Sustainable Development to be held in Johannesburg the following year. Peter flew in from Manaus just hours after *Seamaster* had arrived in the 'river city' after a long journey up the Amazon.

Again, he recounted what he had observed of the wildlife and human activity on the river, bringing passion, urgency and reality to the environment and development agenda of the meeting.

Peter's death on 5 December 2001 at the mouth of the Amazon was a tremendous shock and loss for us at UNEP.

Though best known for his ocean-racing achievements, Peter had embarked on a new and ambitious mission as a global environmental ambassador and was already making an impact.

I am pleased that we have been able to twice honour this remarkable man since his untimely death. In Bali, Indonesia, on World Environment Day (5 June 2002), 1000 delegates to the final preparatory meeting for the World Summit on Sustainable Development paid tribute to Peter's life. Then, in Johannesburg in September 2002, where global leaders adopted a plan of implementation for sustainable development, Pippa, Lady Blake, received from UNEP a memorial award recognising Peter as an oceans champion.

We had begun to discuss with Peter what role he might play in these events. I imagine that he would have been more comfortable in a polar jacket than a business suit and that his presence would most likely have been through a live television link from the Arctic where *Seamaster* was headed next. And, no doubt, in his down-to-earth and insightful way he would have reminded us that we will only safeguard that which we first cherish.

Klaus Toepfer
Secretary-General, United Nations Environment Programme
Nairobi
29 May 2003

Introduction

A true journey of discovery is not to look for a new world — but to take a fresh look.
MARCEL PROUST

Sir Peter Blake, KBE, was the world's most celebrated yachtsman. In a 30-year career, he won every significant blue-water race on the planet. He also won and successfully defended the biggest sailing prize of all, the America's Cup, and slashed the record for the fastest non-stop circumnavigation of the world under sail.

Knighted for his achievements and accorded celebrity status in many parts of the world, Sir Peter turned away from competitive sailing to pursue a passion to help safeguard the environment that he had enjoyed so much.

In 2000, he founded blakexpeditions and, with the backing of the United Nations Environment Programme (UNEP), set out to focus global attention on the need to take better care of planet Earth and its lifeblood oceans, rivers and waterways. His mission was to show people how beautiful and unique the world is and to inspire them to preserve and protect it. Education through adventure and entertainment were the means. Television, on-line technologies and print/publishing were the platforms.

Sir Peter was murdered while defending his vessel and crew against river pirates in the mouth of the Amazon in December 2001.

He had taken *Seamaster* to 70 degrees south latitude in the Antarctic and 1400 miles up the Amazon and Negro rivers in Brazil, to examine the effects of global warming, pollution and exploitation, and was on his way to the mouth of the Orinoco River, in Venezuela, when tragedy struck.

This book is a record of those journeys — Sir Peter's last great adventure. It is a compilation of his daily logs and of the photography that accompanies those logs on the blakexpeditions.com website.

In its endorsement of blakexpeditions and its objectives, UNEP says: 'To adequately address the environmental challenges we face there needs to be a transformation to sustainable lifestyles across all sectors and regions of the world. Critical in this transformation will be the creation of an informed and aware public. Initiatives like your own, utilising sophisticated scientific and communications technologies, the appeal of adventure and the power of storytelling, will be an important part of this process.'

While a record of, and a tribute to, Sir Peter's environmental endeavours, this book is a part of the process that UNEP refers to. It is also a celebration of the passion and commitment that this remarkable human being brought to everything he did.

Not long before he was killed, Sir Peter wrote:

There have been climatic and environmental phenomena on planet Earth before — including mini-ice ages and, every 100,000 years or so, global warming with the ice caps melting.

Never in the past, however, have such massive and potentially cataclysmic changes to the Earth's climate and environment been so influenced by man, nor have they developed at the accelerated rate that we are witnessing today. They have never, either, occurred when the planet is as densely populated as it is in the twenty-first century.

We are, for the first time in history, in a position to directly affect and influence, on a global scale, the environment in which we live — for good or for bad. To date, that influence has, for the most part, been all bad and, as a result, the world is smack on course for environmental and sociological crises.

Global warming is a fact, despite the dissenting views. We are pouring carbon dioxide and methane gases into the atmosphere at a rate that the planet cannot sustain. The temperature of the atmosphere is rising, the ice packs (that have such a fundamental influence on the world's weather) are melting, and we are witnessing substantial climatic changes, more violent and destructive weather systems and rising sea levels.

We are also cutting down the rainforests that are the vital oxygen producers and the carbon sinks that keep everything in the right balance, again at a rate that the planet can't sustain.

And we are polluting and exploiting the waters of the world at a rate that is not only unsustainable but that will have frightening consequences in the very near future (entire species of fish are disappearing and there are projections that there will be no major fishing on a commercial scale within 25 years). The earth's major lakes and rivers are suffering similar devastation.

What are we doing about all of this? At best, very little. At worst, nothing. The warnings are there and the evidence is all around. But the message is not getting through. The environmental rape and pillage continues while we turn a blind eye to the fact that beautiful and unique planet Earth as we know it is in serious trouble — mostly at our hand. We could be next as our food and water run out and our lands disappear.

blakexpeditions is a torch carrier and message bearer for the environment. In our unique exploration vessel Seamaster, we are journeying to the most extreme and environmentally sensitive parts of the planet — the Antarctic, the Arctic, the Amazon, the coral reefs, the great rivers etc. — to see for ourselves what is happening.

We are using the mass media of television, the internet and publishing to share our adventures with as large an audience as possible in order to entertain, stimulate and educate.

Our watchword is sustainability — there are better ways of doing things so that planet Earth can sustain our presence. Our approach, where possible, is to offer solutions rather than to simply condemn.

Our objective is to make people fall in love with the environment, fall in love with planet Earth, and inspire the changes needed to help them survive.

Remember — this is THE most beautiful world, and it is the ONLY one we've got.

On his last great journeys, Sir Peter wasn't searching for a new world. He was patently in love with 'the only one we've got'. But he most certainly was taking a fresh look and did not like some of what he was seeing.

Hopefully, this celebration of the man and his mission will help inspire some of the change he was seeking.

Alan Sefton
Emsworth, England
8 June 2003

I must go down to the seas again, to the lonely sea and the sky,

And all I ask is a tall ship and a star to steer her by,

And the wheel's kick and the wind's song and the white sail's shaking,

And a grey mist on the sea's face and a grey dawn breaking.

I must go down to the seas again, for the call of the running tide

Is a wild call and a clear call that may not be denied;

And all I ask is a windy day with the white clouds flying,

And the flung spray and the blown spume, and the seagulls crying.

I must go down to the seas again to the vagrant gypsy life,

To the gull's way and the whale's way where the wind's like a whetted knife;

And all I ask is a merry yarn from a laughing fellow-rover,

And a quiet sleep and a sweet dream when the long trick's over.

'Sea Fever' — John Masefield

Seamaster

Technical Characteristics

Schooner	With two 27 m masts
Length	36 m
Beam	10 m
Draught	1.5 m to 3.5 m (centreboards and rudders down or up)
Construction	16 mm and 25 mm aluminium (in full survey for navigation in ice)
Sail area	400 m²
Power	2 × MWM 350 hp main engines with tunnel-mounted propellers 2 × MWM 22 kW (220V) generators plus emergency back-up
Range under power	10,000 nautical miles
Fresh water	Produced by desalinator unit

Seamaster was designed by the French naval architects Luc Bouvet and Olivier Petit for polar sea exploration by noted French adventurer/explorer Dr Jean-Louis Etienne.

Built in France in 1989, her reinforced aluminium hull (1.6 cm to 2.5 cm plate, heavier and further reinforced in the bow area, for ice-breaking) enables her to force her way through sea ice approximately one metre thick.

If caught in the ice, her hull design (rounded sections) mean she should pop out on top rather than be crushed. With special insulation and heating she can withstand being 'frozen-in' and be self-sufficient, even in outside temperatures of minus 40 degrees centigrade.

Shallow draught, retractable centreboards and rudders, and tunnel-mounted propellers (stainless steel, five-bladed ice propellers) enable her to operate successfully in minimum depths of water — in ice, close to shorelines or even among the sand banks of the Amazon River.

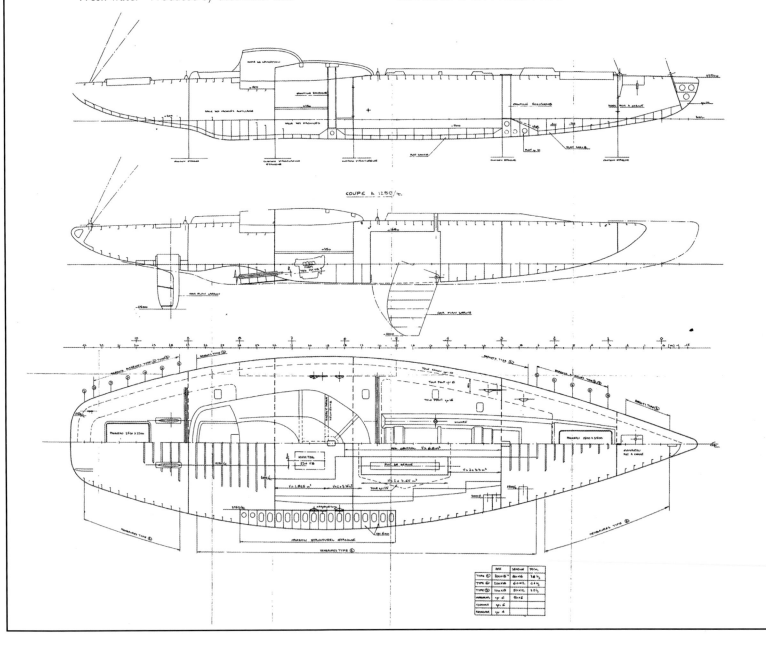

Other facts and figures

Water: 6 tonnes (complete with heater to keep it liquid) plus a water maker that produces approximately 80 to 100 litres per hour from the sea (unless frozen)

Diesel: 50,000 litres

Comms: HF and VHF radio systems, three different satellite communications systems that, as well as voice, enable fax, high-speed data, plus still and moving picture transmission

Navigation: Standard paper navigation charts. Navigation computer with MaxSea electronic charts, integrated GPS units, long- and short-range radars, gyro, fluxgate and magnetic compasses, echo sounders, and Satcom C and Navtex systems

Weather: MaxSea integrated weather, weather fax systems and programmes, Satcom C and Navtex systems, barograph and barometer

Heating: Large, wraparound main saloon windows designed to generate/produce interior heat from sunlight, diesel-fired stove in the main saloon, individual electric cabin heaters

Waste: Antarctic Treaty Regulations standard systems plus two sewage treatment plants, a 7000-litre waste storage tank (that can hold on board all wastes from galley, showers, basins, toilets, etc. for a period of approximately two to three weeks. All non-biodegradable product (plastic, cans etc.) kept on board in large sealed plastic bins for later disposal ashore. Fresh oil for engine lubrication is stored in a special tank for direct pumping to the engines, while used oil from the engines is stored in separate sludge tank and kept for correct shoreside collection. Enough oil storage for more than a year of normal use

Diving: Eight sets of technical dive equipment suitable for ice diving and tropical diving. Drysuits and different wetsuits for varying conditions — including undergarments for sub-zero sea temperatures. Diver propulsion vehicles, dive cameras, and the latest underwater communications and navigation systems (military grade). High pressure air for the dive bottles is supplied by a large compressor in the forepeak (that can fill three bottles at a time) or by a portable compressor for remote filling

Clothing: Icebreaker merino wool thermal wear, and Line 7 Musto sailing/wet-weather gear and survival suits, Line 7 general wear

Survival: Survival equipment for 'at sea' as well as 'in ice' situations, including life rafts, survival suits, emersion suits, EPIRBs (emergency satellite beacons), Antarctic-grade sleeping bags, tents, snow shovels, special boots, crampons, ice axes, climbing equipment, emergency stoves, food packs, extra water, manual desalinator etc.

Reading: A comprehensive technical library plus another bookcase of novels of all different types and tastes

Food: For a minimum of nine months for 15 people. Could probably be stretched to 18 months if we all wanted to lose weight. Includes several hundred steaks, thousands of sausages, chicken, lamb, ham and turkey (for Christmas) plus all those Christmas mince pies that we all dream about for the rest of the year

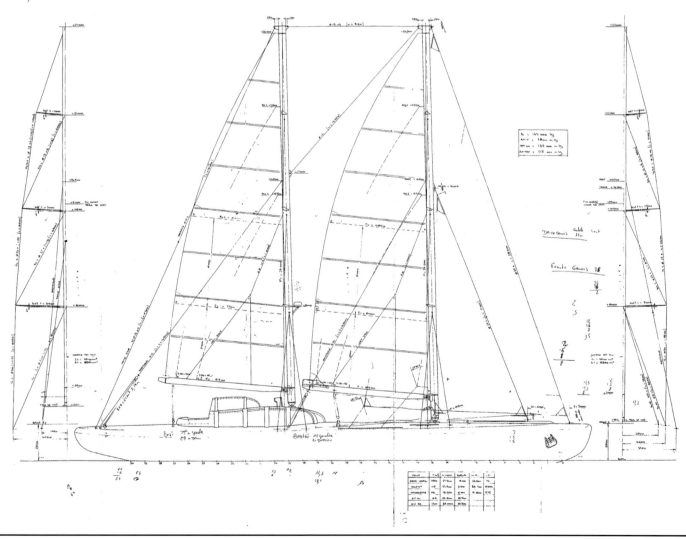

The Journey

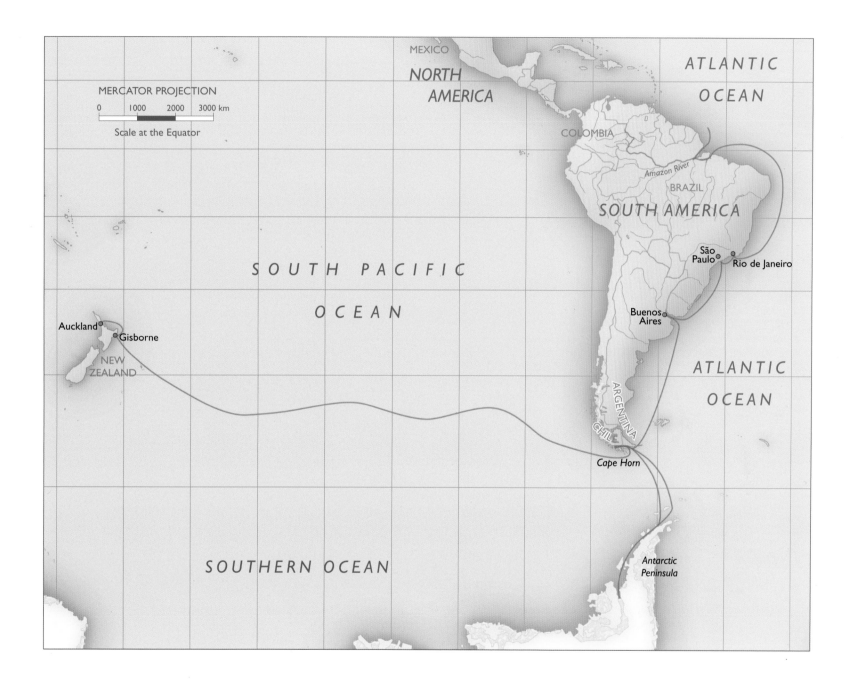

The Southern Ocean and Tierra del Fuego

13 November 2000

●

Location Just south of East Cape

Latitude 38.17S
Longitude 178.24W
Course 190 degrees true
Wind Southerly, 10 to 15 knots
Sea Moderate

First excursion for the expedition team — to get a closer look at volcanic activity at White Island.

We undocked from the Viaduct Harbour at 1115hrs on Saturday 11 November, to the cheers and waves of quite a large group of friends and relations, and people who have helped us over the past few weeks.

A couple of hours later we were on our own as we headed out through the Motuihe Passage towards Cape Colville. The wind was too light for us to sail and the seas calm until we rounded the end of the Coromandel Peninsula, when the big easterly swells and fresher head winds slowed us until we anchored for the night in the lee of Great Mercury Island.

After a much-appreciated quiet night and a good breakfast, we up-anchored and headed out across the Bay of Plenty towards East Cape, on the northeastern tip of New Zealand's North Island.

From there we will follow the route we often took in the Whitbread Round the World Race, when getting south quickly was to have the best chance of being first into the favourable westerly winds of the Roaring Forties before turning left for Cape Horn.

We are slower than normal due to the ice-grids installed over the propeller tunnels, to protect the blades from Antarctic ice — prepared to trade speed now for the extra security they will offer then. Fitting the grids on arrival in Ushuaia (on the southern tip of Argentina) would have been difficult.

At dawn this morning, the lights of homes at

Hicks Bay were away to starboard, and at 0600hrs, East Cape, with its strong tides and currents, was abeam. In the distance, the backdrop to the Cape is one of rugged hills and remote farmhouses, a beautiful part of the country that probably not many people are fortunate enough to view from the sea.

Right now it is drizzling and rather cool but standing watch in the pilot-house — that rather strange little 'bubble' above the main deck-house — is a pleasure and certainly very different from being in foul-weather gear and getting cold and wet on the helm of a racing yacht.

So, here we are making our way down the east coast of the North Island of New Zealand, heading for Ushuaia and the Beagle Canal. On board for the (approximately) one-month trip to Ushuaia are: Peter (the skipper); Don (communications and navigation); Ollie (first mate and diver); Sean (engineer); Janot (second engineer, general hand and diver); Alistair (general crew and support craft); Trevor (doctor); Roger (crew); Michael (crew) and Tracey (cook).

We share 14 bunks in seven cabins. Some are lucky and have their own cabin (for the moment). There are further bunks in the aft area of the vessel but they are full of equipment and stores for now.

Don and I share a cabin and enjoy the company — as well as the DVD movies. I also like to listen to The Goons on my Walkman after a watch. It helps me relax, although the laughter sometimes keeps Don awake.

At the moment, there is a black-browed albatross circling *Seamaster* (it has been with us since soon after dawn) and dolphins alongside. There is rain all around, but we are paralleling the rugged coast north of Gisborne, only a few miles offshore, with the land standing out stark and clear in the background. Shafts of watery sunlight are starting to blow holes in the clouds from time to time.

Customs have just given their approval to stop briefly at Gisborne in order to pick up some spare parts (our last chance to do so). In a few hours we will get the dinghy in the water to retrieve the parts while *Seamaster* waits just outside the harbour.

Then it is south once more into the loneliest expanse of ocean on the planet.

17 November 2000

•

Location The Roaring Forties, approaching the Furious Fifties

Latitude 48.19S
Longitude 167.18W
Course SE
Wind SW 20 to 25 knots
Sea Moderate
Air temp 6 deg C
Sea temp 9.5 deg C

The familiar waters of the Southern
Ocean are just ahead.

Yesterday provided us with our first Southern Ocean gale — with squalls of more than 50 knots in the rain. The seas quickly became quite large, with breaking crests.

Much of the day was spent with only a reefed foresail and headsail set. *Seamaster* marched southeastwards at 9 to 10 knots — not fast but, under the conditions, about right. Compared to the race yachts that I have been on down here in the Roaring Forties, being on *Seamaster* is like being on an aircraft carrier. At times she is right on the top of a crest of breaking, foaming white water and it seems as though the bow of our vessel is in the air on one side of the crest, while the stern is in the air on the other. Most times, however, the waves pass harmlessly underneath.

Last night was clear with a few puffy cumulus clouds about and a somewhat watery moon. The wind eased to the point where we needed more sail. But we will wait until the change of watch at 0600hrs before making a call on whether to shake out the reefs in both the foresail and mainsail. There are some large, really windy-looking clouds coming in from astern that look as though they might even have snow in them. It certainly seems cold enough for snow. We are definitely getting south.

It's a beautiful afternoon. The snow did not eventuate. Instead, the day warmed into a pleasant one for the Southern Ocean, with the surface of the sea flecked with white-caps as far as the eye could see.

There are albatross with us. They seem to go away during the midday period and return in numbers in the evenings. There were two sooty, or light-mantled, albatross circling us a while ago — probably the prettiest of all sea-birds, with various shades of chocolate colouring and very delicate features. They are nowhere near as mighty as the wanderers or the royals, but they certainly look the part in the ocean near and below 50 degrees south.

The type we most often see are the royal albatross — the biggest variety of sea-bird there is with a wing-span that can get to 3.5 metres. Most of the ones we have seen to date are probably not much more than two metres across, but they are still large birds. This is their home, not ours, and they are the most graceful flyers imaginable. They can travel extremely fast or almost hover in one place, all without flapping their wings.

They use the up-currents of air from the waves and swells of the ocean to give them 'lift'. When turning at low level they bank over so that one wing-tip is just brushing the surface of the sea. Quite often they land nearby and watch us sail past — very buoyant and quite at ease on the surface of the sea, even with breaking waves about them.

Over the next few months we are looking forward to having a closer look at the bird, sea and animal life that abounds in the waters ahead:

Wandering albatross; sooty albatross; royal albatross; black-browed albatross; grey-headed albatross; yellow-nosed albatross and light-mantled albatross.

Macaroni penguins; chinstrap penguins; king penguins; emperor penguins; gentoo penguins; Adelie penguins and Magellan penguins.

Southern giant petrel; northern giant petrel; Cape pigeon; Antarctic fulmar; snow petrel; Antarctic petrel; dove prion; blue petrel; Wilson's storm petrel; black-bellied storm petrel; blue-eyed shag; sheathbill; southern skua; McCormack's skua; Dominican gull; Antarctic tern; the pintail, teal and pipit.

Elephant seals; crabeater seals; Weddell seals; leopard seals and Ross seals.

Blue whales (very rare); fin whales; humpback whales; sperm whales; southern right whales; sei whales; minke whales; large-beaked whales; southern bottlenosed whales; orca and pilot whales.

Also, southern white-sided dolphin; Commerson's dolphin and the southern right whale dolphin.

All of this life feeds from the sea, and so is completely dependent on the quality of life in the sea. Until recent times that has been a given and all the species mentioned have thrived. Travelling again through these southern waters, across many thousands of miles of lonely ocean towards one of the most unique and precious places on earth, one wonders why that isn't still the case.

The reality however is that many of those species are under threat from, even endangered by, the influences of man, who is still ravaging and polluting this environment as though there is no tomorrow. All of life (including human) depends on water, and the quality of that water — in the seas, the rivers, the lakes, the streams and the rains. So, we had better start taking more care of it.

We get weather maps several times each day from Wellington Radio and they are showing not too much wind for the next day or so. But being in the Southern Ocean, being in the Roaring Forties (soon to be in the Furious Fifties) it is important to always be prepared. We are continually watching out astern — to the west — for cloud banks and squall lines. Being prepared for what 'might' happen is the most vital lesson in seamanship that one can learn.

Once we enter the 'Fifties' we will need to start keeping a watch for icebergs. There is not much chance of seeing any until we get to 55 degrees south, but a good lookout will still be vital. We have the radar on at night, just in case, even though we think we are alone on the ocean.

On the big catamaran *ENZA*, when racing across the Pacific a few years ago in the Trophée Jules Verne attempt to be the fastest yacht non-stop around the world, we very nearly collided with a piece of ice approximately two metres high, all by itself (we thought). The helmsman swerved to avoid it, not realising that this piece was one half of an old berg that had broken in two. Doing more than 15 knots, we fitted through the gap between the two pieces, but only just. We only realised that the second piece was there after we'd made it through. From that moment on we kept a man on the bow (for the next eight days or so) on iceberg watch.

With *Seamaster* we are not intending to go as far south as *ENZA* (not, at least, until we head down to the Antarctic Peninsula) but it will still pay to 'be prepared'.

The air is clear, the sky is blue. The birdlife is amazing. It's a good place to be.

The Albatross

Why do I mention them so often? Read the following from Ollie and I will be very surprised if it doesn't give you goose-bumps.

Me Albatross

'Greetings my friends. Or are you?

'They call me the Wanderer and I live mostly on the oceans of the Southern Hemisphere. While my friend the dolphin is the master in the ocean, I rule the sky, the wind and the waves.

'The wind is my closest ally, my lifeblood, and he takes me soaring and gliding on vast journeys. Journeys that circle the globe.

'I have 14 to 16 cousins within my close family and we are the largest of all sea-birds. Some of us are quite hard to identify because we look so much alike. Soon you will only see some of us in picture-books, because there are so few of us left. You humans on your long ocean journeys will never be graced by our presence or beauty again.

'Once a year, we visit certain remote ocean islands to breed and incubate our young. You probably didn't know, but once I've found myself a partner, we are a pair for life. We breed from the age of nine to 10 years, on a two-yearly basis. Incubation of the egg is about 11 weeks. Fledging takes a further nine months.

'During this time ashore we usually hang out with all the extended family. Whew, what a crowd! And as you can imagine, there's one hell of a racket with the new chicks about and all of the "goss" to catch up on.

'I actually prefer to be at sea. If there are wind and swells to assist my takeoff and flight (big wings can sometimes be a bit of a drag), I'm in me element. If not, however, I'm quite content to roost on the water and bide my time.

'When and what do I eat? Well, I used to eat a lot of everything — fish, squid and even a few morsels from yachts and ships. In days gone by, the oceans provided a wonderful smorgasbord of all sorts of fare — plenty of it too. Sadly, though, those days are gone. These days it's hard to find a decent feed for yourself, let alone your mate and young.

'Now that most of my traditional feeding grounds have been overfished, I'm increasingly reduced to scavenging. I follow ships and yachts whenever I see them, hoping for a tasty morsel or two. The ocean feast of old has definitely become a famine.

'These days, you have to be careful too. The neighbourhood has degenerated. If you are not careful, and if your hunger gets the better of you, recklessness can cost you dearly. What appear to be tasty morsels can in fact be the bait on the lines of those large fishing vessels that are to be found everywhere. Make the mistake and take the bait — and you've got a gob full of a large, barbed hook. The result — death "by natural causes" (a terrible way to go). I've lost too many of my family, relatives and friends in this fashion.

'At my age (I'll soon be 50), I've seen it all and they're not going to get me. I do my best to spread the word too. Every time a bunch of us get together on the water — family and friends — when there's not enough wind to fly or there's too much wind to fly, I pass on my experiences. I want them to reach my grand old age too.

'I have to be particularly outspoken and forceful with the juveniles, who are so young and feisty. Too many of them go out and learn the hard way, however, and wind up drowned, hanging on the end of a fishing line.

'As you will have gathered, I'm a grandad now, as old as lots of humans, and I spend a lot of time thinking about the good old days in the Southern Ocean.

'I don't often see my old friends the whales any more. They are having it just as hard as we are and some branches of their family are all but extinct. Can't believe they are still hunting them. Why can't they leave them alone? They don't need him in this day and age, except to wonder at his size, power and grace when plying his natural element. I remember the grand banquets as we picked over the left-overs at his feasts. I'm ashamed to admit, though, that I also fed on his remains at times of hunger during his slaughter.

'Today, as I fly with the strong winds to the east, I see and am attracted to a strange-looking vessel close by. Like me, it is using "wings" to travel on the wind. My mates have told me about this vessel. It is very different — could almost have been in that movie *Mad Max*, or *Waterworld*. Its name, I see, is *Seamaster*.

'There are people in yellow suits on board. Waving and beckoning me to go over. I go, because I have heard on the grapevine that these people and this boat are on a mission. They are trying to help me and my friends. Trying to save the whales too, as well as working to stop people polluting and exploiting our backyard. The word is that, like me, they reckon that education is the key.

'I give them a bit of a show — you know, wheelies and the like. I've still got what it takes and can teach those young 'uns a thing or two about water-hugging flight with one wing-tip brushing the waves. As I soar

close by to *Seamaster*, at eye level, they wave again and try to talk my language. Silly buggers. I understand a lot more than they appreciate. They don't have to go making fools of themselves.

'Still, they are our friends and that's something these days. They toss a few morsels so I glide to roost and feed, knowing it is safe for a stopover.

'In those yellow suits, they remind me a bit of my bigger penguin mates.

'I think I'll stay awhile and guide these new friends through my waters. Hopefully they will succeed in their endeavours to make the world understand that all is not as it should be down here in the south. I hear it's not too good elsewhere either.

'We don't want much — just our neighbourhood back to the way it once was. Then we can get on with our lives, happy to co-exist with everyone — humans too, despite everything they have done to us.'

Albert Ross

FOOTNOTE FROM PETER

In my first couple of Round the World races, our yachts, when in the Southern Ocean, would be surrounded by large albatross, day after day, in all weathers. As the years went by (I raced every four years or so through the same waters), I noticed there were fewer and fewer of these great birds. The last time through the Indian Ocean, in 1994, we were lucky to see one large albatross

a week. Their numbers have been decimated, mainly by indiscriminate fishing techniques. And they are being killed at a faster and faster rate. It has to stop or very soon we will have killed off one of the most beautiful and awe-inspiring creatures on the planet.

I have also been fortunate enough to have had encounters with whales that have left me with no doubt as to their intelligence and understanding.

I have watched a large female fin whale come up behind our race yacht, on a light-airs day in the cold of the southern Atlantic Ocean. The whale closed in until its 'snout' was only one metre behind our transom. We could clearly see it examining us with its enormous eyes. Its cream underbelly sported a patch that extended up and over its right eye.

After a while, it turned belly-up and swam under our yacht from stern to bow, the great flukes of the tail wider than our boat. It then surfaced just in front of us and blew — 'whoosh'. Then it turned on the surface and took up station astern of us again, just a metre away. It did this several times.

Our yacht was 24.5 metres long. The whale, we estimated, was approximately 23 metres long. A magnificent giant of the oceans — yet they are still being hunted.

Again, the needless and senseless slaughter has to stop, or the world is going to be a much poorer place for losses of species that can never be replaced.

The majestic royal albatross. With a wing span of more than three metres, it rules the wind and waves of the world's loneliest oceans.

20 November 2000

It's now 0930hrs after an 'everything' night. I'm rather tired this morning and am sure that the rest of the crew feel the same. The ship is quiet down below.

We are in the Southern Ocean, down at 50 degrees south, and have been getting Southern Ocean conditions. After a reasonably pleasant evening sail yesterday in still-rough seas, the wind died completely around midnight, and it began to rain — Southern Ocean rain. We all came on deck to try and stop the sails banging and crashing, and started the motors when nothing much helped. The barograph, which records atmospheric pressure, dropped alarmingly.

Back on course, under motor, with reefed mainsail and foresail and the tiny staysail to steady us, we had little breeze. But by 0230hrs today the wind was building. By 0530hrs it was an 'all hands' alert yet again. We needed to get the mainsail off in a hurry.

The early morning light showed the seas were starting to streak with foam ahead of the squalls that developed very quickly. We needed to gybe (change our downwind course from southeast to northeast). This is a tricky manoeuvre at the best of times. In a building near-gale it can be very character forming.

It went well, except many of the sliders securing the mainsail to the mast broke. We dropped the damaged sail in a hurry — leaving only the tiny staysail. By this time, this was enough anyway. The wind went to 56 knots in gusts, the surface of the sea turning white with spume blowing down the faces of the huge, breaking seas.

We are still running before those seas that now have built in size to be quite awe-inspiring — probably up to 10 metres high with the crests breaking and rolling down their faces. One wave came roaring aboard over the stern whilst we were working in the mid-part of the yacht tidying up the mess from the morning.

We have double-checked the dinghy lashings on the stern, and all items of deck-stowed equipment. So far, so good. The pilot-house door has been closed much of the time to stop the spray driving inside, and to keep the noise of the fury of the gale outside.

1000hrs: Looking out through the pilot-house windows, or harnessed to a strong point on the deck, one can still see the occasional albatross quite unconcernedly going about its morning business of looking for food.

The barograph has risen 20 millibars (mbs) in the past eight hours — an extraordinary rise that makes the gale and vicious squalls easier to understand.

Big waves and strong winds never show very well in a photograph, but believe me, what we are going through has made everyone on board realise what a fantastic vessel *Seamaster* is. She has handled everything with ease, even in extreme conditions.

We have also been thinking of the sailors of more than a century ago — running down the eastings from New Zealand and Australia towards Cape Horn, and then turning left up the Atlantic, heading for Europe with grain or tea. They didn't have the ability to be dry and warm on deck even in the worst conditions (thanks to the marvellous Musto, Line 7 and Icebreaker technical and thermal clothing that we have on board); to be in warm dry bunks after a watch on deck, or to be well fed with hot, nourishing food even when it is blowing old boots and is as cold as charity outside.

The Southern Ocean has earned its reputation. The names for the various latitudes — the Roaring Forties, the Furious Fifties and the Screaming Sixties — were coined by those sailors of old, for all the right (or wrong) reasons.

The nearest land to us at the moment is the Antarctic Continent, not all that far south of our present position. Even though the sea temperature is currently quite warm, we are now entering 'iceberg country' and have stepped up the vigilance, particularly at nights (which, this far south, are getting quite short anyway).

It is a bit of a contradiction that you don't really want to see ice but, then again, you do. Icebergs are fascinating. In my racing days I have been becalmed next to them, raced past them at night, had near misses on a number of occasions, and have spent seeming days on lookout for them. The big ones are majestic, towering at times maybe 130 metres above the surface of the sea.

But while they look magnificent, they drop vast amounts of broken ice into the sea and this is what causes the problems for vessels plying the same waters. That ice drifts away — generally, but not always, downwind of the bergs, and the chunks vary greatly in size. Sometimes those chunks capsize and, unless they are very large, can be difficult to see (they are usually a pale greeny-grey colour, very similar to the ocean anyway).

Having said all that, and given that we will see bergs of all shapes and sizes when we reach the Antarctic Peninsula early next year, we still look forward to encountering some in the open ocean. To witness a berg, a really big berg, at sea, sailing the winds and currents of the Southern Ocean, is something that never leaves one's memory. It is indelibly etched there forever — nature at her most magnificent.

Latitude 49.49S
Latitude 154.28W
Course 065 True
Wind Westerly gale, Force 9 plus
Sea Rough
Air temp 4 deg C
Sea temp 5.5 deg C

Seamaster takes all conditions in her considerable stride.

26 November 2000

●

Location Approx 2200 sailing miles to Cape Horn

Latitude 48.02S
Longitude 126.10W
Course 100/110 deg True
Wind WSW 20 knots
Sea Rough but easing
Air temp 3 deg C overnight
7 deg C daytime
Sea temp 5 deg C
Barometer 1000 mbs

There are seven large albatross with us this morning. Ollie fed them left-over strips of potato and they all landed and sat in the water in a tight ring, squabbling over the feast and obviously enjoying the different fare.

They are royal and wandering albatross, and we are lucky to see them so regularly as we head east. With wing-spans of up to 3.5 metres, they are the most majestic of birds close up — even more so 'on the wing' when they are masters of their element. The alarming fact is that they are likely to disappear if something isn't done immediately to curb the actions of long-line fishermen.

It is estimated that 40,000 albatross are caught every year by long-liners and in drift nets. This is completely unsustainable. These magnificent birds will disappear from the planet unless measures are introduced to halt the decimation. But the evidence is that the message is not getting through. It is not just the larger birds, and animals, that are in trouble however.

In the Antarctic, the land may be iced over and devoid of anything but the most primitive life forms, but the waters are prolific. Vast blooms of phytoplankton, which develop beneath the ice sheets in the spring and summer months, provide the primary source of food for krill — a small, shrimp-like creature whose swarms dye the oceans red by day and shine with phosphorescence at night. Krill is the main food source for five species of whale, three species of seal, 20 species of fish, three species of squid, and many birds, including the penguins. These different predators feed at different stages in the krill's life cycle — at different times of the year, in different places and at different depths, in a delicate balance of supply and demand.

The phytoplankton, then, is at the start of the marine food chain, not just in Antarctica, but in all oceans of the world. The phytoplankton in the oceans also provides much of the oxygen that we breathe. But we are not treating their environment very well. The long-lasting PCB build-up in phytoplankton is increasing at an alarming rate. It is more alarming because the krill eat the phytoplankton and the level of poison increases. The krill, in turn, are eaten by the larger fish, birds and mammals — and the level of toxicity increases further. Where do the PCBs come from? Mainly factory wastes and agricultural products that enter the oceans through rivers, streams and the air.

Dr Mark Orams, a good friend who is a marine scientist lecturing at Massey University in New Zealand, recently presented a paper at the America Cetacean Society's international conference in Monterey, California. Many other top marine scientists took part. In his paper, Mark outlined the findings of a recent survey conducted in the North Pacific — between Hawaii and the US mainland — in which plankton trawls revealed a ratio of six parts plastic to one part plankton over a wide area. Even at microscopic level, plastic does not break down but becomes part of the planktonic environment. Imagine what this means for filter-feeding organisms (most of which form the basis of the marine food chain).

Mark's paper provided dramatic examples of many sea-bird chicks starving to death because the food that their mothers regurgitated for their nourishment contained large proportions of microscopic plastic particles. The plastic entered the guts of the chicks, giving them a feeling of being full. The plastic, of course, does not get digested, so the chicks continue to feel full and therefore do not harass their mothers for food, thereby not producing the regurgitation reflex in the mother. The result — the chicks slowly starve to death.

There are, unfortunately, many other examples of what is going wrong in the natural world around us. The bewildering truth in all of this is that while man is the cause of most if not all of the problems, he has the choice whether to influence environmental matters, for good or for bad. He has the ability and the technology to make immediate and quick changes that will go a long way to alleviating the problems he is causing. Has he the will?

28 November 2000

Location Approx 1830 sailing miles to Cape Horn

Just on dusk, when we had all finished dinner and were settling in for the evening watches, there was a 'whoosh' from alongside and 15 or so southern white-sided dolphins (also known as hourglass dolphins) came in from astern and began frolicking in the bow wave. Quite small, they have very distinctive black-and-white markings and very pointed dorsal fins. They stayed for a while, dashing backwards and forwards, criss-crossing just in front of our hugely strong and unpainted aluminium bow plating.

The southern white grows to a maximum of two metres, and they frequent the Antarctic Convergence Zone, which is close by to the south of us. This is where the cold, north-going Antarctic surface water sinks beneath the warmer subantarctic water. In many places, this line is easily and precisely distinguished by a sudden change in surface temperature. It forms a physical boundary between the Antarctic and subantarctic zones and is fairly constant in position (generally not more than 30 miles north or south of the mean).

This Antarctic Convergence generally forms the extreme northern limit of drift ice, but we are keeping a good lookout nonetheless. In my racing days down here I saw icebergs where there were not supposed to be any and had my share of frights. But that was when speed was of the essence and we pushed our yachts to the limit. *Seamaster*'s pace is much more sedate and, with the radar running 24 hours a day and a sharp lookout on deck, all should be well.

Going back to the very end of 1773 and the beginning of 1774 — that's 227 years ago — Captain Cook was in almost the exact same position as we are right now. He left New Zealand in late 1773, came through the Southern Ocean and went way south, to latitude 72 degrees, before heading north and back to Tahiti. He then returned to New Zealand via the New Hebrides Islands, went through Cook Strait (obvious connection) and once more, later in 1774, was again in our position, heading eastwards towards the bottom of South America — just as we are now.

Cook didn't have the navigational aids that we are fortunate to be able to rely upon. I'm not sure that he even had a sextant in those days — more likely an octant. Also, his method of telling time would have been a wind-up clock, or a very early chronometer, making his navigational feats all the more remarkable. Time is necessary for astro-navigation. You can determine an accurate latitude (north–south position) with a rough idea of time, but to get an accurate longitude requires accurate time — and the early navigators didn't have accurate time.

When Charles Darwin and Captain Robert Fitzroy left England on their ship the *Beagle* in 1831, they (like Cook) didn't have accurate charts to rely upon. In fact, much of the world was still unknown (and that was only 170 or so years ago). As a comparison, the *Beagle* was 28 metres long, had a beam of 8 metres and a draught of 2.75 metres. *Seamaster* is 36 metres long, has a 10-metre beam and a draught of approximately 1.5–3.5 metres (boards up or down). The *Beagle* displaced 238 tonnes, to *Seamaster*'s 168 tonnes (loaded). The *Beagle* crew numbered 75 men — including a technician whose job it was to care for the 22 chronometers aboard, and a manservant for both Mr Darwin and the captain. *Seamaster* has a crew of 10, which includes Tracey as our cook — no chronometer tender and definitely no servants.

For very accurate time, we all wear waterproof chronometers on our wrists, as well as having two permanently mounted Global Positioning System (GPS) units that provide latitude, longitude and time to high accuracy (updated every second from the satellites).

Our charts, paper and electronic, are the latest available, so we always know where the main land masses are, where there might be concentrations of ice, what the weather might be doing, and so on.

Even so, we still carry two sextants and all of the normal tables for celestial navigation, just in case everything else fails. If we were to lose all of our electricity on board, we could still find our way in the more traditional fashion — using sextant, tables and magnetic compass.

Latitude	49.52S
Longitude	117.20W
Course	100 deg True
Wind	Westerly 15 to 18 knots
Sea	Slight with a low SW swell
Barometer	1000 mbs
Air temp	6 deg C
Sea temp	4 deg C

30 November 2000

●

Latitude 49.12S
Longitude 108.20W
Course 055 deg True
Wind Westerly 20 to 25 knots
Sea Moderate and choppy
with breaking crests
Barometer 1004 mbs
Air temp 8 deg C
Sea temp 5 deg C

We are on what might seem an unusual heading because we are positioning ourselves for the expectation of strong northerlies in two days' time. Those northerlies will drive us quickly south. If we opted for the other gybe (we currently have westerlies from astern), we would be on a heading of 150 degrees True, which would take us into light winds to the south, which we don't want. We are covering extra miles in the process, but we are tacking downwind to make the best of the situation. Our direct course to Cape Horn would be 120 degrees True.

One of *Seamaster*'s crew that I will mention frequently is my good friend Don Robertson (alias Captain Rabbit). The Rabbit is a very funny man. I asked him to give me his thoughts on our project so far, and the result has just arrived on my desk in the communications cabin — a computer disk labelled 'Rabbit Droppings':

'Lunch is over, and we are under full sail, making course for Tierra del Fuego at the southern tip of South America. Time for some reflection as to what is happening on *Seamaster*.

On deck, the air temperature is a cool 5 degrees C. We are becoming quite acclimatised however and don't wear the gloves that seemed necessary a week ago, when it was even warmer. Meanwhile, below decks it is luxuriously warm. The design of the cabin top acts like a glasshouse and the sun's rays stream through the overhead glass (or more correctly Lexan), heating the saloon to a comfortable 20 degrees Celsius. The crew that are not on watch are either reading, doing the odd chore or sleeping. All quite civilised.

On first impressions, *Seamaster* could not be called 'a pretty boat'. She always gives the impression of a boat designed for a mission. I am more than happy to be making my first crossing of the Southern Ocean on this seaworthy, comfortable vessel.

I'm sure Peter is finding the same comfort level much to his liking after numerous legs across this part of the world in racing mode. I share a cabin with Peter, which may sound like a very sociable arrangement. It is, except that I never seem to find him relaxing in the cabin and wonder if it is perhaps time to change my socks. Actually that is not the case (I hope). It is that Peter seems to need less sleep than the rest of us mere mortals while he keeps his finger on the pulse of the whole boat. One minute he is engrossed in a conversation with Sean, our engineer, about whatever it is that skippers and engineers talk about, and then he is discussing the water maker with

Janot, a winch problem with Alistair, the provisioning with Tracey, the weather with me, and on it goes.

What, to me, is so impressive about this level of involvement is Peter's understanding, in detail, of all aspects of the boat. Then, just to take up the slack, there is the overall responsibility for blakexpeditions and all that it stands for. No doubt readers are now gaining a better understanding of our mission from Peter's daily logs. Can we change the world? I believe that if we can become more aware of the environmental issues that face us, and are concerned enough, then we can make changes that will make a difference.

I would like to think that my grandchildren would gain as much pleasure from this world as I have (they will be going some to do that!), but also that we have left the planet in their hands in good shape. We can achieve this if we take care of what we have and do something about the warning signs that are there for us all to see. It sounds like a tall order and I must say that I hadn't been especially conscious of all the issues until I spent time talking to Peter and looking at the aspirations of blakexpeditions. I hope that I can make a worthwhile contribution, and still get a bit more sleep than my cabin-mate. Just for good measure I will change my socks.'

I am a little tired today. I don't know why as Trevor and I had a really good watch between midnight and 3 am. We talked about many subjects — both his and mine.

Trevor was our doctor and crew-member aboard *Ceramco New Zealand* in the 1981/82 Whitbread Round the World Race. He took leave from being a cardiologist at Greenlane Hospital in Auckland to race with us. We had our moments in the Southern Ocean as we drove *Ceramco* to the limit downwind in pursuit of our much bigger rival *Flyer*. When, however, I asked Trevor if he would like to come 'for the ride' through the Southern Ocean to Cape Horn again, he hardly hesitated.

So, there we were last night discussing various medical techniques and health issues mixed with accounts of my time working in Beirut at the height of the civil war. We talked of politics and politicians (it's sometimes best to leave politics and religion alone on a vessel at sea), and the issues facing New Zealand, and the world, in the future. We talked of encouraging young people, and of trying to change mind-sets, attitudes really, that have built up in New Zealand over time — attitudes that don't encourage the recognition of excellence or regard competition as healthy. Those are attitudes that must be changed.

Similarly, if we are to do our part for the future

Don 'Captain Rabbit' Robertson.

of those same young people, we need to redirect the attitude of our generation to the world's oceans, seas, lakes and rivers, if we are to leave them with something worthwhile. The seas have always been the ultimate depository of man's waste. Certain parts of the Mediterranean, off the Nile Delta, the waters of the Bosporus, the canals of Venice, have been health hazards for centuries. Until comparatively recently such pollution was relatively localised. Now, though, it has spread around the world's coasts and is affecting the open oceans.

About 44 per cent of the total pollution of the world's waters is discharged directly into the seas and oceans, streams and rivers. Another third is fallout from air pollution. Approximately 12 per cent comes from shipping and another 10 per cent is deliberately dumped. Offshore oil and gas production, you might be surprised, contributes maybe 1 per cent.

Two miracle chemicals of the 1950s and '60s, long discontinued as unsafe in most industrialised countries, still cause severe sea pollution. DDT, from pesticides, and PCBs, used in everything from glues to electrical appliances, are both toxic and persistent. They have been found everywhere — even in Antarctic penguins, Arctic seals, in whales in the Pacific and rat-tail fish found 3000 metres down in the abyssal depths. Third World countries are still

using these chemicals in ever-increasing quantities — sold to them for profit by, in many cases, companies in industrialised countries that have ceased to allow them.

Don't get me wrong, I am not against making a buck or two. But there must be a way to stop this, especially when there are global embargoes on such sales for what should be obvious reasons. It is a bit like selling war weapons to a country and then complaining when the same weapons are turned on the vendor.

Every year, more than three million tonnes of oil contaminate the seas. Only about half comes from ships. The rest is from land-based pollution and less than a third of that is spilt by accident. More than 1.1 million tonnes of oil is deliberately discharged every year by tankers that pump out the oily waters and wash out their tanks before taking on new cargoes.

Every year, fishermen discard about 150,000 tonnes of plastic nets and lines, while countless plastic containers are tossed overboard. The plastic does not degrade easily. Sea creatures eat it or get entangled in it and we have the terrible estimates that up to a million sea-birds and 100,000 whales, seals and dolphins are thought to die every year as a result.

This form of dumping is increasing. Do we need an attitude change?

Reefed down and running before a Southern Ocean gale.

Crossing the
Great Southern Ocean

Trevor Agnew, who was our doctor on *Ceramco New Zealand* in the 1981/82 Whitbread Round the World race, has put forward his thoughts on the changes he has noticed in the Southern Ocean.

There are some striking differences between this crossing of the Southern Ocean in *Seamaster* and my previous experience of the journey 20 years ago on *Ceramco*.

The enduring memories of the *Ceramco* crossing are of the sheer exhilaration as the 20-metre racing machine took off down large waves, at times with the bow wave arching up on either side and extending back to the stern. It was a thrill that we experienced repeatedly, invariably tempered by anxiety as two white-knuckled helmsmen worked frantically to try and stop the occasional broach.

Then there was the cold of sitting for four-hour stretches on the weather rail with waves coming over; the frequent sail changes; the weariness; the solace of time below; the shedding of wet-weather gear in confined space in order to 'crash' for a few brief hours before the sequence was repeated; the difficult choices (which of the two wet sleeping bags is the drier?).

And overriding all of it, the thundering noise as we accelerated down waves, and the scream of the wind in the rigging. It was a mind-numbing time where the weather was everything and the skippers and navigators went hunting for low pressure systems. My experience, I know, is shared with all who have ever crewed in a race across the Southern Ocean and will never be forgotten.

Seamaster is a very different proposition. At 36 metres (120 feet) long, displacing 168 tonnes and with a beam of 10 metres (33 feet), she provides a very stable platform. The pilot-house is secure and dry with a watertight submarine-type door that keeps the weather out. Once inside, you are curiously divorced from the weather. Below, where all is warm and dry, there are fresh towels, showers and a washing machine.

Nonetheless, and vessel differences apart, the majesty and the power of the ocean hasn't changed. We have, to date, been treated very kindly by the weather gods. Even so, we have experienced several severe gales and the speed with which the seas mount and conditions change is awesome.

We have tumbled on deck to reduce sail in difficult conditions, to gybe the vessel and set a poled out headsail. We have felt *Seamaster* lift at the stern and the bow drop as big, breaking seas tumble past, to then see the bow lift skywards again as the wave rushes through. We have been enchanted by the beauty of the sea, by the magnificent glacial colours at the base of breaking waves, and we have been treated to the wonderful company of the ever present albatross.

On this occasion the navigator has taken a course to avoid the low pressure systems and has been largely successful. For this I am very grateful and, if we are allowed to round Cape Horn in several days and traverse another 60 miles in gentle weather before entering the sanctuary of the Beagle Canal, I for one will be well pleased.

For this great ocean has fully earned the respect that it has been given by all the mariners who have ever sailed it.

Dr Trevor Agnew — affairs of the heart, on land and sea.

PETER ADDS

Why is the Horn so special in the minds of blue-water sailors, why has it earned such a reputation? Why is it the most famous (or infamous) landmark in the annals of the sea, commanding just as much respect (or striking just as much fear into the hearts of mariners) as it has through the ages?

Well, it is a most demanding cape to get to and negotiate and is a graveyard for shipping — sail and/or power. The Horn's fearsome reputation is mostly the result of a unique combination of physical and geographical factors that combine to produce almost continuous gales and storms, with accompanying horrendous sea conditions, in one of the most remote and desolate places on earth.

Through most of its passage around the world, the Southern Ocean is unrestricted in its breadth and depth, averaging between 1200 and 1500 miles in width and 2000 fathoms in depth. As this huge river of water approaches South America, abruptly it is faced with a gap of only 600 miles between Cape Horn, at the southernmost tip of South America, and the northern end of Graham Land, a peninsula protruding out from Antarctica.

This gap is called Drake Passage or, simply, 'The Drake', after Sir Francis Drake, the first man to sail through it. During his circumnavigation of 1582–85, he opted for 'The Drake' rather than risk the Spanish outpost in Magellan Strait, the route used by Magellan that lies among the islands north of the Cape itself.

Where the southernmost point of one continent (South America) coincides with the northernmost point of another (Antarctica), the water shallows to less than 100 fathoms. The water mass of the Southern Ocean, rolling unimpeded around the bottom of the world, suddenly finds that it has to squeeze through a gap one-twentieth its size.

Inevitably it accelerates, and whenever waves from deep water run into a shallower patch, they compress and their crests move closer to one another. The result — the wave faces get steeper, and that is precisely what happens at Cape Horn.

One can expect unpleasant seas in the area on these grounds alone. But the Horn also lies at 56 degrees south where stronger winds of up to storm and hurricane force can prevail. This compounds matters somewhat.

Remember too that, until the opening of the Panama Canal in 1913, 'The Drake' provided the last route by which sailing ships could compete economically with steamers. A steamship's engines could not be governed sufficiently to cope with the change of loads caused by the propeller being in the water one minute then turning in fresh air the next, as the ship pitched in rough seas. The result was that, until 1913, a sailing ship, by rounding the Horn, could make just as good time as a steamer between Australia/New Zealand and Europe, or the east and west coasts of the United States.

Nearly everyone that went to sea in sailing ships up to the First World War could expect to round the Horn, and some sailing ships were still doing it in the 1930s. Timing a voyage was of major importance and, with good reason, the preference was to round the Cape during the summer months (from November to March), thus avoiding the appalling winter storms from April to October. Beating around the Horn from east to west in winter, against the prevailing winds and currents, was a hazardous venture, to put it mildly.

Captain Bligh chose to attempt to round the Horn east to west in winter, as a short cut to Tahiti, rather than taking the traditional downwind route around the Cape of Good Hope and under Australia and New Zealand. The *Bounty* battled horrendous conditions for three months as she tried to beat through Drake Passage. Bligh is reputed to have chained his men to their posts. Finally, he had to concede, turn around and run with the conditions, across the South Atlantic, past the Cape of Good Hope, Australia and New Zealand and then up the Pacific to his destination.

The passage from west to east is easier as you are usually running before the winds. Even so, following seas can build up to extreme heights and yachts have been rolled end over end by larger than normal waves.

The legendary Cape Horn — for centuries feared and feted by mariners, all in the same breath.

2 December 2000

Latitude	49.21S
Longitude	99.10W
Course	124 deg True
Wind	NW 35 to 40 knots — gusting 45
Sea	Very rough
Barometer	999 mbs and falling
Air temp	6 deg C
Sea temp	5 deg C

Cape Horn is on the chart at last, after nearly three weeks at sea since we left New Zealand. This is our fourth gale.

0815hrs: I've just sat down at the computer after an interesting night — reefed down the foresail in rising wind then woken by Rodger to say the wind and sea were up further and it was time for more sail reduction.

As I pulled on my sea boots and Musto trousers, Ollie's voice came over the internal intercom requesting assistance. The auto-pilot had gone off-limits and he was hand-steering through the big seas that had quickly developed.

I woke a few crew and we hurried to drop the mainsail onto the boom, then rolled away the headsail and hoisted the small staysail in its place. All this time Ollie was doing a great job of pointing *Seamaster* in the right direction down the face of the now fully breaking seas, using the wheel in the pilot-house without the assistance of the big, powered steering pumps.

The sail reduction steadied the boat down a lot. We slowed to about 8 or 9 knots and were a lot more in control.

It's raining hard right now, the water running off the windows in streams. The pilot-house door is closed, and we can watch the spindrift streaking the surface of the sea. There are huge patches of foaming grey-white sea where the bigger waves are breaking with a roar down their fronts, leaving hectares of frothy white behind. It's only a basic gale at the moment and shouldn't go much above 50 knots in the squalls — so far it has reached 45 knots — but it will probably last much of the day. The albatross are notable by their absence.

The good news is that we are aiming just to the south of Cape Horn. We can sense we are closing in, although still with many miles to go. We also have a real feel for what some aspects of nature are all about. A gale at sea is normally no big deal; a full storm at sea is awe-inspiring. Even now, the conditions make one realise how insignificant we are, compared to the might of the elements.

The square-rigged sailing ships of earlier times used these winds of the Roaring Forties and Furious Fifties to get their cargoes from Australia and New Zealand to Europe as quickly as possible — often racing one another to be first to unload and so obtain the highest prices. It is easy to understand why this part of the globe was their highway.

Just as mountaineers dream about climbing in the Himalayas, sailors muse about Cape Horn, and to get there you have to negotiate the Southern Ocean. The 'Cape of capes' is a kind of altar, a Mecca, a place where man is blooded, a symbol of adversity and achievement, of hardship and conquest. The sailors of old complained and boasted about Cape Horn in the same breath — cursing the experience but loving every minute of it because it was the greatest adventure of their lives.

Cape Horn is also a graveyard for many, many ships and their crews. A journey around the Cape is a trip to the ultimate classroom of the sea. The graduate is a deep-water sailor.

In the past, Cape Horn and the Straits of Magellan were the decisive marks between the world's two greatest oceans — the Atlantic and the Pacific. No Panama or Suez Canal in those days, and for four hundred years there was a mixed-up squabble for rights and sovereignty between Spain, Holland, France, England and Germany — all of whom schemed and plotted to control this remote and weather-beaten outpost of civilisation.

By the last two decades of the nineteenth century, there were more than 10,000 deep-water sailing ships — 5000 British, 2000 Norwegian, 1200 French, 1200 Swedish and 1000 German — almost 10 million tonnes of merchantmen in 1895.

Most of these ships were three or four-masted vessels that carried a few passengers and cargoes such as case-oil, coal, wheat, guano, nitrates, manufactured goods, rice, wood or wool. The ships employed thousands of sailors, and it is from the threads of their records and stories that the fabric of the Cape Horn legends have been woven.

But the opening of the Suez Canal in 1869 suddenly halved the mileage from the Far East to Europe, and when the Panama Canal opened in 1914 it was the end of the days of practical commercial sail. Today, rounding the Horn under sail is predominantly the domain of the racing yachtsman. I am a member of the International Society of Cape Horners — but just a yacht member — having raced around the 'Godforsaken Cape' on five occasions in the past 25 years.

'Ollie' Olphert — first mate and lead diver.

7 December 2000

●

Location 285 nautical miles from Cape Horn

0930hrs: We have just come through a really blustery night — very cold, with squally showers that ripped the surface of the sea into streaks and built the tops of the breaking waves into jagged peaks with little order to them. These broken seas gave us some hard bumps and threw solid water right over the deck.

We suspected a series of strong counter-currents might be the cause, because, within one hour of my going on watch this morning, the sea flattened out, the four to five metre-high swells completely disappeared, and the 40-knot westerly wind eased back. We are now enjoying some reasonably pleasant sailing.

I should have taken more note of the old sailors' superstition about the appearance yesterday of a southern giant petrel. J. A. Latham, in his 1824 publication *A General History of Birds*, notes that the southern giant — 'like others of the Genus, [is] said to be most active and in the greatest numbers, either in storms or at the approach of them; hence their appearance is unwelcome to mariners.' Probably we should be thankful that only one southern giant appeared on our scene.

We were expecting stronger winds overnight, but only of around 25 to 30 knots from the south, not 40 knots plus from the SSW. That sou-sou-westerly is straight off the ice. It looks cold. It is cold.

Cape Horn is directly ahead and the continent of South America is away on the port beam, stretching ever northwards. We can't see the land yet because it is still 140 miles away at the nearest point, but we are closing quickly and hope to be in sight of the Horn by tomorrow evening.

Cape Horn — I don't apologise for mentioning it so often. For sailors who have had to cross an ocean to get here, rounding the Horn is the pinnacle of many a career. We have been looking at the chart for days, seeing the Horn draw ever so slowly nearer. Suddenly the realisation is setting in that it is about to become a reality.

What a thrill for those who have never passed this way before. It is just as big a thrill for me. I will still get a huge kick out of rounding this 'cape of capes' even though I have experienced it five times before — in calm weather and in gales. This time, however, instead of racing on by, I'll have the luxury of being able to turn left and head into the Beagle Canal, to spend time in a splendid place that I could only dream about in my racing days. I used to look through the binoculars as we sped past and think 'one day'.

On the big catamaran *ENZA*, when we were involved in the Trophée Jules Verne non-stop around the world record attempt — English Channel to English Channel, leaving South Africa, Australia, New Zealand and South America to port and Antarctica to starboard — we passed but never saw Cape Horn. The closest we came was approximately 150 miles as we battled our way through Drake Passage in full storm-force conditions.

The wind was screaming out of the north at close to 60 knots as we struggled to get up out of the 60s of the Southern Ocean and into the Atlantic. We estimated the waves to be 18 to 20 metres high — fully breaking — 'Cape Horn Greybeards' as they are known. We couldn't carry any sail (it was too wild) but made our way nearly across the wind and sea with just the windage of the mast and boom driving us forward. It was very, very cold.

We were gradually getting pushed southeastwards towards the South Shetland Islands — the land of ice and snow — for which we had no large-scale charts. Waves were breaking right across the cat's deck. It was awful. All you wanted to do was to crawl into your bunk, pull the pillow over your head and hope that it was all a bad dream that would go away. It wasn't and it didn't.

The conditions became so extreme that we tried the only option available to us — of running with the wind and seas behind us. But *ENZA* immediately accelerated to between 20 and 25 knots down the seas — with no sail set. It was like sailing in mountains, froth and foam and half of the surface of the sea a milky, bluey white. At that speed we were going to be among the South Shetlands in a few hours — so it was not an acceptable alternative. Back on a sou-easterly heading, still with no sails, the only option became hope.

It was a knife-edge situation in which we seriously weren't sure if we were going to be alive to see the sun come up the following day. But then the wind eased slightly, changed to a more favourable direction by a few degrees every hour, and we scooted clear.

It took the enormous experience of all of the crew to see us through to the other side — smiling. I would not have missed that experience for anything.

Latitude	54.48S
Longitude	75.35W
Course	095 deg True
Wind	SW of 17 knots
Sea	Moderate with left-over swell abating
Barometer	995 mbs and rising
Air temp	6 deg C (was 2 deg C at dawn)
Sea temp	4 deg C

Rodger Moore — homework on Antarctica.

8 December 2000

Location 105 nautical miles to Cape Horn

Latitude	55.59S
Longitude	70.25W
Course	094 deg True
Wind	East at 15 knots
Sea	Moderate but lumpy at times
Barometer	1002 mbs and rising
Air temp	5 deg C
Sea temp	4 deg C

Cape Horn just up ahead. The islands to the west of the Horn are showing well on our radar screen — only 38 miles to port — but we can't yet see them with the naked eye from deck level. Alistair has suggested he go aloft to the crow's-nest for a better view, but we are bumping too hard for that at the moment.

Looking at the weather map, there is a big gale coming in behind us that will generate strong northerly winds to these waters in two days' time. It is preferable that we are not still here, so we have two days in which to get into port and snug down in a safe and sheltered anchorage. We should be at Puerto Williams in Chile, and the most southern town in the world, in a little less than that — hopefully in a very sheltered river entrance, secured alongside a 25-metre local charter vessel, by name of *Victory*, which is tied up to the local yacht club.

If we keep up our present speed of 7 knots or so, we should be off the Horn at daybreak. The adventure is beginning. There is an electric charge in the air. We can't wait.

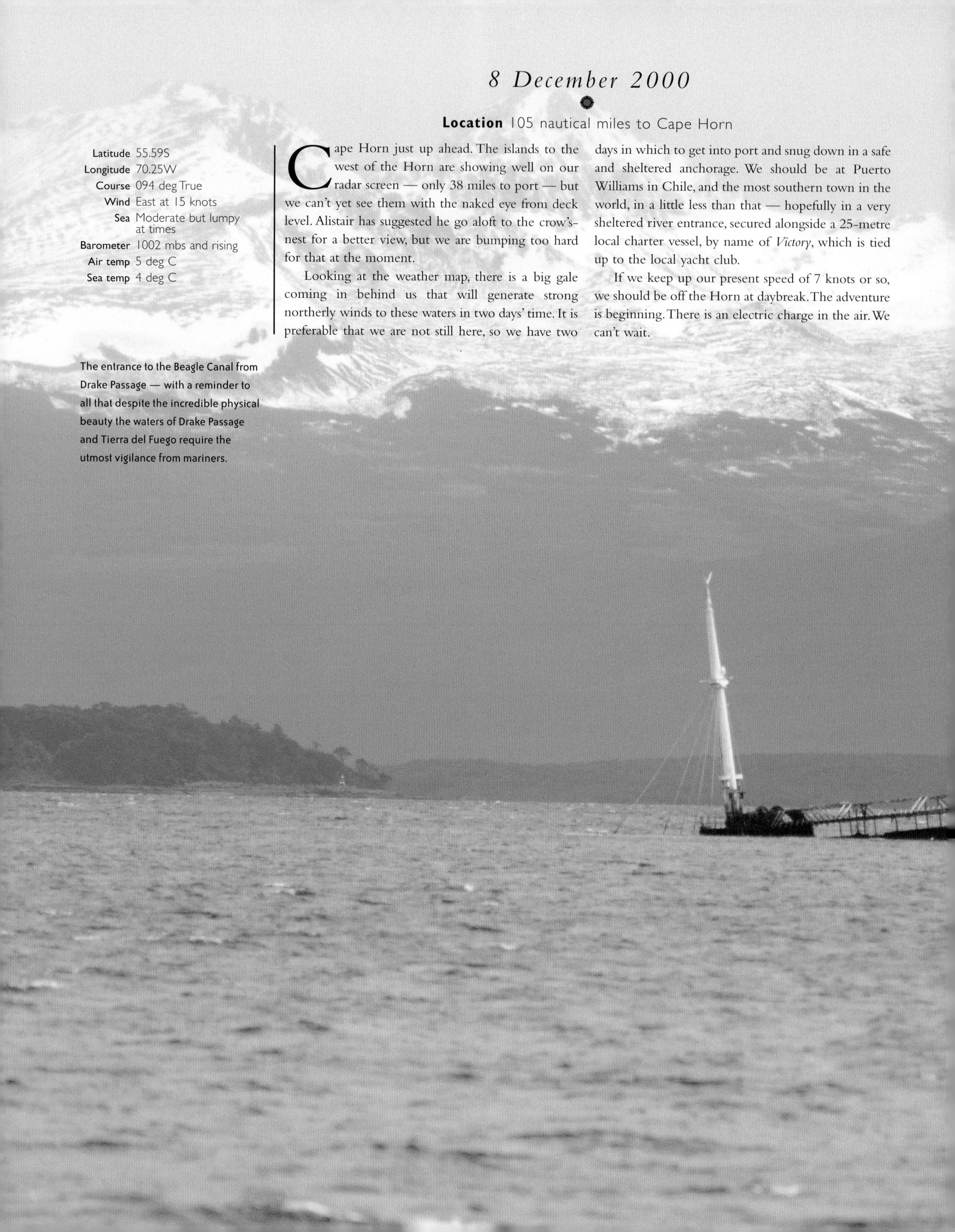

The entrance to the Beagle Canal from Drake Passage — with a reminder to all that despite the incredible physical beauty the waters of Drake Passage and Tierra del Fuego require the utmost vigilance from mariners.

9 December 2000

◆

Location In Paso Picton (Chile), entering the Beagle Canal

1100hrs: We had a grand start to our day when we passed Cape Horn in the dawn — at approx 0345hrs. The visibility was good even though there were passing snow showers. It was very cold on deck at 1 degree C.

I woke the crew about half an hour before and, with most dressed up in their full thermals, including gloves and hats, we watched in awe as the snow-flecked cliffs slid slowly past to port. A Cape Horn fruit-cake and some special coffees with a dash of rum helped keep the cold at bay. Some dolphins were our only escort at that early hour.

It wasn't just Cape Horn that had us captivated, even though, I must admit, I have never seen it with a snow topping before, or looking so menacing in the early morning light. The bonus was the background of other islands, other more distant and jagged mountains covered in white, that continued to unveil themselves as we turned left and headed north towards the Beagle Canal.

We are now in brilliant sunshine and a light northerly breeze — the surface of the enclosed waters blue, smooth and sparkling, with penguins, shags, and other birds appearing everywhere. There are forests and beaches and almost no sign of human habitation — yet.

We all feel we have accomplished something. As a destination, after 5000 miles at sea through the Southern Ocean, you can probably guess that we are not displeased. For me, after racing past so many times, to now be able to stop and look at what I have only seen fleetingly through binoculars fills a void.

Course Variable between islands — at present NW
Wind Light
Sea Smooth
Barometer 1010 mbs and falling
Air temp 12 deg C
Sea temp 5 deg C

17 December 2000

Since arriving in Tierra del Fuego, we have spent time in Puerto Williams but are now in Ushuaia, Argentina, the most southern city in the world. Both places look onto the Beagle Canal — Puerto Williams looks north, and Ushuaia looks south. Both are surrounded by snow-clad mountains. Both share the Beagle Canal as a waterway — one that is divided down the middle by an invisible red line. So, to cruise in Chile we must first of all enter Chile, then apply for a cruising permit — outlining in detail our planned itinerary.

To then pick up a new member of the crew or family coming to join us, we have to journey to Ushuaia, which has the closest airport. This means leaving Chile (passports stamped etc.) and entering Argentina at Ushuaia (customs, immigration etc.). To go back to cruising in Chile, we then need to check out of Argentina (passports stamped etc.), motor the 30 miles eastwards down the Beagle Canal to Puerto Williams, and check in again (passports, immigration, health etc.) — and apply for a further cruising permit. It is a process that we will have to repeat whenever we have to meet visitors or when our current permit expires.

It seems awfully bureaucratic but — when in Rome. We're not complaining either, because the best cruising is in Chilean waters and, when I say the best, it is without doubt one of the most magnificent cruising areas I have been fortunate enough to visit. Additionally, the officials on both sides of the Canal — in both countries — are so friendly that it is a pleasure to deal with them. It just means adjusting your time frames and allowing for all of the toing and froing.

Opposite Seamaster *in Ushuaia.*

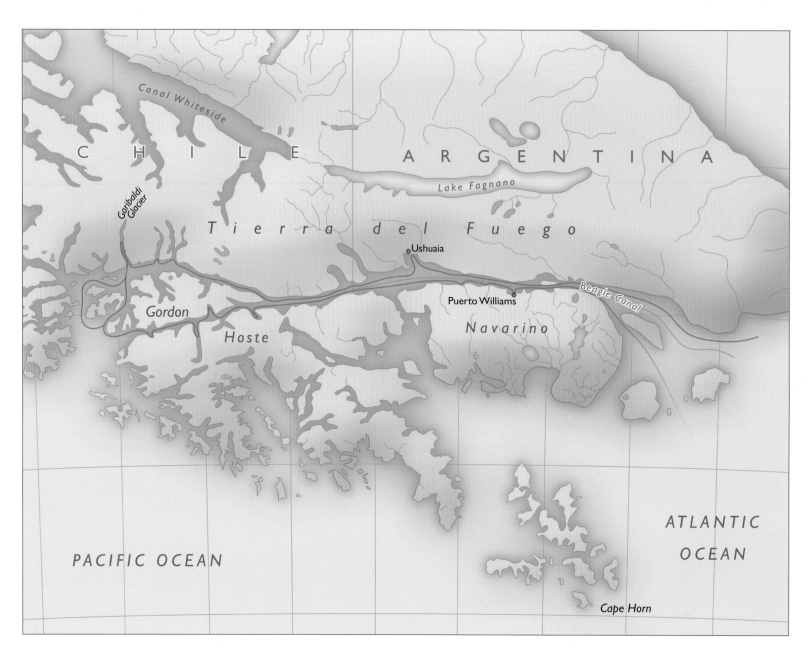

Puerto Williams is tiny, a town of approximately 2500 people, most of whom are military. Fresh food can be difficult to obtain, and the only time some of our crew went to a restaurant in the town they were not exactly impressed. But the town has a charm that is hard to beat. The naval yacht club — an old naval supply vessel resting quietly on the bottom of the river where it was placed 50 years ago — is full of fun in the evenings, when the naval officers and other yachtsmen (mainly French) gather around the open fire in the corner of the saloon and share tales.

I like Puerto Williams a lot. The people couldn't be nicer and the scenery and walks are marvellous. The damage the Canadian beavers (once farmed but now escaped) are doing is not so great — but interesting just the same. To climb through beech forests, alongside mountain streams, to way above the snow-line and look far west along the Beagle Canal beyond Ushuaia, is magical. Mountains drop into the sea on both sides of the Canal — snow clouds mixed with sunshine, forests mixed with spasmodic areas of farmland. The sea is blue-green, the forests dark, the mountain crags black and brown, and the snow dazzling white.

The Chilean authorities have given us permission to visit places with *Seamaster* that have never been visited by a yacht before — places that probably have only been seen by the military, or sealers and explorers of centuries ago. We are privileged to be offered such a gem. Our festive season pause in these parts, before our departure for the Antarctic Peninsula early in January, is clearly going to be a highlight of considerable proportions.

For now, the Christmas spirit is starting to take hold. There is a Christmas tree in the saloon near the galley, complete with coloured lights, one of those musical boxes that finally drives you mad, and gold beads and red tinsel around the perimeter of the main saloon. A large Santa waits in the forward saloon, but we are still expecting the real one on the big day.

We know where we want to be on Christmas day — in Baia Morning, a deep cove just across the Beagle Canal from one of the main glaciers, a high lake at one end with a torrent of water flowing in through a stream. We can drop our anchor and back in under the trees, secure stern lines to the rocks on the shoreline and enjoy. It definitely will not be crowded so that will mean plenty of room for the sleigh!

Brown seals jostling for a place in the sun in the Beagle Canal.

The Weather and Global Warming

'The weather' is one of the most talked-about subjects on the planet — by everyone, everywhere. And 'the weather' as we understand it is a result of moisture in the atmosphere — no moisture, no weather. So, the weather and global warming are closely linked.

If the atmosphere is warmed by 1 degree C, which might seem a small amount but isn't, then it can absorb up to six per cent more moisture, which results in more extreme and changeable weather patterns — stronger winds, greater climate swings, more frequent droughts and flooding, bigger waves, more frequent and more violent hurricanes etc. Pretty much everything in nature is linked to everything else so, if we alter one set of parameters (i.e. allow global warming to go unchecked), this will have a direct effect on other aspects of our environment.

Global warming affects the planet in other ways that most of us might not appreciate. The warming of the atmosphere — even if only slight at this point — is having a huge impact on the Arctic, for instance. More than 50,000 square kilometres of ice are disappearing every year and not returning in the winter. The ice is melting. It won't cause the seas to rise significantly as most of the ice is floating, and so is existing volume in the sea. But it will start to cause the decimation of most of the wildlife that calls the Arctic home — the polar bears, seals, walruses, narwhals, beluga whales, bowhead whales, and countless sea-birds. This is not science fiction. It is already happening.

When we get to the Antarctic Peninsula in a couple of months' time, I am sure that we will find a similar situation, but with a significant difference. The Antarctic is not floating ice, like the Arctic. It is a frozen continent densely covered with ice that has built up over millions of years. When this ice melts, and it is already doing so, there will be the very real prospect of rising ocean and sea levels, and everything that that will mean.

Our aim is to reach as far south as we can into George VI Sound, to penetrate as deeply as the ice will allow and check whether the permanent ice shelves are where they were 20 years ago. Additionally, we will look at what is happening to the glaciers.

Global warming is a fact and its influence is already being felt. For us, in the short term at least, that means changing weather to tolerate and discuss. For the environment as a whole, and for many, many species, the results will be far more serious.

One of the numerous glaciers that tumble into the Beagle Canal — the ice is definitely melting.

Captain's Christmas Log

Written over the Christmas period while in the Beagle Canal

20 December 2000

Peter next to a tree damaged by beavers.

Innumerable glaciers pour down the mountains into the Beagle Canal.

We are anchored in Caletta Olla in the northern arm of the Beagle Canal, tied up by stern hawsers to two large trees at the back of the beach. We arrived in calm conditions yesterday, after a long day of motoring into quite fresh headwinds, and are now backed into the shore facing east, the anchor out ahead of us.

The boys (Alistair, James, Nick and Marc) have been off in the Rigid Inflatable Boat (RIB) to the Italia Glacier, a couple of miles further west. It was one of the most amazing sights they have ever seen, a huge ice face dropping vertically into the Beagle Canal.

It is now blowing hard (saw 45 knots a couple of minutes ago), the wind screaming through the trees behind us and across the masthead, but it is almost calm at deck level, only the odd puff of wind. But the odd puff there means more wind at the bow and white squalls 50 metres in front of the bow whipping the water's surface into a frenzy and throwing spray high in the air to be whirled away a moment later towards the eastern shoreline. It is a very secure anchorage and pretty much as noted in the various pilot and cruising books — except I am not sure that the people writing the books ever came here. The entrance to bay is not at all as described.

We took a walk to see the Holanda Glacier, leaving Ollie, Janot, Trevor and Robyn (Trevor's wife) onboard for safety reasons. The 'walk' was through swamp-land, made more-so by the beavers damming the creeks and the main river. The number of trees they had felled was extraordinary — trunks, branches and stumps everywhere for the entire six-hour tramp. And what a wet 'walk' it was — continually climbing over and around stumps and beaver-felled trees, up steep banks, through thick moss, over streams, under small waterfalls — all the time sort of following the river upwards.

We had a peek of the end of the glacier after two hours and it looked quite close, but it took a further hour to get there.

The glacier was dramatic — various shades of blue (from the palest to the most dazzling shades imaginable) and full of cracks and rifts. Much of the top had melted into peaks of the weirdest shapes. The glacier is receding — like many others in the world. The air is warmer than it once was, even way down here in the Beagle Canal with snow covered peaks all around, snowfalls most days of the year, and tremendous gales of refrigerated air. It is still magnificent but the glacier looks to be a small portion of what it must once have been have been many years ago.

We stayed awhile, marvelling at the view, watching huge chunks break off the front of the glacier and crash into the lake, before starting the long trek back to *Seamaster*. The return journey was just as wet and just as difficult, and we ended up walking along a beaver dam, all around the edge of its lake that must have been hundreds of metres long. The lake had killed off most of the trees. This is the problem with beavers. They chop down trees, small and sometimes very mature, to build their dams. The lakes created by their dams do the rest, drowning the roots of the trees that are left.

Back aboard *Seamaster*, still tied stern-to under the big trees at the back of the beach, with squalls ripping overhead at more than 50 knots. Still quite calm on deck — extraordinary. I hope this bad weather doesn't last too long as there are many more places we want to visit over the next few weeks. I am also looking forward to a dive in better visibility than at Baia Lapataia (part of Argentina) a few days ago.

We have seen surprisingly few birds and almost no sea life at all in recent days, but there are other features that more than make up for this.

21 December 2000

Untied and up-anchored at 0900hrs and set out for Caletta Morning via the Avenue of the Glaciers. Quite remarkable: Holanda, Italia, Francia, Alemania, and Romanche, followed further west by Espania with many un-named glaciers along the route, often hidden round the turn of the deep fiords (senos) off the main channel. The Romanche Glacier had a waterfall coming from underneath the ice face — a veritable torrent gushing out and dropping many hundreds of metres into the sea below. The Alemania Glacier, to the east of Romanche, was enormous — huge ice fields where two or more glaciers join up — with a vast outflow of river water into the Beagle Canal staining the dark, blue-green water a glacial green/white. Huge pieces of ice broke off from up high and boomed down to the seam disintegrating into thousands of smaller pieces as they went, bursting off outcropping rocks on the way down.

We motored the short distance across to the south side of the Canal to Baia Romanche, on Isla Gordon, and into Caletta Morning — a fantastic bay off to starboard just inside the main entrance. Deep all the way in, apart from a kelp patch to port (if there is kelp — then there are likely to be rocks underneath). We sent the dinghies ahead to identify large trees on the shore to moor to with our stern warps. Then we turned *Seamaster* around to face out of the bay, and backed her in, letting the anchor out as we went.

There were blue-eyed cormorants nesting in the cliffs only 30 metres to starboard — many nests with one, two or three young in each, plus two attentive parents who were especially so when the falcons and condors came raiding. They tried to get the parents off the nests in order to get at the eggs. If that failed, they waited for a nest to be empty for a few seconds and then in they went, scavenging the contents of the eggs and then demolishing the nest with their feet, kicking the shredded remains down the cliff to the sea. All of this was taking place just a short distance away from us — nature in her most raw, survival of the fittest. Looking forward, the view was much better — snow-clad peaks of many mountains.

It is necessary to remember a few basic points down here in Tierra del Fuego. Where there are good-size, straight-trunked trees, then there will generally be less screaming squalls when the weather turns. Where there are few trees — watch out. The wind will probably blow you out of the anchorage. As mentioned before, where there is kelp there is probably a rock (not always true, but a prudent way of navigating).

Peter and James Blake looking cheerful despite the gruelling walk to the Holanda Galcier.

23 December 2000

Spent a damp night at Caletta Morning. It poured with rain most of the time. That equated to a lot of snow on higher ground and the white stuff was very much in evidence when we rose and looked out in the morning. Little wind, however, so we were very snug and protected in our anchorage. Today has seen a raft of activity — kayaking, wakeboarding, bird-watching (fascinating), walking, filming and marvelling at how lucky we are to be in this extraordinary place.

Superlatives come easily in this part of the world. Perhaps we might have used a few too many already because, when we motored further west in sleet and rain and then quite strong head-winds with zero visibility, we entered Seno Garibaldi and all superlatives used before went out the window. More than 10 miles in from the mouth, between mountains that we guessed were between 1000 metres and 1500 metres high, the scenery at the head of this seno was exquisite — even in the mist and rain. It was quite dramatic and we weren't prepared for it. The various guides, pilot books and reports don't do it justice. This has to be one of the wonders of the world, and there is no one here but us to see it.

Three huge glaciers dropped into the sea at the head of the seno leaving a mass of ice packed tight in the water and waiting for a northerly wind to set it free on its ever diminishing trip to the Beagle Canal. We went right into the ice pack, testing *Seamaster*'s ice-breaking ability for the first time. Apart from a few scrapes on the bottom paint and a number of thumps, we came through just fine and anchored behind a small island with the glaciers in sight a couple of miles astern.

Ollie, Janot, James and Nick found a large enough floe to stand on — all of them — and towed it back to *Seamaster* with the dinghy. It must have weighed around 20 tonnes. James and Nick then donned survival suits (along with Ollie) and stayed on the floe for quite some time, as well as swimming in the near zero-degree water.

We backtracked down the seno to anchor for the night at Puerto Garibaldi, an indentation in the side of this fiord, in calm conditions. The boys enjoyed further water sports until dinner (amazing how much fun they are having with suitable protection from the cold). A grey fox with a black band on the end of its tail walked calmly along the foreshore, quite unperturbed by our presence. Ollie saw two more just on nightfall.

We kept an anchor watch all night in case of a change in the weather but awoke this morning to a pleasant day. It is now very warm (15 degrees C) and sunny with a moderate northerly breeze. Ollie has been in the RIB with dolphins following right in his wake. He filmed them as they foraged in the thick kelp beds that line the shore.

James and Nick have had further instruction from Marc and Ollie on the finer points of cold-diving and are now in the shallow waters (3 degrees C) near the beach, learning to use their dry-suits and full face masks with internal communications systems. Marc and Ollie are very cautious in their approach — the only way to be, particularly in this part of the world.

It is Alistair's 24th birthday today. He's asleep in his bunk, having been up for much of the night with a stomach bug. I saw him in the galley around 0200hrs and wished him a happy birthday. He'd just been sick again so I didn't get much of a response, just a very weak grin.

I am writing this in the communications room with the weak sun streaming through the overhead windows. The generator is humming quietly in the background, the watermaker is doing what it does best, and we will soon start to think about our next anchorage for tonight — probably Isla Chair, only an hour and a half away. Tomorrow is Christmas Eve so it will become quite busy. We only plan to travel a few hours to find a remote cove for Christmas Day — a cove where no-one has ever been before, but one where Santa's sleigh can get in alongside. The wrapping paper is appearing, the galley scissors keep going missing — it is a good time.

Ollie and James filming *Seamaster* in the Beagle Canal.

24 December 2000

Isla Chair proved to be not so good, so we didn't stay long. The wind came in from the east at 18 knots — straight into the tiny bay in which we were anchored (Caletta Cushion). I wasn't happy with it as a night anchorage and, besides, it was very dirty with plastic bags, old fuel drums and general fishermen's rubbish scattered everywhere. So we motored eastwards to Baia Tres Brazos to anchor outside a bay on the western side of the isla. The RIB went in to check the depths but found them considerably less than the pilot book and there were no reasonably sized trees or rock outcrops to tie to anyway.

Then we hoisted the RIB aboard and headed west, to the north of Isla Darwin — an impressively huge lump of rock — then turned south down Canal Tomson (not open to yachts in the past). After a few more miles heading down towards Baia Cook, we angled ENE into the SW arm of the Beagle Canal with the walls closing in on both sides. It rained and drizzled much of the way. But the sky cleared suddenly and the sun came out — and we were presented with a glorious sight.

The SW arm of the Beagle Canal seems quite different to the NW arm — closer, rockier and greener. We have seen glacial canyons and remote bays behind unexplored islands that we want to return to another time.

We turned right off the main channel into an un-named and un-sounded bay, passed over the entrance moraine left over from days long ago, and entered the inner basin. A squeeze between an island and the shore, with the RIB doing pre-sounding, and we entered an exquisite world never before seen by yachtsmen.

A glacier to starboard dropped almost vertically down the mountain walls, like a frozen waterfall of gigantic proportions. The much larger glacier straight ahead started life high on the plateau above the bay, between the mountain tops that were buried from sight. We turned to port and entered an anchorage more akin to an alpine lake than anything else — completely surrounded by mountain walls and canyons of maybe 1000 to 1500 metres height. Snow, lakes and many, many waterfalls enclosed us. The lushness of the vegetation compared to all the other anchorages had to be seen to be believed — larger leafed trees, brighter greens, denser ground cover, far less evident wind damage, and a beaver dam right nearby.

We couldn't believe our luck. We had found the perfect Christmas anchoring spot.

With the sun beating down on us, and the temperature in the high teens, Marc and his 'flying team' put on boots (and Alistair a pack) and were dropped ashore to climb one of the high points where

they thought they might successfully launch Marc's para-glider. We watched through binoculars as the tiny-sized figures high on the ground behind us spread out the bright red para-sail and then a yellow survival-suit-clad pilot floated off into the afternoon breeze — high over the southern side of the Beagle Canal.

The photos they brought back were stunning to say the least. The surrounding lakes blue in the sunlight — the snow a dazzling white, the sky blue but with many puffy clouds around, the glaciers those marvellous shades of pale blue, the forests various shades of green, the water of our anchorage a dark blue-green tinged with the lighter green-grey of the glacial waters, and *Seamaster* a speck in the distance below — dwarfed by the immensity of her surroundings.

'Christmas Bay' (named by the *Seamaster* crew) in the Beagle Canal. Tierra del Fuego offers some of the most spectacular cruising grounds in the world.

Christmas Morning

0100hrs: James and Nick were really excited about today being Christmas day. Ollie prepared eggs benedict for breakfast and later the main meal of the day — roast, stuffed turkeys with ALL the trimmings. I made a point of selecting some suitable wines.

Looking out from on deck at 0120hrs (in the morning) — the sky was quite light to the south, over the top of the frozen mountains, and it wasn't too cold (around 5 degrees C). There was hardly any wind ruffling the waters where we sat — quiet and still — far away from any ocean swell. The silence was intense. It was a great way to start our Christmas morning.

Santa arrived by RIB from the shore, with red outfit and flowing white beard, booming 'ho ho ho' and with presents for all — but you had to sit on his

knee before you got one. A great meal started at 3.30 pm and finished late with some of us in bed and some dancing to very loud music in the saloon.

Santa has swapped sleigh for Seamaster *inflatable (and looks suspiciously like Captain Rabbit).*

26 December 2000
Boxing Day

Set off at about 10 am — headed east up SW Beagle Canal, then turned right down the 15 kilometre or so seno with a 90 degree bend at the end — not knowing what we might find. Half way up the seno was a really excellent glacier (unnamed) dropping large lumps of ice into the sea. It seemed to be getting bigger rather than receding and was pushing up a lot of gravel on the foreshore. We were able to stop *Seamaster* very close to the shoreline, just off a large blue ice cave of what looked very solid, almost translucent dark blue ice at the back of the cave. Then we headed further up the seno. There being no soundings around the 90 degree bend so we

slowed right down, passing over a couple of moraines but still with approximately 20 metres of water beneath us, to enter a remarkable glacial basin. Two glaciers, lakes, a surrounding of lush trees and a groove through one of the above-water moraine banks where a lake had worn its way to the sea — taking everything with it (trees, rocks, the lot). The scenery was so grand that distances we thought were small were large. A walk ashore through the rocks of the glacial river proved a hike through enormous boulders and large fallen tree trunks. An apparent few hundred metres was in reality a kilometre. It was quite warm even though we were surrounded by huge mountains, all covered in ice and snow. Little wind penetrated this totally enclosed oasis. As far as we knew, we were the first yacht ever to be allowed to officially cruise in this area, to be in these bays.

I have cruised in many parts of the world — the tropics, the Mediterranean, the Caribbean, Scotland and the Pacific — but these last two stopovers are in a class of their own, far and away better than anything I have ever seen.

Most of us turned in early. We have a 0400hrs departure tomorrow towards Puerto Williams where we will clear out of Chile prior to heading to Ushuaia where we will drop Trevor and Robyn off (they are going to explore some of South America before heading back to New Zealand) and pick up Pippa and Sarah-Jane who are joining us for the remainder of our stay in this remarkable part of the world.

Far from his home in Southern England, James Blake surveys a huge glacier.

31 December 2000

Picked up Pippa and Sarah-Jane from Ushuaia airport on 28 December. They arrived late, having had to make a transit stop to refuel. The plane also had a flat tyre that needed changing. But, at least they made it and were here, fit and well.

Then it was back to Puerto Williams to check in and get our new cruising permit before heading down the canal, back past Ushuaia, in pretty much flat calm conditions. It took a while to get to Caletta Olla and tie stern-to under the trees.

We motored across to Caletta Morning yesterday, via the glaciers — not as good as in bright sunshine but still impressive — and are now stern-to again, next to the cormorant colony. We saw a type of falcon on the branch of a tree on the bluff overlooking the basin where *Seamaster* sits. It seemed quite unconcerned by our presence and Don managed to get a few good digital shots before it finally spread wings and lazily flew away — over towards the cormorant nests. It was darkish brown but with lighter patches on both wings. Its head could swivel like an owl's — almost right round (or so it appeared).

James, Nick and Janot (with Ollie and Marc) went for a cold dive along the shoreline yesterday afternoon, it took a couple of goes to get their rigs sorted properly. Pippa and I went for a walk over the hills and had a wonderful view of the Beagle Canal. It was very squelchy underfoot. There were bogs everywhere — particularly high up on the ridges.

Footnote

We had more adventures — including finding and exploring a three-kilometre long seno that wasn't on the chart at all — complete with massive glacier and many waterfalls. We had sunshine and rain, clear skies and heavy mist, some good walks to unknown beaver dams, some foraging along the sea shore. The boys continued their diving programme and, most importantly for me, my family and I had quality time together. At the finish of the 2000 America's Cup defence in Auckland earlier in the year, I thought I would be able to have more time at home and spend more time with the family, but it seems that the opposite has happened. For the next year or so I am going to be onboard *Seamaster* in remote parts of the world. So, I have to make the most of every opportunity I have to be with Pippa and the children, who are growing up fast.

The whole Blake family is here — from left: Sarah-Jane, Peter, Pippa and James.

James Blake and friend Nick Blackman enjoy the icy playground.

SECTION 2

Antarctica

11 January 2001

•

Location In Drake Passage, 110 miles south-east from Cape Horn,
heading towards the Antarctic Peninsula

Latitude 57.00S
Longitude 64.10W
Course 145 deg True
Wind NW light — expected NE by afternoon
Sea Moderate
Barometer 992 mbs
Air temp 10 deg C
Sea temp 4 deg C

Antarctica ahead — 'we can't
wait to get amongst it all.'

We left Puerto Williams, on the island of Navarino in Southern Chile, at 1100hrs yesterday, motored eastwards down the Beagle Canal, past cormorant and seal colonies, and hoisted sails in a light breeze with the open ocean ahead. After a month of smooth waters and quiet bays, to be on a heaving ocean again comes as a bit of a shock to the system.

The Beagle Canal is a wondrous place. We spent many days exploring the waterways and bays that indent everywhere. The glaciers are phenomenal, the waterfalls too many to count, the dolphins so friendly and playful that the youngsters on board for the festive season took to the dinghy to spend time playing with them, even touching their dorsal fins, as they stayed very close alongside, underneath, and behind *Seamaster*. The scenery was the best I have ever seen anywhere. It took one's breath away. But for now, the Beagle and Cape Horn are behind us. The Antarctic Peninsula beckons.

Every member of the crew for the trip to the ice has a subject that he or she will study so that they become the 'resident expert'. My speciality will be ice navigation. Ollie has chosen leopard seals, while others have decided on the orca, krill, phytoplankton, penguins, ice shelves, etc. Once we get over the tiredness that the first day or two at sea always brings, along with a few rather pale-green complexions, our research at basic level will be a lot of fun and an interest for all on board.

We are initially heading towards Hope Bay at the very NE end of the Peninsula, with a stop at King George Island, in the South Shetland Islands, on the way there. The distance across Drake Passage is not great — it's 500 miles or so to the South Shetland Islands — but it can be a furious place. So far we have been lucky and the weather forecast predicts that we might have to motor much of the way.

So we are back at sea again. Our aluminium space-ship is stored for a number of months of exciting times ahead. The forepeak is our 'chiller' and is stocked with whole lamb carcasses that will be hung in the rigging (colder than a household fridge) once we get a little further south. There are further legs of

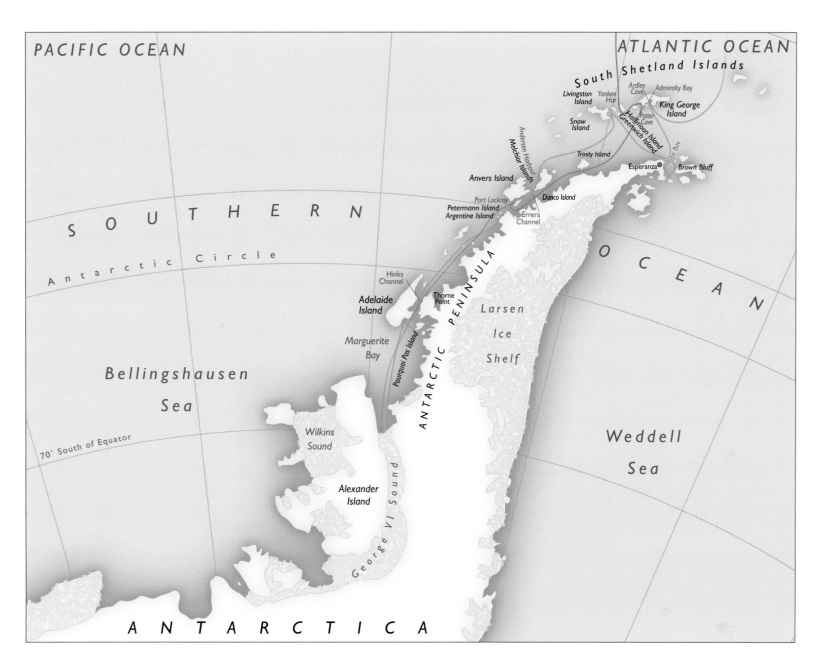

South Shetland Islands

Livingston Island
Yankee Har
Ardley Cove
Admiralty Bay
King George Island

Snow Island
Potter Cove
Halfmoon Island
Greenwich Island
Flipe Bay

Andersen Harbour
Melchior Islands

Trinity Island

Esperanza
Brown Bluff

Anvers Island

Danco Island

Port Lockroy
Petermann Island
Argentine Island
Errera Channel

SOUTHERN

Antarctic Circle

OCEAN

Hinks Channel

Thorne Point

Adelaide Island

ANTARCTIC PENINSULA

Larsen Ice Shelf

Marguerite Bay

Pourquoi Pas Island

Bellingshausen Sea

Weddell Sea

70° South of Equator

Wilkins Sound

Alexander Island

George VI Sound

ANTARCTICA

---

lamb, mountains of beef, boxes of vegetables and fruit, bags of rice and flour, thousands of longer-term tins of food that are our 'backstop', cereals, muesli, many kilos of oats for porridge, and so on.

Our approval from the New Zealand government to go to Antarctica arrived two days ago. There are many 'dos' and 'don'ts' — from how close we are allowed to go to various birds and animals, to cleaning procedures with boots and clothing, and control of on-board wastes. From the moment we cross to the south of latitude 60, we must retain on board all non-biodegradable products. We do so anyway, for every ocean crossing, so this is an easy procedure to follow. There are special sealable bins in the forepeak to facilitate it.

We must also be able to hold all biodegradable waste products on board (food scraps, shower water, galley waste and sewage) when in areas near to breeding sites, or areas of special scientific interest, and can only discharge when well out at sea and away from such areas, and when the wind is in the right direction. We understand and appreciate the reasons behind these regulations and want to comply.

What will the Antarctic be like? Where will we meet our first iceberg? We are already on lookout for them and will take even more care when we cross the Antarctic Convergence later tonight or tomorrow morning. We will wait for the sea to quickly change temperature downwards, for the air to suddenly get cooler, for the sea to change from the present perfect deep blue, with shafts of sunlight disappearing forever into the clear depths, to a much darker green, full of life.

We are waiting to see the first swarms of the reddy-orange krill — the reason for the prolific life here in the cold, and the vast blooms of phytoplankton near the ice edge — the start of the food chain. We have been told of the humpback whales gorging themselves on the krill not too many days ahead of us down the Peninsula. We can't wait to get amongst it all.

13 January 2001

●

Location 6 miles from the eastern end of King George Island in the South Shetlands

Course 140 deg True
Wind Variable 5 knots
Sea state Smooth with a long, low, NW swell.
Barometer 993 mbs and rising
Air temp 6 deg C
Sea temp 1 deg C

Opposite *Seamaster* glides past the iceberg home of chinstrap penguins.

Below 'And we thought we had this place all to ourselves.'

Following page *Seamaster* in 'Iceberg Alley', threading her way through an endless array of bergs of all shapes and sizes.

We are not sure of the ice concentrations ahead of us. The latest set of ice figures, received yesterday on one of our satellite links, was missing the page for our area — and there isn't another broadcast for a further week. So we will probably move to three people on watch from later today, one on permanent ice lookout at the bow, linked to the pilot-house by radio.

The island of King George can be seen on the radar, fine on the starboard bow. We are closing in but are not sure if we will stop here at Admiralty Bay, or whether we will continue on to Hope Bay, another 80 miles or so further south at the top end of the Antarctic Peninsula itself. Much of our planning and decision making now depends upon the weather and, with a forecast of winds freshening from the northeast in 24 hours' time, Hope Bay might not be the place to be.

The *Antarctic Pilot* states: '. . . especially in the early summer, the approach to the anchorage is liable to be found blocked by bergy bits. It is exposed to the very strong katabatic winds that blow down the bay with little warning.'

It's now 1030hrs. A southern giant petrel is keeping us company, pure white from the end of its beak to the tip of its tail. There are Cape pigeons in their chocolate and white plumage darting about in our wake and, over to starboard, a number of gentoo penguins are porpoising along on a parallel course. On the starboard bow, less than 12 miles away through this cool, misty morning, are the cliffs and ice of King George Island.

We are now nearly across 'The Drake' and may soon be allowed to have a dram from the bottle of special whisky given to us by the head of the Argentine navy in Ushuaia for just this occasion. Maybe it would be best with coffee.

1300hrs: Icebergs ahead — showing bright through the mist. Brilliant blues like we have never seen before. Dark blue-greens as though painted by hand. Whites so white they dazzle with their unmarked starkness. Flat tops, rounded tops, old bergs, new bergs, bergy bits littering the surface of the sea and crackling in their demise as we pass through, between and, on occasion, straight over the top.

Escorting us as we weave our way between the bigger 'ghost ships of the Southern Seas' are hundreds of penguins — mainly gentoos and chinstraps — and then the minke whales arrive. We glide very slowly up to a floe that is a floating sunbed for two seals. One of them is a leopard seal. He looks at us disdainfully before rolling over and slipping into the sea to stare accusingly at us as we slide past.

The sun and blue sky and 10 degree C temperatures make the scene the more remarkable. We really can't believe that we are so fortunate to be witnessing so much on our first day. To add to our delight, the mist clears from the frozen King George Island to reveal ice, snow, glaciers, black cliff faces, headlands of green and brown lichen — all glistening in the afternoon light.

2200hrs: We are now in Admiralty Bay on King George Island, a long motor from the sea, and are swinging to an anchor only a few hundred metres from the face of an enormous glacier that regularly thunders pieces of ice into the sea. The Brazilian Antarctic base is nearby across the bay, with the Polish base a couple of miles away towards the entrance.

We have read books about Antarctica, have studied photographs of (supposedly) some of the best scenery, and find that it is much better than we ever thought possible — by a factor of ten. It is rugged, raw, uncompromising, hostile, extreme — and cold. But our impression, after only our first day here, is that it is fantastic and almost beyond description.

The Antarctic Explorers

Antarctica: a land of ice, snow, extreme cold, high winds, blizzards, calms, sunshine, the most extraordinary natural beauty imaginable — full of life, full of intrigue. A land that has drawn man to explore, to suffer the most severe privations in the quest to be 'first' — and to sometimes die in the attempt — 'for flag and country'. A land that is now known — but remains unknown. A land that was once subtropical and is now one of the driest places on earth — a desert — with very little rainfall overall. A land that never warms below the surface. A land with only a recent history involving man. But what a history.

Seamaster communications expert and crew Don Robertson writes:

❝ To misquote Scott completely: 'God, this is an awesome place.' Snow- and ice-covered mountains, glaciers, icebergs the size of houses and then some. Add in the wildlife and it is really awesome.

When Scott made his remark, 'Great God! this is an awful place …', he was in a tent at the South Pole itself, while I am happily living in comfort on *Seamaster*. Some difference.

This frozen continent, the fifth largest, remained a challenge to navigators and explorers for centuries. Early Greek philosophers theorised that a southern landmass must exist to 'balance' the known mass in the Northern Hemisphere. Magellan, Drake and Cook came close to this area. However, it was not until the early 1800s that the blanks started to be filled in on the world map, and conclusive mapping did not take place until the early 1900s.

Following discovery came the great explorers, and while not taking anything away from anyone, for me the journeys of Scott, Shackleton and Amundsen fire my imagination. Here were men who set out on the great journey to the South Pole, some returning, some perishing, while others did not succeed in reaching their goal but survived against all odds. Courage, leadership and self-sacrifice made up their character. What must Robert Falcon Scott have felt when, on reaching the Pole, he made his discovery?

From Scott's journals: '… Tuesday January 16th 1912 … we started off in high spirits in the afternoon … Bower's sharp eyes detected what he thought was a cairn … we marched on, found that it was a black flag tied to a sledge bearer; nearby the remains of a camp … this told us the whole story. The Norwegians have forestalled us and are first to the Pole.'

Scott and his brave party had found Amundsen's tent at the South Pole.

Left **Ernest Henry Shackleton**

Opposite *Endurance*, close to the end as she is crushed in the terrible grip of the Antarctic ice pack.

Amundsen, having initially planned an assault on the North Pole, only to find out during his preparations that Robert Peary had forestalled him, turned his attention to the South Pole. At 3 pm on Friday, 14 December 1911 his party called a halt and with 'five weather-beaten, frost-bitten fists' grasped their country's flag and planted it at the South Pole.

Shackleton, having previously been to the Antarctic with Scott, set out in early 1914 on his own expedition. While the expedition failed to reach its objective, to walk 1800 miles across the continent, it remains a legend in tales of survival after *Endurance* was crushed in the ice pack and all were forced to abandon ship.

Raymond Priestly, who sailed on an earlier expedition with Shackleton, had this to say: 'Scott for scientific method, Amundsen for speed and efficiency, but when disaster strikes and all hope is gone, get down on your knees and pray for Shackleton.' **,**

PETER ADDS

Because we are navigating similar waters and visiting some of the same places, and because we all come from sailing backgrounds, Shackleton is probably our favourite of the Antarctic pioneers, if only because of his remarkable survival story which included probably the most stunning ocean passage achievement of all time.

Shackleton and the other 27 members of the Imperial Trans-Antarctic Expedition were on the other side (eastern) of the Antarctic Peninsula to us — in the Weddell Sea — when, on 18 January 1915, their vessel *Endurance* was beset by ice off the Luitpold Coast.

They stayed with the vessel, locked in the ice and drifting north with the pack, until 27 October 1915, when the pressure finally proved too much for *Endurance* and she was crushed. Shackleton and his party took to the ice and contemplated their options. They were at 69.5S and 51.30W, alone on the ice pack, nobody aware of their predicament, and rescue a very remote prospect indeed.

The crushed *Endurance* was finally released by the ice and sank on 21 November 1915, at 68.38S and 52.28W. Shackleton and party were left on their drifting pack ice, awaiting their chance to launch the *Endurance*'s three boats and strike out for one of the islands to the north.

They had to wait until 9 April 1916, when the ice floes parted enough to give them a chance in the boats. Clarence Island or Elephant Island were their destination, some 50 to 60 miles north of their position.

After an horrific six-day voyage, battling gales, currents and ice, they finally made it to barren and desolate Elephant Island on the NE tip of the Antarctic Peninsula. It was only a rather tenuous, 30 x 15 metre shale beach clinging to towering cliffs, but they staggered ashore and set foot on land for the first time in 497 days

since *Endurance* had departed South Georgia for the Antarctic mainland on 5 December 1914. During that time they had been exposed to just about everything the often-savage Antarctic Ocean could throw at them and, incredibly, the party was still intact.

It wasn't finished however. Elephant Island was too remote to expect rescue. They would have to reach somewhere known to be visited by whalers if they were to have any chance of salvation. Shackleton and Worsely determined that there were three options — Cape Horn, 500 miles to the NW, the Falkland Islands, 550 miles to the north, and South Georgia Island, 800 miles to the NE. All three involved crossing the Drake Passage and, with winter approaching, the conditions would be predictably nasty in the most challenging part of any ocean on earth.

The journey would be attempted by one boat only — the 7-metre open whaler *James Caird*. The crew of six would comprise Shackleton, Frank Worsley (the *Endurance*'s captain and navigator), Thomas Crean (*Endurance*'s 2nd officer), Harry McNeish (the ship's carpenter), John Vincent (able seaman) and Timothy McCarthy (able seaman). They were hardly in the prime of health and were ill-equipped to say the least. The remainder of the party would remain on Elephant Island until rescue could be achieved.

South Georgia would be the destination. It was further in distance but it offered the best prospects of success given the prevailing conditions in Drake Passage, including a current that could carry them 60 miles a day to the east.

The *James Caird* and her crew departed Elephant Island on 21 April 1916. The whaler was built of Baltic pine planking over a framework of American elm and English oak. McNeish had raised her topsides 15 inches with lumber from the *Endurance* but, even so, when fully loaded for the strike north and east, she still had only two feet of freeboard.

For the next 16 days they were subjected to just about everything the Southern Ocean and Drake Passage had to offer — almost continuous gales from SE, SW, N and NW, two full storms with the wind gusting 60 knots, icing so heavy that the *James Caird* nearly sank, and being overwhelmed by a huge rogue wave that left them floundering and bailing for their lives.

Despite all of this, they still made a precise landfall at South Georgia where they staggered ashore late on 10 May 1916, almost back to where they had started in *Endurance* 522 days before. If you think that was enough for anyone — there was more.

The *James Caird*'s landfall was on the inhospitable and unpopulated south-west coast of South Georgia, completely exposed to the westerlies and south-westerlies roaring through Drake Passage. To find help for their comrades back on Elephant Island, they still had to reach the whaling stations at Stromness or Leith Harbour on the northern coast — a trip of another 130 or so miles by sea, around the southern tip of the island and then north along the coast. But Shackleton's men were

past such a voyage and he determined that the only solution was for three of them to cross the island on foot — a trip of only 30 miles as the crow flies.

The only problem was that the crow didn't fly in South Georgia, some of whose peaks climb to 3000 metres. Plus, the island had never been crossed on foot.

After a few days' rest, Shackleton, Worsley and Crean set out for the Stromness whaling station from where *Endurance* had set out for the Antarctic Continent on 5 December 1914. With screws into the soles of their boots to provide grip in the snow and ice, they again embarked on a journey that healthy, well-rested men would have deemed unachievable, if not impossible.

They almost perished in the freezing cold as they clawed their way over 1200-metre ridges, but two days later, in the late afternoon, they strolled into Stromness whaling station and calmly asked for the factory manager. Were those men, or were those men?

As a footnote to the above, the crossing of South Georgia, as far as is known, has been achieved by only one other party — in 1955 by a fully-equipped British survey team under the leadership of one Duncan Carse. Carse was to observe: 'I do not know how they [Shackleton, Worsley and Crean] did it — except that they had to. Three men of the heroic age of Antarctic exploration with 50 ft of rope between them — and a carpenter's adze.'

Shackleton, at the third attempt, and in a third different vessel, returned to Elephant Island in the seagoing tug *Yelchin* (obtained from the Chilean government). On 30 August 1916, the main party was rescued and one of the most remarkable achievements in the history of exploration, human fortitude and endeavour was complete.

Launching the *James Caird* at Elephant Island for the 800-mile voyage to South Georgia.

14 January 2001

●

Location 10 miles north-west of Hope Bay at the entrance to Antarctic Sound
(at the top of the Antarctic Peninsula)

Latitude 63.20S
Longitude 56.53W
Course 145 deg True
Wind NNW at 10 knots
Sea state Confused and lumpy
Barometer 990 mbs and steady
Air temp 3 deg C
Sea temp 1 deg C

Above A dusting of fresh snow and ice.

Opposite Janot (left) and Ollie find a place to park while waiting for the shore party to return from a closer look at the penguin colonies at Brown Bluff on the eastern tip of the Antarctic Peninsula.

Following page Magnificent and majestic — and aground in 100-metre deep water off Hope Bay at the entrance to the Antarctic Sound (on the northern tip of the Antarctic Peninsula). This is where the big bergs escape the Weddell Sea to sail the high seas of the Southern Ocean until they melt and break up.

The wind in Admiralty Bay increased dramatically during the night and by 2 am was blowing a steady 45 knots plus from the north — straight off the huge glacier at the head of the bay. Janot called me to discuss our situation. We had lots of heavy chain out, and the anchor (very big) was well bedded in the glacial moraine bottom. We had room to leeward if we dragged — more than a mile. But the question was, if we dragged would we then be able to retrieve the anchor and all the chain.

We started the generator to make sure we had lots of instant power if needed, then we started the main diesels to keep them warm. There are heaters in the main engines that warm them up when the generator is running, but we wanted to make sure. Just as well we did. The starboard engine had an airlock that required attending to.

The wind by this time was gusting 50 knots at the masthead and closer to 70 knots at deck level. The spray, straight off the glacier, was hitting the saloon and pilot-house windows and running in torrents. Our anchor held but we decided to wait for a lull and then up-anchor and depart to sea, just in case conditions worsened.

They didn't. At 5 am the wind suddenly eased 10 knots and the metre-high breaking waves diminished. By 6 am we had 8 knots of breeze and a reasonably pleasant morning in the making. Conditions were now perfect for an orderly departure, so we headed out between the stark, ice-clad cliffs of Admiralty Bay, pointing south once again.

We are now motoring towards Hope Bay — a three-kilometre deep indentation at the top of the Peninsula. Hope Bay is off to the west side of 'iceberg alley' where many bergs broken off from the ice in the Weddell Sea to the east of the Peninsula come through Antarctic Sound on their journey out into the South Atlantic. All this afternoon there have been rows of bergs of infinitely different shapes and sizes lining both sides of our course as we head south. Many are grounded in shallow waters (if anyone can call 100-metre deep water shallow) and there are a great number of smaller bits that we are weaving between. This means we have an iceberg watch on the bow at all times — looking out for the bits that are hard to see from aft in the pilot-house.

A large red fishing boat — a ship really — moved north on the other side of the bergs earlier in the afternoon. We understand that they are after the Antarctic toothfish, a highly sought-after species that, in the past three years, has been so totally decimated that there are severe doubts that it will ever recover to former numbers. This mirrors the demise of cod in the North Atlantic, but it is happening much faster. And it is not a problem that is exclusive to cod and toothfish either. It is happening to all species. Far, far more fish are now being taken from the sea than are naturally being produced.

Today, almost one billion people around the world depend on seafood for their basic protein. At the present rate of catch, there will soon not be enough harvested to go round, let alone feed the extra tens of millions more people who, in 20 years' time, will be expecting seafood to be their staple diet. If we are not careful, and if we keep doing what we are doing, there will soon be very few fish at all left in the sea. This is now recognised fact.

15 January 2001

Location At Brown Bluff — right at the top of the Antarctic Peninsula where it meets the Weddell Sea

Leaving Hope Bay behind yesterday, we entered Antarctic Sound and saw 'iceberg alley' at its best. We were weaving between very large bergs — blues, greens, some covered in penguin and bird droppings, some of impossible shapes, some still flat-topped, some that had turned upside down in recent times, some full of bright blue caves. All made from incredibly old ice that, in most cases, was probably far older than mankind itself. Seals hunted in the intense turquoise waters close to the edge of some bergs and penguins — Adelie, gentoo, chinstraps — were everywhere.

We are now at anchor in the shallow waters at Brown Bluff — about eight miles down the eastern end of the Peninsula — a high, brown rock-face of many different hues. Adelie penguins are nesting as far as the eye can see to our left and to our right. Many have their homes high above the water — a long march over the shale slopes from the 'beach'. The land is stained pink, no doubt from the krill that is the penguins' staple diet. The smell, even from several hundred metres away, is rank and strong.

There is continuous traffic through the water past *Seamaster* — outbound and inbound. The large fluffy chicks that are standing around need feeding, so the parents are busy right now. There is also continuous traffic on the shore — penguins entering and leaving the water, making their way to and from their nest sites. It is a place of great activity.

A very large leopard seal (we estimated it to be approximately four metres long) has been cruising backwards and forwards just outside the line of grounded ice floes — waiting to pounce on penguins returning from fishing or about to leave the beach. The penguins on the shore are highly agitated and not entering the water — and who can blame them? Those coming home suddenly go crazy as the seal gets amongst them. We watched as, only a few metres away, the leopard grabbed an unfortunate Adelie and shook it violently back and forth, effectively skinning it. The leopard then appeared calmly on the surface, looking at us with penguin feet sticking out of his jaws. He munched happily for a while before going back for seconds.

Latitude	63.30S
Longitude	56.54W
Conditions	Snowing
Wind	Light
Sea	Calm
Barometer	983 mbs and dropping
Air temp	Plus 3.0 deg C
Sea temp	Minus 1.0 deg C

Above **Penguins, penguins everywhere.**

Opposite **Ice flows grinding ashore off Brown Bluff.**

The other penguins are now very uneasy about entering the water to go out for food. They make their way from their nest sites high above the beach, probably taking an hour or more, to stand in an increasingly bigger group on the sea's edge, watching for the tell-tale signs of danger lurking. Then, as though someone fires a starter gun, they are off — straight out towards the many small icebergs littering the outer limits of the bay. The same sequence is repeated time and again at about 15-minute intervals as the next groups join the building queue.

The returning birds all make high-speed approaches to the gravel shore, almost frantic as they are about to exit the water then visibly relaxing once safe back on the pebbles. Many obviously haven't made it. The bottom is littered with skeletons and pieces of the unfortunate ones that have fallen prey to the killing machines that station themselves just off the beach.

This is all part of the life-and-death cycle of nature in the raw — survival of the fittest in one of the most remote parts of the world. At least these same penguins are now totally protected from a much more dangerous enemy — man. Yet, only 150 or so years ago, we were killing all species of penguins, and seals, and boiling them down for the oil contained in the rich blubber that keeps them warm in the harshest of climates imaginable. The oil was used to light lamps in towns and cities. Many species of penguins and seals were hunted almost to extinction. Thank goodness we learned in time and thank goodness we won't make that mistake again!

Danger lurks in the form of a leopard seal and the penguins are reluctant to take to the water.

Following page In the mist of the morning *Seamaster* ghosts past a magnificent iceberg.

21 January 2001

Location Half Moon Island

We have still been passing the most enormous icebergs imaginable — many more of them than when we entered 'iceberg alley' a few days ago, and much, much bigger. Huge, blue, new tabular bergs; craggy, worn, old, castellated bergs; bergs that have turned upside down; bergs on their sides — all with one thing in common. They are immense.

The bergs comprise billions of tonnes of frozen water being released into the oceans — but first they will sail their ghostly paths through currents for a year or two, or more, gradually diminishing in size; very old water that was laid down as the snowfalls of millenniums ago, full of the nutrients and microscopic life that are so important to the beginning of the marine food chain.

The view we have on this clear but freezing-cold evening, as the sun is heading for the horizon, is one of enormity — both in size and in age. Nature at her grandest in a form impossible for man to replicate.

Chris Coffin, a good friend from the United States who is helping us with blakexpeditions and who is on board for a brief visit to the ice, has been studying icebergs and has this to offer:

Latitude	62.35S
Longitude	59.54W
Conditions	Damp with drizzle
Wind	Calm
Sea	Calm
Barometer	990 mbs and falling
Air temp	5 deg C
Sea temp	2 deg C

'Many people have asked me why I want to go to Antarctica — 'just a bunch of penguins and ice'. They are partially right. There are a lot of penguins and certainly a lot of ice, But they are wrong on the 'just'. Since our first iceberg sighting on our way down to Hope Bay, I have continued to be amazed by the 'ice sculptures' floating in the Southern Ocean and the Antarctic Sound. Whether a tabular berg or a small floating 'bergy bit' shaped as a swan or whale, they are amazing. The sea and wind carve these blocks and each is highly individualistic and has unique colouring, from a traditional white ice to a deep blue only created by intense pressure over long periods of time. There are cathedral bergs with tall spires, with large arches, and some with ski slopes that the penguins slide down. There are bergs with blue-ice 'beaches' — slightly submerged ice plateaus where the seals and penguins play.

They are all beautiful and they come in all sizes (as well as shapes). The bergy bits range from a square metre to 10 square metres or so (no real limit defined). Our most recent 'Sea Ice Edge Report' (used for navigation) noted three large icebergs, one 20 x 20 nautical miles, another 3 x 14 nautical miles, and one 8 x 29 nautical miles. Just amazing!

We have added a new dimension to our study of these bergs. While at Half Moon Island, we donned our drysuits, full-face masks, and the rest of our scuba equipment and went diving on a bergy bit just off our bay. The berg was about 15 metres by 30 metres with a maximum of 3 metres above the water. It was in a little over 20 metres of water and hung up. That made it about 25 metres tall from bottom to top.

As we entered the water, there was a feeling of excitement because no one on our team had ever been next to one of these. We were careful to make sure we weren't diving under a ledge in case it dropped off while we were close to it. Approaching the berg, we could feel the water temperature drop, especially when we were less than 3 metres away.

At first, in poor visibility, the berg appeared milky/bluish white. Then, as we approached the face of the berg at about 6 metres below the surface, the artwork was revealed. We were greeted with a smooth, concave, and also dimpled surface. There were crystal-clear, almost completely transparent shafts of ice going right through the berg, and layers of blue ice where pressure had done its work. There were smooth cut-outs, like those created when you melt an ice cube under warm water. There were channel cracks that went deep into the ice, likely spots where the berg will break later in its life.

Thank you, God, for providing us with such majestic beauty!'

Amazing ice sculptures — carved by wind and waves.

Don ('Captain Rabbit') has decided to implement a scheme of his own involving the sale of icebergs, and has sent the following letter to some of his friends:

'I have been lucky enough to meet the Executive Directors of the Solid Block Investment Company. This company specialises in a resource that has never been tapped — icebergs. In this part of the world, these magnificent blocks vary in size from the regular half acre to as large as 1000 square kilometres.

The blocks come with full building permits and enjoy the unique status of being the only real estate investment that has multiple sea views and changing locations.

Full details of the company and the directors are being sent to you from the Long-&-Short-of-It Investment Brokers who are arranging banking facilities in the Cayman Islands.

In the meantime, please send, as a token of your good faith and a sign of interest in making 234% return per week, the sum of US$50,000 to our bankers.

There is no time to lose. Be in while the bergs are at 60 south. We cannot be responsible for your investment if you wait until they reach warmer waters.'

Seamaster on a beautiful day at Half Moon Island (in the McFarlane Strait between Greenwich and Livingston Islands in the South Shetlands).

23 January 2001

⬡

Location Andersen Harbour, Omega Island

Latitude	64.18S
Longitude	62.55W
Wind	Southerly 15 knots
Sea	Smooth
Barometer	980 mbs and steady
Conditions	Sleeting
Air temp	2 deg C
Sea temp	1 deg C

Andersen Harbour, Melchior Islands. This harbour is formed in the gap between Omega and Eta Islands. We are anchored towards the head of the bay in quiet conditions, surrounded by high ice cliffs and rolling snow-covered ice hills that would support a ski resort in any other part of the world. There is no one else around — just us. The ice cliffs look as though they have been worked on by a massive ice cream scoop.

An ice floe, aground in the bay just astern of us, capsized this morning, breaking into many pieces as it rolled over. As a result, the bay is littered with lumps of ice everywhere. The ice cliffs that surround us are full of caves and holes and vary from snow white to pale blues, to those patchworked in pale green lichen.

I'm not going to apologise if we continue to be surprised and amazed. It is that sort of voyage — one of personal discovery — and we are never sure what we will find around the next corner. Just when we think we are viewing nature at her ultimate, we are staggered by the realisation that there is no 'finite' in nature. There will always be something new to discover that is better yet.

To live here permanently would be unthinkable for us humans. We wouldn't be able to survive without considerable external assistance. Even now, in the Antarctic summer months, if we were left ashore in our daily work clothes we would probably be as

stiff as boards by the morning. We would not be able to survive even one night — imagine what it must be like in the dark winter months?

But this is home to the enormous amount of life that we see, and the animals and birds not only survive — they thrive — and this time of the year is when food is most plentiful. This is their time to raise their young, to breed, and to grow fat ready for the next winter just around the corner.

In more recent times, however, man has entered that equation. We influence the state of the oceans that produce the food that these creatures depend upon. And we pillage the fish stocks at levels that cannot be sustained — even for our own good. We are upsetting the balance of nature like never before. Dr Sylvia Earle, a remarkable ocean research marine biologist and scientist of great standing, has the following thoughts on ocean conservation:

'If I could choose one thing to do with my life, that would make a difference, it would be to try to protect as much of the wild ocean as possible, actually, the wild planet as a whole. We are dependent on nature and we somehow, when we live in cities, forget where oxygen comes from. We forget that we are connected to systems that shape the character of the planet. The ocean in particular is our life support system. It is an ancient ocean, ancient systems, and we are newcomers. If we do in our lifetime whatever is possible to embrace these wild areas and the creatures who are our fellow citizens on this ocean planet, to take care of them, that would be the best gift we could have for future generations.'

'The ice cliffs look as though they have been worked on by a massive ice cream scoop.'

25 January 2001

Location Danco Island, Errera Channel

1900hrs: We up-anchored at the Melchior Islands around 0900hrs and didn't get here to drop anchor off Danco Island until 1730hrs. It was only 30 miles or so but, as we motored slowly southwards down Dallman Bay towards the Gerlache Strait, the cry of 'Thar she blows' came from Janot, high up in the crow's-nest. This sent the the divers and cameraman scrambling into their drysuits.

We lingered near a number of whales for a few hours, first a female humpback and her calf moving very slowly on the surface, then several minkes. We stopped the engines, turned off the steering pumps, echo sounder and generator, and just drifted in the clear, cold, morning air.

A pair of minkes came up right next to us and stayed alongside for quite a while — so close that when they 'blew' we sure knew about it on deck. The spray was covering the lens of the big camera and the smell was — well, as you would expect — very fishy. What a marvellous experience. We were all on a high for quite a while afterwards.

Seamaster is now anchored off the northern end of Danco Island in about 35 metres of water — shallow enough to hopefully stop the bigger bergs that are making their way out of the channel from bumping us. The smaller ones are scraping along the topsides as I sit and write this.

The view from on deck is — well, it is unbelievable. The channel is like a mirror, the high mountains all around reflected in the dark surface of the water. All of the icebergs are reflected in the same way and the bay is littered with ice as far as the eye can see.

The gentoo penguins on Danco Island appear to have had a very successful breeding season with most adult pairs raising two chicks. Many of the young are already in their final plumage. Not too many weeks now before they will be having to fend for themselves. To climb slowly around the rookery — split into many separate areas, some right on top of the island — meant keeping a watchful eye out for the skuas. These beautiful, multi-brown sea-birds are the scavengers, ever watchful for the opportunity to raid a penguin nest and grab a young chick.

We followed the gentoo paths up through the snow — quite deep furrows that are their tracks to and from the sea, way below. It was comical to see several on the track going up and a number on the same track, going down. They didn't even acknowledge one another as they passed. Don and I walked up a furrow in the snow that was only a few metres across from their main thoroughfare. We were walking side by side — humans and penguins. They gave us a cursory glance, but that was about all.

It was amazing to see how fast they went, and how good they are at climbing the steep and rocky hillsides that they call home. When they reached the nest site they were greeted by ravenous chicks that were much smaller than the parents, wanting as much food in as short a time as possible. We sat and watched them for a long time.

Latitude	64.43S
Longitude	62.36W
Wind	Calm
Sea	Mirror-like
Barometer	988 mbs and steady
Air temp	12 degrees C
Sea temp	0.5 degrees C

Above **Alistair, Jackie, Marc and Janot.**
Opposite page **Gentoo penguins.**
Left **The view from the deck is unbelievable.**

30 January 2001

Location Port Lockroy

Latitude 64.49S
Longitude 63.29W
Wind Very light and variable
Sea Calm
Barometer 980 mbs and falling
Air temp 16 deg C
Sea temp Minus 1 deg C
Conditions Fine with some high cloud

The young gentoo penguins were relaxing in the sunshine. They can really relax too — spread-eagled face down on the shingle or rocks, their big feet and wings spread, fast asleep with seemingly not a care in the world. We counted 25 young in a 'creche' being looked after by eight adults. Neither the adults nor the chicks were the slightest bit concerned about our presence.

Ken and Jim from the British base here came to dinner on board *Seamaster* last night. One of their jobs is to keep a check on visitor influence on the penguins. So half of their island is open to visitors and half is closed (as a control). They told us that there appeared to be no noticeable difference in penguin behaviour over the past four years between the visited compared to the unvisited sites. Mind you, the gentoos seem a very relaxed bird anyway.

This will not, however, be the case much longer. The young are developing fast and in a few weeks will go into the water for the first time. For some it will be the last. The leopard seals, building up their own reserves for the coming winter by eating as many of the penguins as possible, will be waiting. It will be a leopard seal banquet and the sea will turn red.

Imagine being a penguin — a lovely, fluffy chick. You avoid being attacked by skuas in your early years, you hope that Mum or Dad don't get taken by a leopard seal and not come home with the food, and you finally make it into adulthood. Then, on your first swim, you are greeted at the water's edge by a killing machine intent on no good.

Approximately 40 per cent that hatch don't make it — nature is not kind. But as long as man keeps away from the mass slaughter of yesteryear, the penguins will continue to thrive. Their only natural enemy should be the leopard seal. Man should not be a factor. The problem, however, is that we still are. Maybe we aren't knocking the penguins on the head and turning them into fine leather for shoes and oil for our machines, as we were not too long ago. But we are now attacking them in a far more insidious way — slowly destroying their habitat. The future for all the animals, birds and fish in the Antarctic is looking bleaker than ever as global warming and pollution make their marks.

As we head further south, the ice and snow on the land are thickening up. The scientific view, however, is that there is not as much as there used to be — that there is more exposed rock than ever before. Global warming is having an effect, there is no longer any doubt about it. Will it be enough of an effect to cause the oceans to rise? The latest thinking is 'Yes', that a rise in sea levels globally of at least a metre is almost guaranteed.

There will be those that may not agree, but the informed consensus is that global warming, accelerated by the increased burning of fossil fuels and the consequent release of enormous quantities of carbon and other nasties into the atmosphere, is already having a serious effect on the world's climate.

A warmer atmosphere for the Antarctic may not mean a lot in the short term (say the next 10 years), but in the long term (the next 100 years) it could be disastrous — and accelerated global warming is not the only problem we are causing. Toss in pollution through indiscriminate dumping, and exploitation through the pillaging of fish stocks and the chopping down of the rain forests, and you have a right old witches' brew for disaster.

Above The British base at Port Lockroy.

Right Gentoo penguins with nothing to fear from *Seamaster*'s skipper.

2 February 2001

●

Location At anchor at Thorne Point

The anchorage we are now in — just a gap between a couple of small islands and the shore — is very peaceful. It is normally solid ice at this time of the year.

The large inlet leading southwards down the narrows inside Adelaide Island is normally not navigable, but this year it is — for the first time in memory according to a ship's captain we met two nights ago. He has been in this part of the Antarctic (on passenger ships) every year for the past 25 years, and has never seen it like this. He told us that temperatures here on the Peninsula were, on average, now 1.4 degrees C warmer than 25 years ago. We also understand that there is (comparatively) little ice further south towards the George VI ice shelf at latitude 70 degrees south — our destination. We will have to wait and see for ourselves.

Looking at the mountains as we came south today, the huge granite slabs and pinnacles (nunataks), it is interesting to reflect on how long it has taken for the earth to be shaped the way it is and the different forms it has taken, about the arrival of life on the planet and how it has developed so diversely over so many millions of years, and the 'fit' of each species and why.

This shaping, which has taken since the beginning of time, arrived at a wondrous and sustainable balance of elements and species. But one very dominant species — man — emerged and is now altering that balance. Man is now so superior to everything else that he can do what he likes, or at least he thinks he can. Not so. As Dr Sylvia Earle has stated:

> In our lifetimes, we have witnessed what is literally a sea change. Our generation came along at a time when natural ocean systems were largely intact. In a few decades, our species has squandered assets that have been thousands of millennia in the making — and we're still doing it! Even children have witnessed changes caused by trashing beaches that were pristine a few years ago. What we must do is encourage a sea change in attitude, one that acknowledges that we are a part of the living world, not apart from it.

Andy (our cameraman for the television documentaries) was hoping to film a leopard seal in action with the penguins leaving the shore. A couple of leopard seals came around all right, but were very camera shy. Marc (one of our professional divers) kept turning Andy around to face the seal, but the seal made a point of staying behind Andy — often much less than a metre away.

Leopard seals are not known to be dangerous to man but, when you see how they deal to unfortunate penguins, it is a good idea to treat them with the utmost respect. They are powerful, extremely fast and have a mouth full of very sharp teeth.

Latitude	66.57S
Longitude	67.12W
Wind	Fresh southeasterly (katabatic)
Sea	Calm at anchor but rough at sea
Barometer	998 mbs and rising
Air temp	6 deg C
Sea temp	0 deg C
Conditions	Fine and sunny

Above **A tranquil anchorage in the Argentine Islands where normally there is only ice.**
Left **The business end of a leopard seal.**

Animals of Antarctica

Whales

There Leviathan,
Hugest of all living creatures, in the deep
Stretched like a promontory sleeps or swims,
And seems a moving land; and at his gills
Draws in, and at his breath spouts out a sea

Milton, *Paradise Lost*

There are 10 species of baleen and toothed whales commonly found in Antarctic waters. They are:

Baleen

Blue (*Balaenoptera musculus*)
Fin (*Balaenoptera physalus*)
Humpback (*Megaptera novaeangliae*)
Minke (*Balaenoptera acutorostrata*)
Southern right (*Balaena glacialis australis*)
Sei (*Balaenoptera borealis*)

Toothed

Orca (*Orcinus orca*)
Southern bottlenose (*Hyperoodon planifrons*)
Southern fourtooth (*Berardius arnuxii*)
Sperm (*Physeter macrocephalus*)

The ones we would most like to encounter are:

Blue whales

True giants. The largest animal in the history of life on earth — as large as the largest dinosaur, and several times its mass. Blue whales can achieve lengths of 30 metres (100 feet) or more and weigh close to 84 tonnes. Seeing a blue up close is supposed to be one of the most exciting spectacles in nature.

The blue comes to Antarctica to feed on the vast resource of krill that thrive here as the ice fields melt during

the summer. They may consume more than eight tonnes per day. It is estimated that, at the height of the summer, the total weight of krill in Antarctica is equal to five times the weight of all of the humans on the planet. No wonder there is so much life in these waters.

A humpback whale taking a closer look at *Seamaster*.

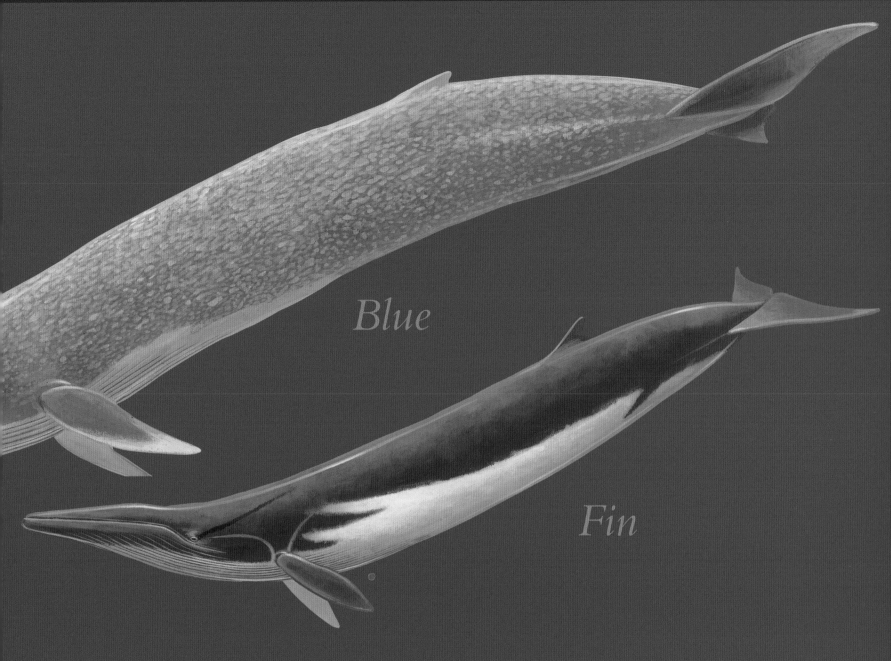

Blue

Fin

At the end of the Antarctic summer, when krill is no longer abundant in these waters, the blue migrates north to still unknown breeding grounds, living off its blubber and gathering in small groups for mating. The females breed only once every three years. The young whales feed on their mother's milk, which is so rich that they can put on weight at between four and five kilograms per hour.

The blue is almost completely reliant on krill for its diet and, given the huge amounts that it consumes, is the first species to be vulnerable to changes in the environment that have a detrimental effect on the essential food chain.

The blue was a prime target for whalers, and had by the 1950s been hunted almost to extinction. According to one authoritative source, only about 1000 to 5000 survive today and it is not known if that number is increasing.

I have never seen a blue but hopefully that will change. It is staggering that, even though the blue is a highly endangered species, it is still being hunted, when the chance arises, by some of those who, even in these informed times, choose not to accept the consequences of their actions.

Fin

The fin whale is the second largest of all whales, reaching lengths of 20 metres (66 feet) and weights of up to 50 tonnes. Long, sleek and hydrodynamically perfect, fin whales have been built for speed, and have been called the greyhounds of the ocean.

The fin usually prefers to feed north of the ice and does not migrate as far south as the blue. The attraction of going south however is the same — huge quantities of krill. The fin's diet is not as almost-exclusively krill as the blue's though. It also eats small schooling fish.

Fin whales can burst to speeds of 25-plus knots to catch prey. They have been protected since 1978 but are known to be taken by the Japanese in their 'scientific whaling' programme. It is estimated that only about 80,000 remain.

Humbback

*He is the most gamesome and light-hearted of all
the whales, making more gay foam and white water
than any other of them.*

Herman Melville, *Moby Dick*

The most curious of all whales, which is what brings the
humpback into frequent contact with man and boats — a
trait which has contributed to its downfall as a species.

The humpback can weigh as much as 32 tonnes and
reach 20 metres (51 feet) in length. Bulkier in shape and less
streamlined than the blue or the fin, it also has very long
pectoral flippers. The head is covered with bumps called
tubercles, each of which carries a single stiff hair rather like
a cat's whisker. The hairs are probably sensory in nature.

The humpback makes the same north–south
migrations as the blue, but it generally stays close to
coasts and breeds in shallow water. It is the only whale
known to use a feeding technique employing bubbles —
which it exhales at depth, with others, to form a bubble
net that traps or confuses the prey and allows the whales
to 'gulp em up'.

By the early 1960s, humpback numbers had been
reduced to around 1000 to 3000 animals.

A humpback struts its stuff
for an appreciative
Seamaster crew.

Minke

The minke is a lightweight when compared with the blue,
fin or humpback. It weighs in at around seven tonnes and
measures around eight metres (26 feet) in length.
Probably because of their size, they tended to be ignored
by whalers until the early 1970s but, between the
1974–75 (Antarctic) summer and the whaling moratorium
in 1985, they became the whalers' prime baleen whale
target in Antarctic waters.

The minke makes the same north–south migration as
its relatives and also feeds mainly on krill when roaming
the edge of the ice pack. Little is known, however, about
how it gets to and from the ice.

Sperm

The sperm weighs in at around 30 tonnes and measures
around 14 metres (46 feet) and is the largest of the
toothed whales. It was a principal target of the whalers in
Antarctic waters in the second half of the eighteenth
century and the first half of the nineteenth.

The sperm-whaling industry collapsed around 1850,
due to the greatly reduced numbers of sperm to be found
and to a reduced demand for whale oil. But it became a
target again in the 1950s and the first half of the 1960s
when an estimated 5000 animals a year were taken, until
hunting was halted in 1979.

Orca

The orca weighs around eight tonnes and is around
seven metres (23 feet) long. It is much more diversified
than the others in that it can be found in all oceans, from
the tropics to the ice. In Antarctic waters, orcas feed
mainly on penguins and seals.

Whalers in the Antarctic paid little attention to the
orca and numbers in Antarctic waters are estimated at
more than 200,000. Russian ships killed
nearly 1000 in the late 1970s,
however, and hunting was
subsequently banned.

To have been next to some
of these magnificent creatures;
to have looked into their eyes;
to have seen them in mid-
ocean; to have witnessed them
hunting under the pack ice for
food — just a few metres away
from where we stood; to have
watched them gather in a group
and hear them talk and sing to each other;
to have seen mother and calf together; to know that
some stay together all their lives; that some
communicate over many hundreds of miles; that they
are some of the greatest travellers ever — means I have
great trouble understanding why, even in these so-
called enlightened years, the whales are still being
hunted for profit.

Humpback

Minke

Sperm

Orca

Fur Seals

The Antarctic fur seals were all but wiped out but have recovered remarkably well. They appear intelligent, are very streamlined and amazing swimmers, and have quite a sense of fun. There is no doubt that playing is part of an average day for the young ones. They roll and twist and frolic in the shallow waters, often appearing to have mock battles — and then curl up next to, or on top of, one another when back on the shore.

They all have very large brown eyes, fine faces with small protruding ears, and very long whiskers. They can move quite fast on land compared to other seals — with their hind feet useful for walking as well as swimming (don't get between a mature fur seal and the sea). In the water they are very fast and can change course very rapidly.

Adult males grow to almost two metres long, are stoutly built, with heavy neck and shoulders. Their bulky appearance is enhanced by a striking mane of long shoulder fur. They can weigh over 100 kg. Females are only 1.5 metres long, are more slenderly built, have no mane and weigh less than 50 kg. Their fur consists of a dense, velvety underpelt about 2.5 centimetres long — waterproof and virtually windproof — with an outer layer of coarse guard hairs.

The world population of the Antarctic fur seal is now estimated to have reached more than 300,000, but when you consider that the South Shetland Islands alone, within four years of their discovery in 1819, yielded 320,000 fur seal skins to British and American sealers, the total population today is still very small. They were so nearly wiped out.

There is no real reason why they should be hunted at all any more. Yet what is astounding is that it has been agreed (by whom, I have to ask) that some sealing can continue within the Antarctic zone — i.e. south of latitude 60 degrees south. 'Someone' has decided that it is all right to hunt various types of seals because there are enough of them to not threaten such species with extinction. I would like to bet that this 'someone' has not sat and watched the seals for hours as we have, has not had the one-on-one experiences that we have, has not marvelled at how magnificent and well adapted these animals are, has not witnessed them having fun together, playing and obviously enjoying one another's company. This is identical to the thinking in some countries (that should know better) that commercial whaling should again be allowed, even if the rest of the world has decided it is wrong.

Antarctic fur seals enjoying the sun.

Me Emperor Penguin

'Assume I am an emperor penguin.

'I am the biggest penguin of all. I weigh up to 40 kg (90 pounds) or more, twice as much as the king penguin, and I can be more than one metre tall (up to 42 inches). I need this body mass as insulation against extremes of temperatures and weather.

'I will probably never touch solid ground in my lifetime, which can be as long as 50 years. My mate and I will always breed on sea ice, sometimes as far as 160 kilometres (100 miles) from the open sea itself.

'There are approximately 40,000 of us breeding pairs in the world — scattered all around the edge of the Antarctic Continent but using only about 40 breeding colonies, which are all on the rim of the continent. We mate around March/April as the days darken to twilight. My mate lays a single egg then transfers it to me while she goes back to the sea to regain her fighting weight.

'I deliberately stack on the weight, probably around 10 kg, prior to this time, gorging myself in preparation. My favourite food is fish (95 per cent of my diet) and squid (three per cent), with a small amount of crustaceans. I usually hunt for my food in the twilight zone at about 50 metres (165 feet) below the surface of the sea, but I can dive as deep as 450 metres (1500 feet). I can stay underwater for up to 18 minutes or so without needing to take a breath. I can also swim on the surface at nearly eight kilometres per hour.

'Throughout the depths of winter, my male friends and I stand together on the ice — come hail or snow, storms or blizzards, with the eggs on our feet. The cold is intense but we have a flap of skin that covers the egg to protect it from the elements. We shelter each other in enormous huddles, our backs to the wind and driving snow, packed so tight that 10 of us adults can fit into a square metre. This cuts our heat loss in half but, boy, are we hungry when our chicks hatch on our feet in mid-winter after two months of incubation and no food.

'Miraculously our mates, who have fattened themselves up at sea during this period, now return and take over parental duties. Even though I have lost half of my body weight, I still give the new chick its first meal of a secretion of fat and protein from my crop. Then it's time for me to trudge the distance to the sea to feed, a journey that might take several days.

'Our chick soon moults into its first suit of down. Fed at first by its mother, then by me (once I've put on weight again), the youngster joins a crèche when about six weeks old and fledges (in the spring) when about five months old, when the shortest walk to maximum food is available.

'In a hard season, when the sea ice doesn't crack and expose the sea, many chicks will die. But, if all goes as it has for ages, the sea ice will split open just long enough to allow our new generation of emperors to slip away before Antarctica closes in again.'

Ollie

PETER ADDS

Penguins in general have become the symbol of Antarctica. They are ancient birds. Fossils reveal that they were once nearly two metres tall. They were first seen by a Welshman in the sixteenth century. He called them 'pen gwyn', which is Welsh for 'white head'. The name stuck.

Penguins have such fine, dense feathers that their skins were once put to a number of uses in the world of fashion. The early Antarctic explorers and, more recently, Antarctic scientists, used king penguin skins for fancy slippers. The thick layer of fat beneath penguin skins (2 cm thick in the case of kings) was also sought after.

In 1867, one company alone is reported to have collected 115,000 litres of blubber from 405,600 birds. It was the kind of slaughter that eventually aroused naturalists to press for legislation against such practices.

King penguins were killed in large numbers on the island of South Georgia, for their oil. The king is now protected, as are all penguins, thank goodness.

The emperor penguin — probably the most loved symbol of Antarctica.

5 February 2001

Location Pourquoi Pas Island

Latitude 67.45S
Longitude 67.43W
Wind Light and variable at anchor — fresh easterly elsewhere
Sea Slight
Barometer 995 mbs and steady
Air temp 3 deg C
Sea temp 0 deg C
Visibility Unlimited

A day on the 'beach' for a group of Weddell seals — all part of the summer fattening process.

We are back at our 'anchorage' under Pourquoi Pas Island, between a couple of underwater rocky reefs — probably glacial moraines — in about 30 metres depth of water. We are surrounded on all sides by an underwater ridge of 10 metres or less that keeps the bigger icebergs out.

There were a number of bergs stranded around the edge of our 'basin' last night, giving us a feeling of protection. Some have floated away on the high tide and are lying stranded, closer to the rocky shore. The ice falling off the ice cliffs only a few hundred metres away fills the bay with brash from time to time. This spreads out and comes knocking and scraping past *Seamaster*'s hull. This is no place for a painted fibreglass yacht.

Pourqoui Pas Island is named after the ship of the French explorer Jean Baptiste Charcot. He organised a French national expedition to the Antarctic in 1903 and charted large parts of the Antarctic Peninsula region. This work was to be of great importance to navigators in the years to come.

Charcot returned in 1908, in *Pourquoi Pas*, the most modern polar ship of its day. Besides exploring and charting further coasts and islands, he tested a lot of new equipment, such as electric lamps, anti-snow blindness goggles, a petrol-engined motor boat and different types of clothing. Charcot was a very humane person and was known as 'the polar gentleman'. He was one of the first to point out the dangers of overharvesting the whales.

On Anchorage Island we found southern elephant seals. There were about 19 females (cows) to the one male (bull) and a number of young. These elephant seals are not known to breed so far south. They would normally be found on the subantarctic islands where there are beaches and tussock to lie on. So, we can now add a new breeding site to the list — one a long way further south. Is this another sign of a different climate developing?

The southern elephant is the largest seal in the world, with bulls, at up to 4000 kg, substantially larger than the cows at around 900 kg. Their food consists mainly of squid, plus fish caught in deep dives that last in excess of 30 minutes and have been recorded to depths of 1000 metres. Pups are born in mid-October, and during the four weeks of lactation may gain weight at a rate of up to 9 kg a day, while the cow may lose 135 kg in the process, starving all the time.

The southern elephant seals were decimated by man's need (and greed) for more and more oil.

6 February 2001

●

George VI Sound beckons. We want to see what has happened to the George VI ice shelf that fills the channel (the Sound) between Alexander Island and the mainland at the base of the Antarctic Peninsula. Indications are that it has receded dramatically, especially over the past eight to 10 years. We probably won't make it to the face of the ice shelf itself. It is dropping so much old ice into the sea as it recedes and the channel is full of it. We are, however, going to give it a go.

We are in the middle of Marguerite Bay as I write this — heading south and about to turn to starboard to round the Flyspot Islands.

The calm sea that we are motoring in is normally a mass of fast ice, but not this year. For the first time that anyone can remember, it is totally ice-free. There are, however, many magnificent bergs never far away, always in sight like pale ghost ships. Many have piled onto the shallow areas around various islands and reefs and will end their days there, gradually decaying and eventually leaving nothing to show for their having been. The bits that are continually breaking away from those magical white-blue cliffs are a nuisance that we need to constantly watch out for.

The mountains away to port, near Windy Valley and our destination, nearly 60 miles away on the starboard bow, are showing crystal clear in the midday sunshine. We could see the high peaks of Alexander Island over 100 miles away before we up-anchored this morning.

Latitude	69.15S
Longitude	69.12W
Wind	Light southerly
Sea	Slight
Barometer	995 mbs and steady
Air temp	1 deg C and falling
Sea temp	0 deg C
Conditions	Very pleasant but getting colder
Visibility	Unlimited

Ice carvings on a grand scale in Marguerite Bay.

7 February 2001

Latitude 69.52.4S
Longitude 68.48.5W
Wind Light southerly
Sea Calm
Barometer 998 mbs and rising
Air temp 1 deg C
Sea temp Minus 1 deg C
Visibility Unlimited with a blue haze over distance
Conditions Amazing

1600hrs: All we can see now to the south is snow and ice — miles and miles of it.

To the west and east as I look from the pilot-house is more ice, plus distant high mountains and glaciers. To the north, behind *Seamaster*, are patches of sea — full of icebergs.

We are 7.6 miles short of latitude 70 degrees. This is as far south as we can get. No vessel could go further, not this year. Probably no vessel has ever been as far south in this arm of George VI Sound. In previous years, where we are now would have been frozen solid. So would the rest of the Sound through which we have just passed with comparative ease.

In 1974, the permanent ice shelf was where we are moored now. The shelf has, however, receded at approximately one sea mile per year for the past 26 years or so. So, this year, that shelf is at least another 25 miles further south through the ever thickening and permanent sea ice that fronts it.

It is far too deep to anchor — probably 100 metres or more — so *Seamaster* is tied to the edge of the thick sea ice, a much better alternative in the circumstances.

Getting here was interesting, threading our way through quite heavy concentrations of ice at times. *Seamaster* crunched through and over some of the very flat, low-lying sea ice as we tested her ice-breaking capabilities. It's quite a strange feeling to purposely speed up to between 6 and 7 knots and plough up and onto the ice, break a path and carry on, leaving some of our blue bottom paint behind in memory of our passage.

There were sections, sometimes of a few miles, where there was no ice at all — just open water in which we could maintain normal cruising speed. Finally, though, and as expected, the big ice began to close in and there were few lanes of open water. We had to wend our way backwards and forwards the last miles through this ice to reach our destination late this morning.

It was a real thrill to suddenly come to a great expanse of open water, having just been hemmed in, and to then see the line of solid ice and snow stretching the 18 miles or so right across the Sound a few miles in front of us. And there to greet us was a solitary emperor penguin, plus Adelies waddling along in twos and threes. Seals were dotted about on the ice, asleep. A whale blew to starboard.

Alistair, Janot and Marc went ashore to prepare for us to come alongside the edge of the ice. We then aimed *Seamaster* at the 'shore' and went straight in, riding well up on the edge. We kept the motors engaged ahead to stop her sliding back off while the big bowline was

Above *Seamaster* dwarfed by a 500-metre high berg that is aground in Marguerite Bay — in 1000-metre deep water.

Right The sea ice barrier stretches for miles on either side of *Seamaster*'s parking spot.

looped around a convenient large lump of old blue ice maybe 20 metres back from the shore.

Seamaster now has two bowlines holding her to the ice and a stern line secured to a climber's ice anchor screwed into the surface. We are able to get off and on *Seamaster* using a large fender as a step.

It is fantastic. The high mountains on either side look close, but are in fact a long way away. The air is blue with distance and the wildlife is the best we have seen since arriving in Antarctica.

A large female leopard seal cruised along the edge, 'spy-hopping' (looking for an unwary penguin too close to the ice edge). She stayed awhile to watch what we were doing. Andy was later looking at two emperor penguins through his binoculars, and saw the leopard seal leap onto the ice and grab one of them.

I was standing on the ice right by *Seamaster* when a Weddell seal suddenly exploded out of the water next to my feet. I thought for an instant that it was the leopard seal back for a visit, but the first Weddell was immediately joined by another who appeared to take great exception to the fact that *Seamaster* had pinched his parking spot, and told us so.

The Weddells, in their rather ungainly but obviously efficient way, quickly moved off across the ice to join a colleague already asleep behind a small ice hill right next to our anchoring bowline. They are there now all asleep and not the slightest concerned about the creatures in yellow or their big grey polar yacht.

An iceberg we estimated at around 60 million tonnes passed a few hundred metres astern of us, drifting slowly on the current coming from under the sheet of sea ice. It was part of a veritable conveyer belt of bergs being spawned by a large glacier away to our east amongst the blueness of the distant mountains.

Seamaster — moored to sea ice and as far south as she can go in George VI Sound.

8 February 2001

●

Location Alongside the sea ice in George VI Sound

Latitude 69.52S
Longitude 68.48W
Wind 10 knot southerly
Sea Calm
Barometer 994 mbs and falling
Air temp Minus 5 deg C at night (presently plus 4 deg C)
Sea temp 0 deg C
Conditions Excellent
Visibility Unlimited — probably more than 100 miles

Above **Skipper and boat at 69.52 degrees South.**

Opposite **Antarctic seas require careful negotiation. We did most of our navigation during daylight hours as the smaller bergs that are continually on the move create hidden dangers. We nervously attempted night-time navigation only when we had to.**

While the others were involved with diving, I had a telephone call to make to Nairobi — to the headquarters of the United Nations Environment Programme (UNEP). Environment ministers from more than 80 countries were gathered to talk through the problems of global warming and other ecological issues.

UNEP asked blakexpeditions to talk to the meeting, live by satellite phone from our present position here at the bottom of the Antarctic Peninsula, to describe what we had found over the past few days and weeks. To be here on *Seamaster*, on a piece of sea that no one has ever been on before (because it is normally frozen) really brought home what is actually happening to the ice in this part of the world.

It was quite extraordinary to be standing on sea ice in my survival suit, describing what I could see to an important group of people many thousands of miles away in a completely different environment — a very real example of the potential of modern communications.

Talking about the environment in general is a passion of mine. Even so, I would never consider myself a 'greenie'. But to be here in Antarctica on such a beautiful day, amidst this most incredible scenery, and be able to say what I really felt was very special, particularly when those government representatives listening in Nairobi effectively hold the ecological future of this planet in their hands. Or do they?

It is very necessary that their hearts are behind making a difference in the way we care for this world of ours, but often they are hamstrung by constraints

(political and commercial) that are difficult to overcome. So it is now going to be more and more up to individuals who will accept nothing less than what is needed to enable nature to accommodate our presence on the planet.

That is the reason for blakexpeditions and what we are doing. We want to educate and encourage as many people as possible to want to make a difference, and we are using all of the modern communications technologies to do so. To be part of the United Nations Environment Programme, and have them officially on board with us, is a constant reminder that, while we are only a few individuals with certain ideals, there are others who also think the same way. And, between us, we can all help to bring about worthwhile change.

The divers say that the water is very cold and that there is quite a strong current running a few metres below the surface. The visibility for their second dive, for Andy to film the phytoplankton, was down to only a few centimetres without lights.

Our echo sounder gives a depth here of 965 metres — to a rocky bottom. No wonder the immense icebergs, that need many hundreds of metres of water to float in, have no trouble doing so here. Their journeys will see them travel north out of the Sound, the lucky ones spending a few years sailing the cold of the Southern Seas before fading away to become part of the oceans once more. The unlucky ones will be grounded to break up in the comparatively shallow waters at the bottom end of Marguerite Bay. It was like an iceberg graveyard as we passed through on our way here.

9 February 2001

●

Location George VI Sound

Latitude 69.54S
Longitude 68.57W
Wind Light southerly
Sea Smooth
Barometer 990 mbs and falling
Air temp Minus 4 deg C
        minus 7 deg C at night
Sea temp 0 deg C
Conditions Foggy

1000hrs: We decided to move at around 2330hrs yesterday. I was asleep when Alistair came and suggested that it might be a good idea to depart as the huge iceberg that was off our stern all day was on the move and was closing in on our berth alongside the ice. We quickly retrieved the shore lines and steel stake and eased away to the east. Where we were moored was quickly obliterated by the berg.

With the sun setting, we motored along the edge of the ice until we reached a spot that looked friendly. We then drove *Seamaster*'s bow onto the pack so that Alistair and Janot could climb down and sledge-hammer the stake back into the ice to act as a securing point for our bowline.

Immediately, a large leopard seal cruised by. Crabeater seals were everywhere, but very wary of the leopard (I am not surprised). Then a few minke whales

Above **A Weddell seal basking at 70 degrees South.**
Right **Weddell seals playing under** *Seamaster*'s hull.

came right alongside and went under *Seamaster* — disappearing under the sea ice to feed on the krill.

All of this activity, and more, has continued overnight. Even though the air temperature stayed between minus 6 and 7 degrees C, the surface of the sea has shown no signs of freezing. We think that has to do with the current that is flowing from the south under the ice at this point but that we reckon originates further north, in the Southern Ocean, around Alexander Island.

To be alone on watch and hear the sharp blows of the whales nearby, and to have them return time and time again; to see a leopard seal try to catch a crabeater seal by chasing it out of the water and following it onto the ice right next to our bow (with the crabeater hissing and bubbling at his larger foe); to follow the seven or eight seals as they frolicked along the edge of the ice in the misty early morning light — right under our bows — with no hint of concern: just perfect.

There is a thick mist this morning — spreading ice onto the upwind faces of all of the rigging, the masts, the ropes and the dinghy. Any water on the deck is slick ice.

1230hrs: The minke whales are coming past in increasing numbers — sometimes in the distance, sometimes right alongside. They surface and blow loudly several times before submerging below the ice sheet to feed. After 10 to 15 minutes they return and repeat the process.

There are more leopard seals eyeing up the smaller crabeaters asleep near the edge of the ice. The resident leopard has turned on a fine performance, trying (we think without success) to catch an unwary crabeater. He came within a few metres of us as he stalked along the edge of the ice — 'spy-hopping' with his long neck extended so that he could see over the edge and sight his prey. He tried sneaking up on a group of seals gathered some way from the sea to sleep in the sun, and managing to get very close. He grabbed one by the tail, but the crabeater got away (the crabeater can move much faster than the leopard seal when out of the water).

The leopard then spotted an emperor standing right in front of *Seamaster*'s bow. He snuck along the fringe of the ice — carefully popping his head up every so often to check the emperor's whereabouts, then he leapt up onto the ice to make the kill. But the emperor displayed a surprising turn of speed and escaped to safety. The leopard was unsuccessful yet again.

We keep having to remind ourselves that, while leopards killing seals is not pretty to watch, it is all part of life's cycle in the wild. The penguins are part of the natural food chain in this part of the world.

That chain starts with phytoplankton (all the small, single-celled plant life, much of which grows on the underside of the sea ice). Nutrients from the land (trapped in the ice) — nitrates, silicate, phosphate and iron — enter the sea. Sunlight is added (in the summer months) and the phytoplankton develop to become the essential food source for the Antarctic krill and other zooplankton (the animal plankton). Either directly or indirectly, all other animals, ranging from the 30-metre long baleen whales (filter feeders) to birds, fish and squid, depend upon the zooplankton for life-giving sustenance.

The minke whales are gorging themselves on the krill right now. The seals are doing the same — putting on as much blubber as possible in preparation for the lean winter months ahead. Even the leopard seal, that likes to eat penguins, fish and the occasional crabeater, also eats krill — using its sharp teeth as a sieve to strain the krill from the water.

Latitude 69.343

Longitude 69.08W

Wind Very light southerly

Sea Calm

Barometer 980 mbs and rising

Air temp 14 degrees C in the cockpit at 1800hrs

Conditions Sunny with cloud

W talks. The cracks offer noises that sound like a door with squeaky hinges opening, or a rumble that could be traffic on a nearby motorway. Then it is suddenly gone, as quickly as it came. The distant glaciers produce hushed rumblings from time to time. Then quiet envelops us again.

There is no doubt that the ice pack is disintegrating. Huge chunks are breaking away all the time and drifting north out of the Sound. The slab we are tied to right now is kilometres long and, we thought, several kilometres wide. During our walk today, however, we found that, while it is certainly very long, its width has been drastically reduced by a big crack that has developed maybe only 200 metres in front of us and stretching sideways as far as the eye can see. This crack is now between one and two metres wide in places with clear, dark, liquid sea filling the gap. This piece of shelf will soon break off and follow the rest. It has been here for a number of years, but this is its last.

You can also see evidence of the summer months on the trapped bergs nearby. Great long icicles, like clear stalactites made of diamonds, hang by the hundreds inside caves in the ice and all around the overhanging edges. We break off pieces to suck, like ice lollies but with no flavouring, just crystal-clear water.

1800hrs: We are adrift again. Just as I was suiting up for my first Antarctic dive, Don remarked that we were away. I wondered what he meant until I looked ahead and saw that almost the entire ice shelf that we had been walking over this morning was breaking into quite small pieces — all at once. Don said he felt the ice, just prior to the break-up.

As I write this, we are drifting northwards once again, still attached to a piece of drift ice the size of a cricket pitch, but we will shortly need to up-stake and move to a new mooring for the night. The sky is blue with large patches of cloud. The visibility has improved enormously and it is quite warm on deck. The glacier nearby is as clear as it has been — stretching upwards and away into the mountains. The sea is blue, the bergs dazzling white. It's a great afternoon. Ollie has just gone for a swim in a pair of shorts and his orange Hawaiian floral shirt. Nobody else is keen to follow.

Tomorrow we are planning to leave George VI Sound, or at least to make our way through the broken ice and try to make our exit. We will tie up to a berg for the night if the wind lets us and then carry on at full light the following day. The next two days will be days of careful watches, berg avoidance, and a critical check on the weather. There have been many big bergs floating past us while we have been here over the past week, along with significant patches of sea ice breaking loose. It will be interesting to see if we have a reasonably easy exit or have to test *Seamaster*'s ice-breaking capability some more.

The number of bergs going by and the break-up of the old sea ice all around us has made me aware that getting out of the Sound might be a lot more difficult than getting in. The entrance to the Sound has, at times, been choked with ice, right across its 32–kilometre width.

Right Ice lollies — of crystal-clear Antarctic water.

Following page 'All around us the ice quietly "talks". There is a continual hiss of the millions of age-old air bubbles released from the ice into the air. It is a similar sound to that of freshly poured champagne.'

14 February 2001

Location At sea

After a night of drifting, with the pack disintegrating all around us, we started engines at 0930hrs and headed north.

With Alistair up in the crow's-nest, we found our way around the western end of the first line of ice without any trouble. The rest of the Sound ahead of us was blocked apart from a narrow gap right near the shore. Beyond that was a stretch of a few miles of open water — then more ice, solid from side to side.

We pushed and probed until Alistair identified the narrowest point through which we might be able to break through and escape. Making sure that everything below decks was secure, we built up speed and rammed the 1–1.5 metre sea ice that was blocking our way.

Seamaster rode well out of the water, her bow rising at an acute angle, until we ground to a halt with the forward third of the vessel sitting on the ice pack. Slowly, with 168 tonnes of boat weighing down on it, the ice broke into large lumps and parted. *Seamaster* settled back into the water.

We backed off a touch and then surged forward again under full power, straight at the next blockage. The result was the same — *Seamaster* climbing up onto the ice and then forcing it apart with her weight.

With everyone hanging on — particularly Alistair, 25 metres above the deck in the crow's-nest — we repeated the process time and again until, finally, we had punched our way through and were free.

It took us another four hours of weaving our way between bergs and brash ice, with the odd lump of very hard glacial ice, before we reached comparatively open water, but we had escaped the Sound and *Seamaster* had really proven her pedigree as a polar exploration vessel.

Our time in the Sound, moored to the ice pack at a point further south than anyone has been before, was an experience that none of us will ever forget. Thank goodness, though, that we are not going to have to stay for the winter.

Latitude	68.52S
Longitude	68.35W
Wind	Light and variable
Sea	Moderate with a low NW swell
Barometer	984 mbs
Air temp	5.2 deg C
Sea temp	Minus 1 deg C
Conditions	Fine with cloudless sky

Seamaster pushes and probes her way through the brash ice in George VI Sound.

Latitude	67.11S
Longitude	67.35W
Wind	Southerly of 10 to 15 knots
Sea	Smooth
Barometer	983 mbs
Air temp	4 deg C
Sea temp	0 deg C
Conditions	Partly cloudy with a very cold southerly breeze

Photo opportunity against a stunning backdrop of very old ice that has been formed by the immense pressures of its journey to the top of the sea. From left: Marc, Ollie, Don, Alistair, Jackie, Peter and Janot (seated).

W unnamed island just south of The Gullet, near Hinks Channel. The names may not mean much, but the view from here is grand.

We are facing the south but, with the wind sending eddies around the high craggy cliffs of our island, we are also often pointing all ways. Right behind, to the north, is Mount St Louis, reaching 1200 metres and blocking out all satellite communications. To the east, through the clouds and overlooking a huge white-blue glacier of immense proportions, are the Gravier Peaks, reaching between 2000 and 2500 metres. West of us, over the top of more glaciers and on the other side of The Gullet, is Mount Reeves — also around 2000 metres high.

This surely is a grand place. It is, however, normally completely cut off by solid, unrelenting ice. Near here last year a British Antarctic supply vessel was stuck for five weeks — held by the ice. The previous four years, it was completely impassable. This

relative ease, just as *Seamaster* did. The Antarctic Peninsula is certainly a different place this summer.

The chart for where we are shows this island as only a dot the size of a tiny fly speck, but it is much more than that. With the cold southerly wind behind us, we were looking for somewhere to spend the afternoon and night. This spot, with all its physical magnificence, fits our mood perfectly. We are probably the first vessel to ever anchor in this remotest of places.

The summer is definitely going. On the east coast of the Peninsula, in the Weddell Sea, the pancake ice is starting to reform already — a prelude to the coming freeze. So we have good reason to keep moving north. In a few short weeks' time, no more movement will be possible by a vessel such as ours. The biggest natural happening on our planet is under way. Antarctica will, in the winter months, double in size — as it does every year.

19 February 2001

●

Location Next to the Ukranian base, in the Argentine Islands

The old British weather station Wordie House is close by so Don and I set off in the RIB in the still but crisp morning air and found a place to land where the water was deep, right near the front door of this now-protected historical site.

Inside, it was like going through a time warp, almost as though the meteorologists had left only yesterday: old communications equipment, manual typewriters, dog logs (they kept dogs here in the 1950s), and the daily logs for 1958 and 1959. That was quite a while ago now, but reading some of the log entries made us realise how fortunate we have been with our expedition.

They also had fine weather at this time of the year in 1958 but, by the end of February that year, the ship coming to pick up the team was beset in ice down near Rothera, the present British base, where we were only a few days ago in open-water conditions.

The team here then had gale-force southeasterly winds for a week with driving snow and severe icing of all surfaces, followed by northerly gales. They must have used a lot of coal to keep warm — some of which is still here.

Wordie House is in excellent condition and even though it is now visited by many people from the small cruise ships, it has obviously been well respected. It is, I understand, maintained by the UK Antarctic Heritage Trust which has, along with its New Zealand counterpart, set out to make sure that the physical history of this continent of ice, snow and extraordinary exploits isn't lost.

Latitude	65.15S
Longitude	64.15W
Wind	Calm
Sea	Mirror-like
Barometer	1000 mbs and steady
Air temp	5 deg C
Sea temp	0 deg C
Conditions	Perfect
Visibility	Forever

20 February 2001

Latitude 65.10S
Longitude 64.08W
Wind Variable 5 knots
Sea state Slight northerly chop and a 1 metre SW swell
Barometer 996 mbs and steady
Air temp 6 deg C
Sea temp 0 deg C
Conditions Perfect
Visibility 100 km

The Antarctic Peninsula — an extraordinary place and one where, if you are fortunate enough to be here even for a brief time, it suddenly hits home how important this extraordinary continent is to the wellbeing of the rest of the world. You realise that you are part of something far greater, more magnificent and intricate — and more fragile — than you ever imagined.

You also understand that the environment must be appreciated and nurtured for all the right reasons, that it is what makes this planet of ours different to anything else in the known solar system.

Seeing all this wildlife in its natural environment is very rewarding. What is not so rewarding is to receive notification in the past couple of days from the Antarctica Project, a great group that is endeavouring to monitor and publicise what is actually happening to the wildlife south of 60 degrees south, of the terrible damage that the 'illegal' fishermen are doing to the birdlife in this part of the world.

It is estimated that the total sea-bird catch for the Antarctic zone is between 106,000 and 258,000 birds over the past four years. This includes some 22,000 to 68,000 albatross, 5000 to 11,000 giant petrels, and 79,000 to 178,000 white-chinned petrels.

All scientific evidence is that these levels of depredation are completely unsustainable for the species and populations concerned. And, if this isn't enough, a survey at Bird Island in South Georgia found an unusually large amount of fishing hooks, presumed to be debris from long-line fishing vessels.

Even worse, an analysis of regurgitated material from wandering albatross chicks showed that 79 per cent received food containing line and/or hooks. What will it take to convince authorities in all countries that their fishing vessels must employ different practices?

Don is passionate about the wildlife we see around us every day. These are his very pertinent thoughts:

'One day man will visit other planets far away from our own. And if we are very lucky we may even find life there. We don't know what that life will be like, or what form it will take. In fact, the only thing we can be pretty sure about is that it will be nothing like us. The way they communicate with each other will probably be so alien that we may never be able to fully understand it. They may not build cities, drive cars or fly in aeroplanes. But they will probably be so different that this will bother us a lot more than it bothers them.

They might be very much larger than us. They may not walk and talk. But we will still be able to tell if they're intelligent by their ability to communicate with each other and their behaviour towards each other, no matter how different it is to our own. It will be an amazing moment as people look in awe on these creatures so very different to us in every way. People will devote their lives to understanding them, to communicating with them, to just admiring them for their difference. What we hopefully won't do is fire great steel harpoons into their bodies and then flay the flesh from their still warm carcasses.'

Whale tale. These pictures were sent to the Antarctic Humpback Whale Catalogue. The catalogue can identify individual whales anywhere in the world by the markings on their tails.

2 March 2001

Location At sea in the Neumayer Channel

1530hrs: Port Lockroy is only an hour or so ahead, around a few corners. It was used by the whalers of long ago. Bones still litter the beaches there, testimony to man's actions of the past for all to see.

The place was named by Jean Baptiste Charcot in 1904. His expeditions were privately funded and his explorations and discoveries have been ranked as some of the most important in the history of Antarctica. He was a great leader and a scientific observer of note, and even back then, he was concerned about how the whales might fare if man continued hunting them in earnest. Much of what he predicted is coming true. However, he was not the only early explorer to put forward his concerns about man and the environment.

Apsley Cherry-Garrard was a man amongst men. He was with Scott on his final expedition in 1911, but not one of the party who perished returning from the South Pole. Cherry-Garrard wrote a book entitled *The Worst Journey in the World*. This covered a side-expedition that he and two others undertook in the winter prior to the Pole attempt. The men with him were 'Uncle' Bill Wilson and 'Birdie' Bowers — both of whom perished on the way back from the Pole with Scott only a few months later.

Their aim was to search for emperor penguin eggs to endeavour to prove a connection between reptilian scales and feathers. They set off from their base camp at Cape Evans on Ross Island in the mid-winter of 1911 to walk to Cape Crozier, where the only known breeding colony of emperors was thought to be. This was a distance of some 105 kilometres each way. As Cherry-Garrard stated in his book: '. . . and so we started just after mid-winter on the weirdest bird-nesting expedition that has ever been or ever will be.'

It was an awful journey. 'Antarctic exploration is seldom as bad as you imagine, seldom as bad as it sounds. But this journey had beggared our language: no word could express its horror,' Cherry-Garrard wrote.

They eventually collected six eggs, broke some on the way back, and finally made it with just three eggs — after five weeks in the snow and ice with the temperatures down to minus 61 degrees centigrade.

'Polar exploration is at once the cleanest and most isolated way of having a bad time which has been devised,' said Cherry-Garrard. He had, however, proved himself to himself. His account of that terrible journey includes the following, which is as pertinent today as it was then:

We cannot stop knowledge: we must use it well or perish. And we must do our tiny scrap to see that those who do use it are sound in mind and body, especially in mind, of good education, with a background of tradition, a knowledge of human nature and of history; with a certain standard of decency which inspires trust; with disinterestedness and self-control.

Plato said the good ruler is a reluctant man. The really wise man knows what an awful thing it is to govern, and keeps away from it. Our problems are not new: they are as old as the men who hunted the prehistoric hills. When they hit one another on the head with stones the matter was confined to a few caves: now it shakes a crowded world more complicated than any watch.

Human nature does not change: it becomes more dangerous. Those who guide the world now may think they are doing quite well: so perhaps did they do.

Man, having destroyed the whales, may end up by destroying himself. The penguins may end up like the prehistoric reptiles from which they sprang. All may follow the mammoths and dinosaurs into fossilized oblivion.

Latitude	64.44S
Longitude	63.17W
Wind	Light and variable
Sea	Slight
Barometer	977 mbs
Air temp	7 deg C
Sea temp	I deg C
Conditions	Perfect — sunny
Visibility	150 km

Seamaster at Port Lockroy amid the remains of the 'bad old days'.

Latitude 63.54S
Longitude 60.46W
Wind Northeasterly, 25 to 30 knots
Sea Rough outside harbour
Baromete 988 mbs and steady
Air temp 0 deg C
Sea temp 0 deg C
Conditions Blizzard
Visibility 150 metres

1800hrs: The snow is swirling past *Seamaster* and piling up all over the decks, in the ropes, and filling the dinghies and cockpit. The blizzard is getting everywhere. To go out through the pilot-house door is to be instantly coated with white. We are anchored in 70 metres of water, in behind the ice cliffs of a 350-metre high headland. The shoreline is only 200 metres away, but is rarely visible.

The day started well with calm at dawn. There were a few breaks in the sky to the east, but low cloud over the mountains nearby. An iceberg that had wandered into our bay overnight remained grounded in the comparatively shallow water just astern of us — with lumps falling off into the sea from time to time. The many fur seals headed off early to feed and were still away as we raised anchor at 8 am — motoring westwards to clear some rocks and stopping next to three humpback whales lying on the surface.

The remains of their krill meal — the bright pink 'shells' — were scattered across the water all around us. The whales were making slow circles — still feeding — with their huge mouths open to strain their food through the baleen plates. We left them to it and turned north — then northeast — heading towards Mikklesen Harbour on Trinity Island.

An hour later, the now familiar cry of 'Thar she blows' rang again. Four humpback whales had been sighted right ahead. We slowed then circled around, stopped both main engines and turned off the generator, the steering pumps and depth sounder, and went into silent mode — just sitting and watching as *Seamaster* rolled gently on the short swells coming from further north. After a while, all four humpbacks approached us, moving very slowly. They came right alongside, sometimes submerged, sometimes on the surface, then went under *Seamaster*, rolling upside down and exposing their white underbellies. Their huge and very distinctive flippers gleamed pale yellow-white.

We could see close details of the blow-holes, of the barnacles growing on their backs and heads, and even on the very tips of their tails. Their eyes looked at us in a knowing way. We were looking at them very closely, all exclaiming at the experience of a lifetime. In turn, they were examining us and communicating with one another all the time. Our hydrophone picked up their conversation, but they wouldn't have needed any device to know what we were saying about them. Time and again they circled around, came back next to us or passed right under our stern, blowing from time to time with very distinctive snorts. Then inhaling with a tremendous gasp before closing the blow-hole and easing back under the surface. They sometimes stopped right alongside — so close we could almost touch them — looking at us and at our vessel. Occasionally they popped only their heads vertically above the water, almost like a spy-hopping leopard seal. An hour later, they suddenly formed a line abreast — side by side — and slowly moved off, heading south.

We watched some humpbacks breaching yesterday. After today's experience, our cup definitely runneth over. One could not help the impression that the humpbacks today were as interested in us as we were in them. They were relaxed that we were there, almost as though they knew we were interested only in observing them. We had no other more sinister motives.

Remains of a whaling station on Trinity Island — probably more than 100 years old.

6 March 2001

●

1200hrs: The dawn brought more evidence that the Antarctic summer is drawing to a close. *Seamaster* was covered in snow. It was piled deep in places, and the chimney from the big diesel heater, poking up above the pilot-house, was one of the few items still clear.

We lit the heater. Even though the interior of *Seamaster* wasn't particularly cold, with the snow thick on all the windows, it was like being in a snow cave — with wood trim. The saloon became really warm and dry in less than an hour and, now that Ollie and Marc have been at work with the snow shovels and fire hose, much of the upper works are clear again.

As we approached a small inlet on the island, where there seemed to be a gently sloping gravel beach protected from the waves, Ollie spied a leopard seal on the hunt, very near the shore. He recalls:

‘Andy and I have had a particularly pleasant day filming penguins in the shallows at a wonderful little pebble beach in a bay at Mikklesen Harbour, Trinity Island. We were hoping for an underwater shot of the leopard seal, the species that loves penguins almost as much we do, but not for the same reasons. We had seen one on approach to the beach, it came to investigate the Zodiac, and we wondered if today would be our lucky day for underwater footage.

The tide was out when we first arrived so the penguins were mostly lying around or out fishing. As we were the only source of activity, it wasn't too long before our inquisitive leopard came to visit, to check out what we were up to. She approached to within metres and gave us her friendly nod before heading back to the outer edges of the bay.

Later in the afternoon, with the incoming tide, many of the penguins were arriving back ashore after feeding. The new chicks were honing their swimming techniques alongside us. The sound of such activity in the shallows must have attracted the leopard, and before we knew it, what looked like a runaway torpedo came hurtling towards the shore to rest about a metre from the edge (to our relief, missing all the penguins). Here was our leopard lying just beside us, within arm's reach.

Cameras running, we chose to stay glued to the spot (maybe because we were frozen with fright) and as she had had no success in the hunt, she gave us the once-over and then slowly turned and made her way back into deeper water. What an experience, to be up close to such a fearsome-looking creature.

A little later, as we continued filming and before we could even turn around, she came in again and grabbed a penguin alongside us, quickly retreating to the deeper waters. We jumped into the Zodiac and followed, to watch events unfold.

Much to our surprise, the leopard continued playing with the poor penguin, like a cat with a mouse, sometimes with the penguin in her mouth, sometimes resting alongside it or just swimming slowly after it. She did not appear to want to inflict the fatal bite and often let the penguin go. If it swam away, she would follow. It was not pretty to watch so, after 30 minutes, Andy and I decided that we had had enough. We'd got to film the leopard in action and maybe there would be other opportunities to come.’

Latitude 63.54S
Longitude 60.46W
Wind Northeast of 15 knots
Sea Slight roll at anchor
Barometer 988 mbs and steady
Air temp 2 deg C
Sea temp 0 deg C
Conditions Snow easing
Visibility Poor but improving

A leopard seal playing with a hapless penguin, like a cat with a mouse, before finally making the kill.

10 March 2001

●

Location Potter Cove, South Shetland Islands

Latitude 62.14S
Longitude 58.40W
Wind 30 knot easterly but easing
Sea Slight
Barometer 990 mbs and rising
Air temp Minus 2 deg C
Sea temp 0 deg C
Conditions Abysmal, with driving sleet and snow
Visibility Very poor

1800hrs: We left Trinity Island yesterday, headed for Discovery Bay on Greenwich Island. As evening approached, a large patch of packed brash ice, sea ice and icebergs appeared ahead, blocking our path.

There were four hours of daylight (or twilight left) and only 35 miles to go — and the corner of the ice reef hopefully was only eight miles or so ahead. We decided to press on, still hoping to reach Discovery in time for dinner — even though we were heading 90 degrees away from our desired course.

We headed northeast for nearly three hours to try and get around the ice but there was no way through. The 'patch' extended as far as the eye could see from the deck and it was too rough to have a man go up to the crow's-nest to check further.

The wind rose as the evening progressed until it was 35 to 40 knots from the east — driving before it fine sleet that covered everything. There was so much ice in the water that we were continually having to take avoiding action. Clothing on deck was full cold-weather gear. The spray from the bow wave was turning to ice crystals as it blew over the boat. The winches, and most of the ropes, were frozen stiff, and with ice falling from the sails and rig, it was important to be wearing goggles in case the shards hit you in the face. Gradually the decks became sheets of ice, the seawater froze on the lifelines as it left the now steep waves as heavy spray, and forward visibility was reduced to less than 100 metres or so.

So there we were — trying to find a way through floating ice of all sizes, in a gale, with driving sleet, in the middle of the night. We kept two crew on the bow with the searchlight, looking for bergs. Marc, Alistair and Janot shared this role. They were harnessed on and in full survival suits, and they were regularly covered with spray from the bow going under.

Further aft we had several lookouts, all helping spot ice and direct the helmsman. Ollie and Don worked the radar and navigated, trying to find a way through the pack. It was vital to always have an escape route and not get hemmed in, or be unable to return the way we had come.

We didn't find 'the corner' until much later and, rather than the escape we were seeking, it proved to be the start of a narrow lane in a much bigger sheet of broken ice than we could ever have imagined. At times the floes pinched in on both sides so that we had to slow right down and squeeze through the narrowest of gaps, not exactly sure how or if we were going to make it until the very last moment.

By midnight, however, we had finally cleared the last funnel between the two sheets of compacted ice, and passed behind (to leeward) an enormous berg that was only just discernible in the driving sleet (even though it was only a few hundred metres to windward), and motored up Maxwell Bay at the southern end of King George Island.

We entered Potter Cove on radar and using our electronic MaxSea charting system that has proved so valuable in all our exploring to date. We could not see the land until we had actually anchored soon after 0100hrs — just off the lights of the Argentine base of Jubany.

By this morning *Seamaster* was iced up on deck with the temperature at minus 5 degrees C, the sleet and snow reducing the visibility to near zero. We have stayed where we are for the day. We have hardly ventured outside, the big diesel heater in the saloon keeping downstairs very warm and cosy, while the wind and sleet have hammered the outside.

We hadn't intended to be at sea last night, but we always knew this would sometime be an inevitability, and so we were prepared for it. We could have hove to, clear of most of the ice to the east, and waited until the dawn, but to be in a gale in the Bransfield Strait, at night, in heavy ice conditions, was not the place you would have wanted to be.

I have raced through the Southern Oceans a number of times and had near misses with ice as well as seen many bergs, but I have never had a night like the one we have just experienced. It will certainly be recalled as one of the highlights of our journey, but one that I will be pleased not to repeat too often. We are very fortunate to be in such a strong, well-found vessel. *Seamaster* came into her own last night. Only equivalent ice-breakers would have attempted such a passage.

We hit one large lump of clear ice, very difficult to see even in the full light of day, let alone at night-time. It thumped under *Seamaster*, hit the big steel centreboards and then the propeller guards, which no doubt saved the props from damage. The crew checked below the water as a matter of course, but all was fine. This was what *Seamaster* was designed and built for. We rarely deviate for small brash ice any more — we just chomp through it.

Opposite Iceberg watch — 'baby, it's cold outside.'

The air temperature is well above zero — but this has brought fog to the area. The Chilean base a few hundred metres away is often hidden from view. The rocky island just off our stern is no more than a dark blob at times as the fog lifts a little, then disappears as the fog descends again.

The massive, solid ice 'pack' that we had to find a way through a couple of nights ago has grown considerably larger as enormous quantities of ice from the Weddell Sea linked up. This ice pack has moved close to the shores of the South Shetland Islands and the edge is just outside Maxwell Bay. It is now beginning to fill the whole of the Bransfield Strait — the piece of water between here (the South Shetlands) and Antarctic Peninsula proper. However, a change to strengthening west and northwest winds over the next few days should keep a navigable passage reasonably clear along the shoreline — we hope.

It is very early in the year for the big freeze to begin in earnest — but maybe this is how it starts. We are now seriously considering having to move south down the islands in the next day or so, as we really don't want to be forced to spend the winter here, interesting as it might be.

15 March 2001

●

Location At Triangle Point, near Yankee Harbour on Greenwich Island

Above The Chilean base in Ardley Cove, King George Island in the South Shetlands.

Opposite Instructions from the skipper to the bow watch.

1200hrs: More rain accompanied by a blustery northwesterly wind had *Seamaster* tugging hard at the anchor overnight. We had a very firm hold and didn't drag at all, but the lights of the Chilean base shining through the gloom were a welcome feature to check our position against from time to time.

As I write this, we are at sea, having left King George Island in mid-morning. We have had a very pleasant motor-sail in patches of bright sunshine down the leeward side of the South Shetland Islands — all uninhabited except for the occasional 'scientific' stations. Some islands are showing more green than ever, but it is only moss. It is too cold and there is too little sunlight for even stunted trees. If the warming experienced this year continues however, larger plant forms may not be many decades away. To starboard is Greenwich Island. Yankee Harbour, just around the corner now, was a favourite for sealers and whalers back in the early 1800s.

1700hrs: We have anchored under the lee of Triangle Point instead. The wind is still curling into Yankee Harbour, but we are very snug in behind some rocky outcrops and the ever present ice cliffs. Two humpback whales have just circled us, probably a mother and her calf, both blowing in unison and staying very close together.

1900hrs: We were up for a walk, so took the red inflatable into Yankee Harbour and landed in the lee of the spit, right next to a large Weddell seal snoozing just above the water's edge. Gentoo penguins in their black and white uniforms were strutting everywhere, or lying around asleep in hollows amongst the stones. There were several fur seals — the females very placid but the males taking exception to our presence. One came towards me at the run, roaring with his mouth wide open. The skuas stayed very close to us, but the giant petrels patrolled on the wing — up and down the spit — rarely landing. There was one try pot rusting away on the foreshore and we came across whale bones and driftwood throughout the walk.

A cloud stretching from horizon to horizon came up over the island to windward, so we have just had a fast and bumpy ride back to *Seamaster*, in case the weather changes for the worse.

Sea Rough
Barometer 997 mbs
Air temp 3 deg C
Sea temp 4 deg C
Conditions Overcast
Visibility Good

Opposite Time to reflect. 'Not all
that we have encountered has
filled us with joy.'

Following page 'The natural world,
the environment that means so
much to all of us, is truly a
wondrous place.'

snow for three days and she was all iced up again.

We were snug and secure at our anchorage off Triangle Point but all through our last night there we could hear the ice cliffs calving huge quantities into the shallow waters at their base. Only the smaller brash reached us, clinking along the side as it flowed past on quite a strong current. There was only the occasional solid thump from a larger lump.

The following evening, the wind changed direction and started gusting more than 30 knots. The sea quickly became quite rough and we were now on a lee shore. We had no choice but to shift to a safer spot under the lee of Glacier Bluff in Yankee Harbour. Within 10 minutes of re-anchoring, the wind dropped to 4 or 5 knots and swung to the southeast. It seemed as though the worst was through, but it still snowed hard and the decks were more slippery than ever.

We commenced securing for sea, but the decks were so icy that the work outside — the stowing of dinghies, kayaks and fenders — had to wait. The heater was on in the saloon, so everything was warm and dry down below despite the ice and frozen sludge building up over all windows.

We left our anchorage at Glacier Bluff around 0600hrs yesterday, as the dawn started filtering through the heavy snow. We had to use the snow-shovels to clear some areas of the decks of the drifts that had built up overnight — particularly the cockpit, which was deep in fine powdery stuff.

Once out through McFarlane Strait, and a narrow, winding and turbulent channel with a 3-knot current against us, we then met the Southern Ocean swells. They have diminished since we crossed the 100 metres line and now are only causing a not unpleasant rolling motion from time to time.

The reason for leaving so early was to get as many miles as possible north of the South Shetland Islands before dark this evening. We haven't seen any small lumps of ice in the sea since clearing land but there will no doubt be some big bergs around until we are north of the Antarctic Convergence sometime tomorrow.

So far we have made great progress on our way back to South America. Cape Horn is only 250 miles ahead, with another hundred or so on to Ushuaia. But we may stop at Puerto Williams in Chile as our first port of call and tie up alongside the yacht club in the shallow river. This will be the best place to remove the propeller ice grids that we have had on since Auckland. There is no doubt they have saved the propellers from severe ice damage on more than one occasion but, once back north, we would rather regain the speed that they cost us through the extra drag they create.

As we leave the Antarctic behind, this from Janot:

Last night, I was on watch, by myself in the wheel-house, surrounded by a dark and rainy night, and questions came to my mind: what did I learn in Antarctica, and what will I remember about this experience?

I learned a lot about a lot of things: about myself, about my friends, about wildlife, about beauty. I enjoyed the plenitude of those moments we were lucky enough to share with the seals, the whales and others.

I have just one regret — it was too short. Like the Arctic, where I spent one summer, two years ago, I think I need to spend a whole year in this place to be able to understand all of the systems, the cycle of life and the deep relationship we have with such a different world, which is part of ours, and such an essential part. I need more time to integrate all that I sense, to mature my analysis, to make sure I looked through the right lens, that I did not alter the reality, being dazzled by the bright beauty of what I saw.

I will remember mostly feelings, strong feelings about pureness, about beauty, about life; feeling blessed, to be one of those rare people lucky enough to come to such a special place and, finally, the most frightening of all — the feeling of the vulnerability and fragility of this wonderful place that is threatened by our mistakes and our lack of knowledge, by our thirst for energy or power.

20 March 2001

◆

Location At sea, approaching the Beagle Canal in Southern Chile

Wind	SW 25 to 30 knots
Sea	Moderate
Barometer	1025 mbs
Air temp	6.5 deg C
Sea temp	4 deg C
Conditions	Overcast
Visibility	Poor

We are presently sailing in a very fresh wind with whitecaps everywhere. This follows a night of near gale-force conditions and rough seas. *Seamaster* was jumping around like a small dinghy at times, but making good speed even though our sails were well reefed.

The islands north of Cape Horn are off to port as we head towards the eastern entrance to the Beagle Canal, with Puerto Williams planned as our first stop back in South America. We left here two and a half months ago. Since then we have had a most extraordinary and rewarding time 'down south'. But we are pleased to be back.

When we set out on this, the first voyage in a five-year programme of expeditions to some of the most remote locations on the planet, we really weren't sure of the outcome. Now that we have had time to look, to learn, to listen and, most importantly, to think, we have gained an appreciation that perhaps we didn't have before. And we are even more fascinated by what we find around us. The natural world, the environment that means so much to all of us, is truly a wondrous place.

Not all that we have encountered has filled us with joy but, then, we didn't think it would. The most important objective for this and future expeditions we undertake is to help 'make a difference' to how we all perceive the environment, to explain why it matters, and to outline the reasons why change is necessary in a number of vitally important areas. I think we've made a good start.

There is a legend that says:

> On the occasion of a great forest fire, all the animals sought to escape. Only one little hummingbird was gathering a few drops of water from the river and flying high to drop them on the fire. They asked the hummingbird what use was it to do so little. The hummingbird answered — 'If everyone were to do just a little!'

Think about it.

The Amazon and the Rio Negro

5 September 2001

Sarah-Jane Blake on passage from Buenos Aires to Rio de Janeiro.

Seamaster alongside the Yacht Club Argentino in Buenos Aires.

Seamaster undocked from alongside the Yacht Club Argentino in Buenos Aires at 10 am on Saturday, 1 September — destination, north to Brazil and on to the Amazon.

It was raining and completely overcast with very poor visibility as we motored out into a stiff head wind and choppy sea that only increased the further down the Rio de la Plata (River Plate) we went. With vast amounts of brown water flowing seawards out of the Parana River — the second-biggest river in South America — and into the de la Plata, against the incoming wind, the going was quite lumpy. All hatches stayed firmly shut to keep out the short steep waves that kept breaking on deck.

The lack of visibility and increasing rain didn't make for a bright departure, but all of the crew were excited. The next big adventure was under way. A few unsettled stomachs during the night cleared up the next day when we turned left after passing Punta del Este at the southeastern corner of Uruguay, and freed away to the north.

As I write this we still haven't seen the sun since before leaving Argentina. We have been at sea for more than four days and it rained solidly for the first three. The lightning had to be seen to be believed. I have been around the world many times, have been through more intense electrical storms with thunderclaps so loud that they would shake the boat, but this trip takes the prize for length of display — two days and two nights with very little let-up.

Being in the pilot-house or on deck was like being surrounded by huge flash guns that lit the world around us from horizon to horizon. Forked lightning flashed its jagged lines horizontally across the sky, for miles at a time, leaving a distinct smell of ozone in the damp air. Sheet lightning played incessantly above and through the dark clouds. Even at midday we had our navigation lights on as it was twilight for much of the time. Thunder rolled continuously overhead like kettle drums from another dimension. For the new members of the crew, this was an experience they won't forget. The might of nature can be very humbling. It certainly made us feel very small in comparison to the enormity of the power surrounding us.

The Antarctic expedition was the most memorable experience of my career to date. It has, and will continue to have, a lasting effect. I have to go back. The Amazon and Orinoco Rivers will produce other feelings — maybe.

Apart from Marc, none of us have been there before. To again be able to go to one of the most critical environmental areas of the planet and become part of it, even for just a little while, will be very rewarding. We feel very fortunate to have the opportunity, especially as our crew, through our television documentaries and our website activity, will be millions — not just the 15 that are manning the watches at the moment.

In the Amazon, we plan to make our way upstream for 1000 miles to Manaus, a large, modern city that is at the hub of Brazil's massive river system. Here we will branch right into the Rio Negro, another of the world's great waterways, and forge our way northwest upstream to San Gabriel, which, we expect, is about as far as we will get before the river becomes unnavigable.

The *Seamaster* crew will then split into two, with a 'Jungle Team' going on through the Rio Casiquiare, the system of natural waterways that links the Amazon river system with that of the Orinoco.

The Amazon originates in the Andes of Peru (not far from the Pacific Ocean) and makes its way eastwards right across the South American continent — mostly through Brazil — to the Atlantic Ocean. The Orinoco originates in the Guiana Highlands and then wends its way northwest and north, along the border between Columbia and Venezuela, before it veers northeast through Venezuela to empty into the Caribbean.

While the Jungle Team threads its way along the Orinoco, *Seamaster* will retrace her course, back down the Amazon to the Atlantic, where she will turn left up the coast of Brazil and head to the mouth of the Orinoco, to pick up the other half of her crew as they complete their journey.

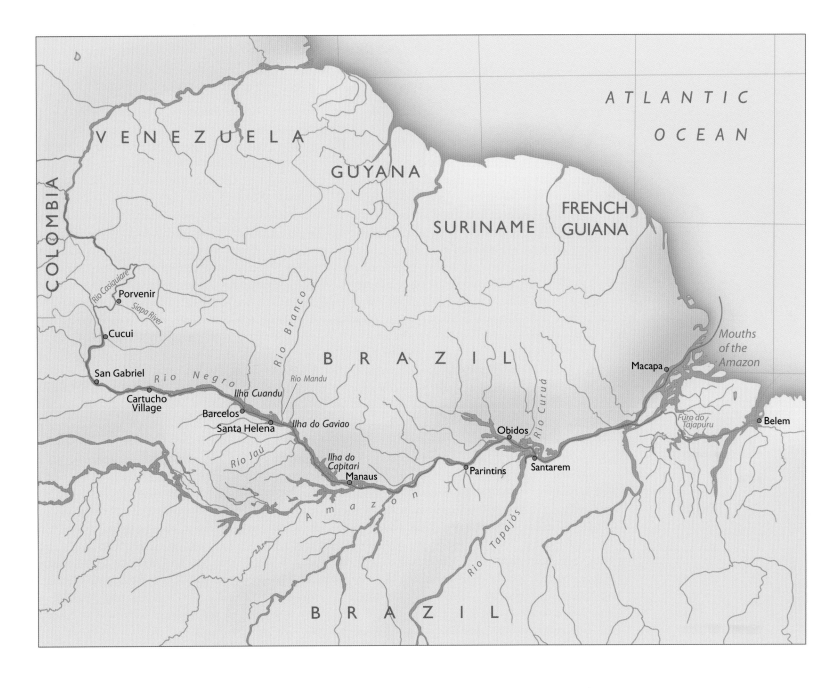

Why are we doing this? The reasons are similar to those that took us to 70 degrees south on the Antarctic Peninsula. It is part of our mission to visit the 'pulse points' of the planet and report on what we see, on what we find, and on what we learn through our adventures on this very special vessel of ours. Rather than reading about it, we want to 'see for ourselves', form our own opinions, and share our experiences with as many people as possible.

Is the ice melting in Antarctica? Are the forests of Amazonia being destroyed and, if so, what will be the outcome of such destruction? How will it affect you and me, and our children, and their children?

It has taken me a long time to even start to understand the term 'global warming'. The more I have got to grips with it and have come to understand and appreciate what it means, the greater has become my concern about what we are doing to this planet of ours.

Goose-winged and reaching towards Rio de Janeiro.

Janot cools off as conditions improved and temperatures rose.

We are currently enjoying the best conditions to date on this part of the journey. We are under full sail with a blue sky, wind on the beam and on course for the most eastern corner of Brazil. From there we ease away to the left and head along the northeast coast of Brazil towards the mouth of the Amazon. Belem, on the southern side of the river's great estuary, will be the starting point for our Amazon adventure.

Since we wrote our last log we made our entry into Brazil at Sao Sebastiao and then anchored for the weekend at Ilhabela, a very beautiful island, where we were made most welcome at the Yacht Club Ilhabela.

Then onward to Rio de Janeiro where we were alongside at the Yacht Club Rio de Janeiro and once again made to feel very welcome. Interest in blakexpeditions was high, from the press through to a group of local Optimist sailors, which only served to heighten our keenness to get started. What have we been doing since Antarctica? Essentially, getting *Seamaster* ready for her second expedition in conditions that could not be more different.

Seamaster is an exploration vessel designed primarily for extremely cold climates. She can safely withstand minus 40 degrees centigrade temperatures, and can 'winter over', completely self-sufficient, should she become frozen in when exploring the ice regions of the planet. The enormous amount of insulation incorporated into her construction, however, also means she should be a good vessel in the intense heat of the tropics, so long as we manage to keep the sun from the decks and improve the ventilation throughout. So, awnings to cover almost the entire deck have been made and new extractor fans will provide a 10-knot breeze throughout the interior; specially moulded scoops mean we can keep the hatches open even in driving rain, with insect netting covering all openings. Additionally, the ice grids that protected the propellers in Antarctica were removed in Ushuaia, to improve performance through the water (less drag and we don't expect ice in the Amazon anyway!). Extra refrigeration has replaced the aft divers' shower, to keep the salad and vegetables fresh, and a special water purification system, custom designed and built, will enable us to safely drink the river water when the tropical downpours don't provide enough to top up the tanks.

All of the crew have been inoculated against yellow fever, rabies, typhoid and hepatitis A and B, and are now up to date with all those other jabs that you have as a child but may tend to forget about as you get older. The 'potions and lotions' to avoid being bitten by mosquitoes fill the passageway shelves. The special clothing developed by Line 7 is still in the boxes down aft — waiting for the weather to warm up. The high anti-snake boots take up space in most cabins, along with special hats, ponchos, sandals and general bits and pieces. Still to come are the hammocks, for sleeping under the awning on deck. We will purchase these, along with other essentials, in Belem in a few weeks' time.

Of course it will be very different to Antarctica, and not only climactically. There were, for instance, no shops way down south, whereas the Amazon is populated and we will never be very far from a small village. Still, there is a long way to go — approximately 3500 miles north and then west — to the river city of Belem, not too far south of the equator and our next destination.

Leaving Ilhabela.
From left: Ollie, Santiago (Maccall), Leon, Sarah-Jane (Blake), Peter, Rob, Charlie, Diego (Maccall), Robin, Rodger, John (Morgan), Geoff and Janot.

On the south bank and 70 miles inside the mouth of the Amazon, Belem is a city that took us by surprise with its population of an estimated two million people and high-rise buildings piercing the sprawl of the many shanties.

The wet-weather gear and survival suits of Antarctica have been cleaned and stowed and we now have wet-weather 'ponchos' to take their place — light and airy and the most suitable for the daily tropical downpours. To dress for watch is much simpler than down south too — a T-shirt and shorts, that's all.

We are now taking our anti-malarial tablets every day, and the insect repellent will soon be a must. The sun burns very quickly, so hats and the new lightweight Line 7 clothing to keep us covered up during the hottest time of the day are very welcome.

Keeping the food fresh poses different problems, but the two large refrigerators installed in place of the divers' shower help with the fruit and vegetables, and the freezers in the forepeak are full to the brim with meat and other frozen items.

To keep to schedule as we push the long way westwards against the Amazon current, we will be motoring day and night (when the river is wide enough). But there will be times when we will be restricted to daytime only and a good deck patrol will be essential when we anchor for the night in some remote areas.

Initially we will be in the main river where we will encounter a great deal of traffic. After Manaus, however, that will all change. The traffic will reduce primarily to local river craft and ferries, and we will get the opportunity to make side excursions into tributaries that have rarely been visited.

Our guide is Miguel Rocha da Silva, who was the guide for Jacques Cousteau when *Calypso* spent 18 months here in 1992–93. Miguel is a wealth of information and will be an invaluable addition to the crew. Our pilot for the 1000-mile leg up the Amazon to Manaus is Joseph. Our cook Paulo is already in the galley preparing his first lunch for the crew. He has a restaurant in Manaus and will be good to be with in the marketplace when we are buying our supplies over the next few days.

We are presently anchored just off the yacht club to the south of the town — in very shallow waters with all types of extraordinary and often brightly painted river craft passing in a continuous stream day and night.

The full deck awnings that we had made in Buenos Aires over the winter months have this morning been unfolded and fitted. They look like they will do the job admirably.

What a river. A few facts and figures will provide some perspective to our journey and why we are here:

- The Amazon is the world's largest river in volume of water and second longest (after the Nile), travelling 6577 km (4087 miles) from source to ocean. Of that distance, 3615 km (2246 miles) are in Brazilian territory.
- The river is navigable by oceangoing ships for 3885 km (2414 miles) upstream, as far as Iquitos in Peru.
- The Amazon rainforest is the largest equatorial forest in the world and occupies approx 42 per cent of the area of Brazil.
- It contains 30 per cent of the remaining forest in the world and is larger than the whole of Western Europe.
- The Amazon comprises one-tenth of our planet's plant and animal species and produces one-fifth of the world's oxygen.
- The river collects water from more than 1100 tributaries as it travels more than 4000 miles from the Andes to the Atlantic.
- It drains an area of over seven million square kilometres and is estimated to carry 20 per cent of the world's fresh water.
- At the mouth of the river, water flows into the Atlantic at 160,000 to 200,000 cubic metres per second — a flow greater than the world's eight other biggest rivers added together.

Statistics like those take some getting to grips with. We have much travelling to do — all against the river current — if we want to see it for ourselves.

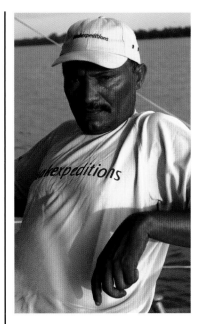

Joseph — *Seamaster*'s river pilot for the Amazon leg from Belem to Santarem.

The colourful river ferries rafted together at Belem — all built of wood rather than metal to reduce the impact of tropical heat.

On board we have:

Don ('Captain Rabbit'), from New Zealand, once again with digital camera at the ready for *Seamaster* log photos, and my back-up on navigation and general organisation.

Rob, from New Zealand, and *Seamaster*'s delivery skipper. He has spent the past weeks and months writing up a systems manual for all on-board equipment — working with Janot and Alistair to fully understand the inner workings of *Seamaster*.

Marc, from the United States, and first mate **Ollie**, from New Zealand, two more key hands and the expedition's lead divers as well as taking care of much of the logistical planning. Marc has spent most of his time since Antarctica planning the details of this expedition, liaising with the authorities in Brazil and Venezuela, and identifying the route — both on the big river and, later, through the jungle waterways to the Orinoco River. Ollie's masterminding of the winter refit is already paying dividends.

Janot, from France, the ship's engineer as well as a key crew-member and another of our expert divers. Janot also has a natural way with languages and does much of our interpreting.

Alistair, from New Zealand, another of *Seamaster*'s key hands, has the responsibility of keeping an eye on the younger members of the crew while also ensuring the smooth running of our small craft.

Rodger, who is Alistair's father and another Kiwi, still pinching himself from the sail north, which was a far cry from the bash and crash of his previous journey with us through the Southern Ocean from New Zealand to Cape Horn.

Geoff, from New Zealand, general hand, currently is helping Paulo with provision lists and stowage plans, while salivating about the prospect of some of the fish dishes for which the Amazon is famous.

Leon, yet another Kiwi, is a newcomer to the crew but also a talented television director/producer. He is currently developing the theme for our next television documentaries, co-ordinating with the film crew in England. They don't join us for another few weeks so Leon will be in charge of documentary footage until they do.

Charlie and **Robin**, two 18-year-olds from Britain, who are starting on a 'gap' year in their education that will be different to most.

Franck, from France, who will be taking photographs for a worldwide agency as well as working with individual newspapers and magazines.

John, a friend of Alistair's from New Zealand, who joined us in Argentina, is only supposed to be with us to Manaus, but we hope he will stay longer.

Right *Seamaster* — off Belem — and resplendent in her new awnings with equally new hammocks strung in the shade beneath.

Below Rob Warring, our delivery skipper.

●

Location Belem

It's Sunday aboard *Seamaster* — a day off for many of the crew and a day on which to attend to personal needs — like sleeping late, visiting the market, reading a book, swimming in the yacht club pool, or simply doing nothing much at all.

The generators still need their oil and filters changing in preparation for the hot days ahead, however, so Alistair and Rob have been sweating it out in the engine room, making sure that everything is in order.

As I write this, Paulo is in the galley preparing lunch (the main meal of the day) and some of us have just returned from a morning with our guide Miguel to the market. The best time for this was to start early, so at 0800 we were ashore and ready to go. Fifteen minutes later, we were at the edge of the market, which sprawled through several streets but focused on the many fishing boats jammed together at the dock, alongside the large, under-cover fish section of the facility.

Not surprisingly, we saw fish that we have never encountered before — some very small, some huge, some (like the piranha) with very sharp teeth and legendary biting power, some that eat only fruit and others that are far more voracious and a lot less discerning. There were diminutive shrimps to the largest pirarucu, that can reach three metres in length (there were large, thick white fillets of this enormous Amazon River fish on sale alongside the considerably smaller — but still large — fruit-eating tambaqui). Prices seemed very cheap to us, ranging from approx US40 cents to US$1.60 per kilo for the overall range of fish.

Many of the small fishing boats were deeply laden, their crews getting the on-deck charcoal barbecues going for lunch. Most were wooden, perhaps no more than 10 metres long, with very little freeboard showing above the river. Some were brightly painted, others had obviously seen little, if any, paint for many years. Most of the spindly masts were held up by cords tensioned by old-fashioned deadeyes — discs made from wood with holes that the tensioning line is passed through.

We now understood why these craft give a very poor echo on our radar screen — there is almost no metal to reflect the radar beams. These boats rarely carry lights, either, so we will have to be extra careful when we head upriver. The Amazon is their highway and there are large volumes of traffic plying the huge waterway between here and Manaus, 1000 miles upstream.

We wandered outside and through the many and varied fruit and vegetables stalls — made from rough timber, sacks, cardboard, plastic and tin — Miguel getting us to try things we had never tasted before. We

bit into the tiny yellow flowers of the small, green jambu plant and found that our mouths were tingling and almost fizzing from the effect for the next half hour or so. We sampled strange fruits that were very refreshing, and scraped the brown 'powder' from around the outside of the nut of the jatoba fruit (enclosed inside the very hard outer husk that had to be broken with a hammer in the first place). The powder tasted strong and sweet. I'm not sure if I will add it to my list of favourites.

There were racks of spices, cheeses, vegetables, fruit, nuts, clothing, meat (cooked, raw, salted — of rather strange hues), and the Belem equivalent of 'fast food' stalls. There was a woman who offered us the magnificent pale, grey and silver skin of a boa constrictor, complete with head and a full set of very sharp teeth for 60 reals (about US$24). You could get a smaller skin without a head for 20 reals.

There were stores that stocked cast-iron, charcoal-fired clothing irons, huge spun-aluminium pots, a mangle, gas stoves, shoes, boots, jungle medicines, hats, bags, and so on — and 33 rpm long-playing records from way before my time.

People in the market recognised us from a local television programme last night, so they also knew, from the same programme, that we were interested in buying additional hammocks. We eventually arrived at a good deal and seven hammocks were carried away to be placed in the boot of the car while Miguel went in search of an extra bag of oranges, some small but very special fish, and some tropical herbs of distinctive flavour. We came back to *Seamaster* loaded with the many items.

The deck now sports a lot more hammocks, strung out of the sun under the awnings and in the cool of the breeze. They certainly will prove their worth.

Fishing boats with fresh catches for the market in downtown Belem.

Miguel advises Peter about the local fish species.

2 October 2001

●

Location Heading for the Rio Para

We up-anchored just before sunrise this morning. Daylight comes very quickly here with only a few minutes separating dark from full daylight. The sun was a blazing orange disc behind the high-rise buildings of Belem, creating a surrounding hazy reddish glow.

The outgoing tide gave us a good push as we motored away down the river. After negotiating a narrow and shallow channel, past islands with sandy beaches, and overgrown ruins and chimneys showing through the canopy of trees, we turned south-westwards up the Rio Para — a long day ahead of us to our next anchorage just short of the point where the river becomes a number of narrow fingers. We are heading for the narrowest.

The river was calm to begin with but now there's a short, steep chop following us along. The river was full of quite thick, brown silt at the anchorage in Belem, but here in the bigger river, whilst still brown, the water is much clearer. Janot and Rodger have the river-water sterilisation system in operation and, so far, it is working really well. The tanks should soon be full again.

We are very conscious of waste, and both our toilets incorporate high-quality sewage treatment systems. But these are normally used in sea water with natural chlorine produced by an electrical charge through the salt water. The river, however, is fresh water, so, to continue treatment, we now add a measured quantity of fine salt to the water in the toilet pan after use, to produce the chlorine as before. Needless to say, we have a lot of salt on board.

A number of craft passed us earlier in the morning, most heading for Belem. They included a barge loaded with lorries that was probably at the end of its 10 to 15 day trip from Manaus. There are no suitable roads linking these far-apart cities, although some are planned, so the river is the delivery route.

1230hrs: We are in narrow channels between some islands — small villages to starboard nearly hidden by the trees. Coconut palms protrude above the rest of the dense foliage; trees with red and yellow flowers are common. A double barge loaded with logs sits waiting to leave. Fishermen in their dug-out canoes come alongside wanting to know if we will buy their shrimp. Other river traffic converges on the narrow sections so the on-deck watch has to keep a good lookout, including for fishing nets that are difficult to see.

Paulo is cooking thin fillets of pork for lunch, using the on-deck barbecue for the first time. Cooking in the open will certainly help keep the saloon cooler. Our chef also appears from time to time in the cockpit with jugs of strange-looking juice — cold and refreshing and often containing ingredients unknown to us. His latest concoction is a very deep red in colour — the juice of the assai berry, a fruit about the size of a large blueberry, from the assai palm that grows in the jungle nearby. We are eating and drinking well.

1330hrs: What a visual feast — the very narrow but quite deep channel between Ilha da Jararaca and Ilha do Murumuru was lined on both sides by small houses, mainly thatched, with rickety wooden jetties. Many had large satellite television dishes. Some of the houses were of two levels, brightly painted but with no need for glass in the windows. Most were on short poles, built over the water. Obviously the closeness to the ocean means that the changes in river level are influenced more by tide than by whether it is the wet or dry season.

The tide this close to the river mouth is still helping us upriver at over 10 knots, but it will soon turn against us for the rest of the afternoon. Our next anchorage is still about 50 miles away and we are unsure that we will make it before dark.

There will be a full moon to assist us later but unlit craft will still be a problem, as will the large rafts of plant matter floating downriver. Maybe the searchlight is about to get its first workout since that miserable night in Antarctica when we were caught in the ice, in a gale, at sea — *Seamaster* frozen over, and the lookout on the bow in survival suits with eyes freezing shut. The contrast could hardly be greater.

Paulo — hard at work in *Seamaster's* galley with 22 mouths to feed.

3 October 2001

Location Furo do Tajapuru

0900hrs: The anchor came up with the sun still well below the eastern horizon and a full moon in the western sky providing us with a golden path. A light breeze ruffled the surface of the river. The island just to windward, behind which we had sheltered for the night, was becoming less of a dark wall and we could begin to pick out details of the fishermen's houses down near the water's edge.

We are now into the narrow Furo do Tajapuru, snaking our way through the jungle in a generally northwest direction towards the main Amazon River. At 1 deg 12 min south latitude, we are only 72 miles south of the equator.

Floating islands of one of the floodplain plants, not unlike a water hyacinth, appear in patches. We weave to avoid the larger clumps. Pink river dolphins surface briefly nearby from time to time. Brightly coloured washing hangs from clotheslines of many of the houses. In most that we pass, children are waving from the open 'windows', or they gather to look at us from the ends of their jetties. I wonder what they must think of such a strange craft.

Many dug-out canoes head out from the shore to greet us, most paddled by small children, some with mother and baby in the bow. All of the people look very healthy and well dressed, but then there is not much need for more than the minimum of clothing in this part of the world. Surprisingly, some are wearing short-sleeved jumpers.

The most amazingly lush vegetation comes right down to the river, much of it growing in the water. There are the large assai palms with the red berries, enormous mauritia palms with their bright yellow fruit, banana palms, palms that produce palm-oil, and mango trees covered with fruit.

Brightly coloured butterflies and large moths are becoming more frequent, along with a few wasps, or hornets. We have so far encountered very few mosquitoes (the fewer the better). We all apply anti-bug cream in the evening when *Seamaster* comes to a halt.

The big black urubu birds (a type of vulture) are wheeling overhead, while smaller swallow-types zoom in and out of the rigging or perch on the stays, singing with a high, clear note. It is all extremely beautiful.

The canoes often come really close. Two of them hitched a ride for a few miles (they said they were on their way to the next 'town'). They hooked a piece of wire around one of *Seamaster*'s stanchion bases and were dragged along at 9 knots. Eventually, one of the paddlers fell out and had to be rescued. Maybe we should have invited them aboard but our pilot and our cook — both local people — advised against it. No harm was done apart from a wetting.

Typical riverbank dwellings in the Furo do Tajapura tributary — the Amazonians either carve a space in the jungle or build on stilts over the water.

Location On the river

A number of the pink river dolphin appeared just before dark and stayed around all night. These ones were a rich medium pink and quite extraordinary. They grow to about 2.5 metres in length, can weigh up to 150 kg, and are the main predators of fish in the Amazon, often heading away from the main channels into the flooded forest (at high river) in pursuit of their prey. Their eyesight is reportedly not too good but they are masters in the use of their built-in sonar, which is more useful anyway in the muddy brown waters of the river.

Coming out of the Furo Ituquara, where we spent the night, we had to weave our way between the long nets laid by the fishermen in the pre-dawn hours. Most people seemed to be up and around with the coming of the sun. No doubt they go to bed soon after it sets.

We are now heading up one of the main sections of the Amazon, pushing against a 3-knot current, and expect to make a further 80 to 100 miles before once again stopping for the night. The river is so big that we could keep going after dark, but stopping and looking and listening and smelling and taking it all in is why we have come here.

The river is wide at this point — wide and brown. We have been passing numerous canoes and many small fishing boats all day. A good lookout has to be kept for nets at all times. They often stretch for many hundreds of metres across our path. We have also passed numerous log-carrying barges heading down the river. Much of the logging of the Amazon trees is, supposedly, illegal, but there is little done about it. Joseph, our pilot, has advised us that mosquitoes will be out in force tonight, and that even he will be putting on the insect repellent.

The afternoon was very warm, with temperatures in the shade around 35 degrees C. Copping the full glare of the early-afternoon sun, our exposed deck, even though painted a pale cream, was registering 59 degrees C. Thank goodness for the polar insulation beneath the decks to shield the accommodation.

Rodger Moore has spent many months with us now, often to be found sorting out generally unsavoury plumbing problems in the bilge. Having a father and son (Rodger and Alistair) in our crew actually works very well. Both have a passion for what we are doing. Here are Rodger's thoughts on the Amazon to date:

'Here I am, one year since my introduction to *Seamaster*. What an experience! First, the four-week crossing of the Southern Ocean and the rounding of Cape Horn and the cruising time in the Beagle Canal. Then the sail from Ushuaia, past the Falkland Islands, to Buenos Aires. Then the great sail from Buenos Aires up the coast of Brazil to the entrance of the Amazon.

The crew is now working like a well-oiled machine — a great bunch of people. The boat has been transformed to handle tropical conditions and I am in my newly purchased hammock, sitting/lying while I make notes.

We have chosen various topics of interest to study and make comment on while we are here. Mine is Amazon history and exploration.

The Amazon changed forever with the arrival of Europeans in the fifteenth century — first the Portuguese and then the Spanish. The Spanish made two trips down the Amazon after plundering the Incas in the Andes. The Portuguese, in 1637–38, were the first to travel upstream. There was a signed treaty between these two nations, but the boundary was stretched in favour of the Portuguese because of their presence in the Amazon basin. After the initial rush for the elusive gold had failed, the quest became intellectual enlightenment. The 'green hell' of the conquistador became the 'paradise' of the naturalist.

Awareness of immense botanical riches in the Amazon grew, and the next serious explorers, in the eighteenth century, were the scientists. Among the first was a Frenchman, Charles Marie de la Condamine, who came to resolve an argument over the precise shape of the earth. He took leave from his employment, planning to be away for two years but staying ten.

The next great explorer was Baron Alexander von Humboldt, who catalogued more than 12,000 plant species, most of which were new to science. He also entered the natural canal system that links the Amazon and Orinoco river systems (the Casiquiare) and, in a very arduous journey, tracked it for 322 kilometres.

Another, Henry Walter Bates, in 1848 came and documented close to 15,000 insects. His 1863 publication *The Naturalist on the River Amazon* is still regarded as one of the best contemporary accounts of Amazon natural history of his time.

These scientific explorers gave a changing Europe more than just catalogues of plant and insect life however. When de la Condamine returned to France in 1745, he took with him the first example of latex sap from a rubber tree, an important element at the beginning of the Industrial Revolution.

Then there was a remedy used by the native Indians for malaria — a bitter-tasting alkaloid called quinine, obtained from the red bark tree that is a native of Peru and Ecuador. An Englishman took

Opposite *Seamaster* about to leave a breathless Furo Ituguara.

seeds of the tree to India, where they flourished, and quinine became a worldwide treatment for malaria. The drug was made into a tonic. The colonials added gin to mask quinine's inherent bitterness — and the world-famous G&T was born.

Hardwoods, including mahogany and teak, were exported in large quantities. Chocolate made from the seeds of the cacao tree became a popular drink amongst teetotallers, notably Quakers such as the Cadbury family.

Nothing, however, prepared the Amazon for the follow-on affects of Condamine introducing latex to a Europe starting in on the Industrial Revolution. Like quinine, rubber was known to, and used by, the Indians long before the Europeans arrived. Its value in the newly industrial world was huge and its value

in the marketplace was strictly controlled by government and private companies, who maintained a tight rein on exports to control prices, while also exploiting a completely unprepared and hapless workforce. The native Indians were forced to tap the raw latex from the trees and prepare it for shipping, under fear of torture and death. Their lives were incidental to the ever-increasing lust for profits.

Rubber ruled supreme for 30 years, between 1880–1910, until rubber plants were eventually smuggled out of the Amazon to British colonies around the world and the monopoly held by the rubber barons was broken.

The city of Manaus, for which we are headed, was one result of the rubber boom. It is thriving today but for different reasons.

5 October 2001

●

Location Off the entrance to the Rio Curua

1100hrs: The higher land to starboard is in contrast to the marshy ground that began the day. Escarpments 200 metres high flank the northern side of the river. There are a number of jungle-clad volcanic cones rising among them. This was obviously once an area of great upheaval in days long forgotten. Similar times could be returning — but not for reasons of volcanic activity.

The river here is between three and 4.5 kilometres wide, and up to 60 metres deep. We are plugging away into the current — 2 to 6 knots of it most of the time but 5 knots yesterday evening. That slows your progress considerably, and is something we will have to put up

with for the next few weeks as we progress towards our first goal of Manaus. We are pleased that we are here during the dry season, with a slower flow. It must be quite interesting at the peak of the rainy season.

On Ollie's watch in the middle of the night, he found a bat hanging just above Franck's hammock — hanging there and examining the hammock's occupant. We had passed cattle farms in the late afternoon yesterday and Marc thought it had probably come from nearby there. Franck didn't have his mosquito net in place, but from now on nets will definitely be on all hammocks at night.

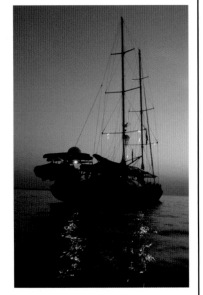

At anchor in the Rio Curua.

Pushing current in the main stream of the Amazon with Marc on bow lookout.

Even though there may be few insects at the moment, the potential problem of vampire bats is worse. They are known to carry rabies and leptospirosis. The mosquito nets should keep them away. We all take our anti-malarial tablets every day, but there is nothing to take to help prevent against the risk of dengue fever that will become more and more prevalent the further we travel up river. The correct grade of insect repellent and the wearing of long-sleeved shirts and trousers tucked into boots will give the most protection.

We left before sun-up this morning, motoring in a wide, brown stretch of water with the hills and mountains now giving way to low land once again — a dark-green line of jungle with the much brighter green of the grasses and reeds bordering the river's edge, plus long sandy beaches.

We have seen a container ship as well as a number of passenger boats that call into the small villages at the side of the river, and a cruise ship from the Bahamas. Paulo told us that it costs only 140 reals (about US$55) to travel the six days from Belem to Manaus on one of the local boats — sleeping in your own hammock — or twice as much for a cabin.

Around the middle of the day, Ollie mentioned that we were coming level with another small river entrance that led away parallel to the main river for a number of miles, past Ilha Gurupatuba and up to the town of Monte Allegre, before rejoining the Amazon again.

We launched the RIB and headed off — planning to meet *Seamaster* upriver a couple of hours later. It was an interesting time, motoring past small farms, seeing children playing in the river, pigs and horses cooling off in the water, and large green and black iguana lizards that watched us as we sped by or lazed in the branches of trees and hardly opened an eye when we stopped to look. The vultures circled overhead or sat staring from the tops of trees. There were numerous large, snow-white herons, flashy kingfishers, black Amazon cormorants and one green parrot. We even came across an iguana swimming across the river entrance, surrounded by a number of pink dolphin and the smaller grey dolphin.

The afternoon has been another hot one with *Seamaster* motoring downwind and directly into the sun. As relief, we have anchored early off the entrance of Rio Curua. The younger members of the crew have put on their boots and are off in the RIB to look further upriver and possibly ashore. The pink dolphins continue to play around us, snorting in a very distinctive way that is quite different to the clean 'whoosh' of the common dolphin. They are an extraordinary, almost unreal colour, like something out of a cartoon. Ollie has the hydrophone in the water and the rest of us are sitting in the shade in the cockpit listening to the sonic clicks. It adds a whole new dimension to what we are looking at.

Marc is itching to get into the water and swim with the dolphins. He says: 'If the dolphins are present, the piranhas aren't.' It's an interesting theory!

The sun sets after another long, hot day on the Rio Curua.

9 October 2001

●

Location Santarem, in the Rio Tapajos

Opposite Another glorious sunset on the Rio Tapajos.
Below Peter, helped by Marc and Alistair, prepares for his first dive in a lagoon off the Rio Tapajos.

A day of diving — our first in the Amazon. Miguel brought Carlos, a long-time friend and local scuba diver, aboard to go over the charts with us and help identify the best dive spots.

My notes from the session indicate:

Dive spot 1 Caiman (alligator family) and tropical fish

Dive spot 2 Caiman, turtles, black piranha and anaconda (I'm not sure that I will dive this one until Ollie has had a good look around first and returns in one piece)

Dive spot 3 Much the same as #2

We up-anchored from the city of Santarem at dawn and motored a few miles upriver, dropping anchor again off a sandy beach that stretched away as far as the eye could see. Before going ashore, Marc gave us all a briefing on what to be aware of and what to look out for. He outlined how to avoid confrontations with snakes — and what and what not to do if bitten. Anti-snake venom was in the day-pack.

The kayaks, dive gear, dive bottles, water containers, cameras and rucksacks were all carried a few hundred metres over some dunes, through a small stream that came up to our shorts, and along a track through the trees. Our destination was a sandy area beside a small lake with a crystal-clear stream flowing out of it.

It took a while to get the divers (including me) into our gear. The last proper dive we'd had was in Antarctica. Interestingly, that meant that the air we were about to breathe from the scuba bottles had come from the ice at the bottom of the world.

Carlos advised us that the caiman were amongst the reeds 'just over there', the anaconda — up to six metres long — were slightly further round the edge of the lake 'over there', and the piranha were generally 'everywhere'.

We set off in a clockwise direction around the not-very-deep lake (probably three to four metres at most), mindful that we were likely to encounter some life forms that we hadn't met before (well, I was anyway).

We did find a turtle or two, buried in the mud of the bottom of the lake and waiting out the daylight hours in seclusion, and there were numerous brightly coloured 'aquarium' fish keeping within the shade of the overhanging trees around the lake's edge. We also saw a school of piranhas, which didn't look too threatening, and Ollie came across a small caiman lying on the bottom — watching him. Of the anacondas — no sign (thank goodness).

I'm not particularly squeamish, but when the visibility turned out to be quite poor — our fins kicked up the bottom into a thick brown fog — and my imagination started working overtime, I am not sure I could say that I enjoyed it as much as I might have.

Location Rio Tapajos — near the small town of Alter do Cha

Since leaving Belem nine days ago, we have been amazed by the beauty of the river scenery, by the friendliness of these shy people, by the life in the water and, even though we have yet to encounter it first hand, by the life that we know we will see on the edge of the jungle, particularly after Manaus.

The Amazon has evolved over a long time — too long for us to comprehend. As in the rest of the world, forests and jungles were cut down to provide space to grow crops, for fuel and because the trees were a readily available cash crop. Now roads have been forged through the wilderness areas of the planet, opening up large tracts to easy access for forestry and mining.

Oil and gas are to be found in some of the most remote parts of the world, from the Antarctic to the Arctic. These oil and gas (and coal) deposits, fossil fuels formed many millennia ago, are huge stores of carbon. They have remained in the ground — until now. To feed man's voracious appetite for energy, they are being tapped and burned — as fuel for transport, industry and the raft of other 'essentials' of modern life.

While the resulting emissions are causing global problems, such as the seemingly omnipotent global warming, delicate ecosystems, such as the Amazon that have evolved over millions of years, are also under threat from the 'harvesting' process.

Here in the Amazon, the timber, minerals and fossil fuel sources are not the only easily available 'resources' to be exploited. Most of the bigger animals here are already gone — or nearly so. Many others are following the same fate. The world market for endangered species, be it jaguar pelts or boa constrictor skins or live parrots, is increasing.

Making a quick dollar is generally the motive behind the deforestation, the mining, the stripping, the cutting down, the shooting, the capturing and so on. But, because this is happening to some far-away forest, jungle, ice shelf, whale, jaguar, life in the sea or in a river, and because it doesn't directly affect us on a daily basis, we choose perhaps not to care enough.

We should. This Amazon basin in its present form, for instance, is vital to all of us. For every five breaths that we take, no matter where we are in the world, the oxygen for one of those breaths comes from here — i.e. one-fifth of all the world's oxygen is produced by the plant life in the Amazon.

The Amazon jungle also regulates climate, smoothes out water flows after heavy rain, and contains more biodiversity — plants, animals, insects, birds, all life — than any other one place on the planet.

To cut it down for a short-term financial gain would be foolhardy in the extreme, but there is a plan

Safety briefing from Marc (Hertel) before the team's first dive — in a lagoon off the Rio Tapajos. From left: Peter, Don, Rob, John, Geoff, Rodger, Carlos, Charlie, Miguel, Robin, Alistair, Marc.

Following page A local fisherman catching piranha in the lagoon off the Rio Tapajos where the *Seamaster* team enjoyed their first Amazon dive.

afoot to do just that and, if it goes ahead, the government-sponsored 'Advance Brazil' plan will mean the loss of 40 per cent of the jungle.

The results will not just be the loss of a large part of the 'lungs of the planet' and the destruction of a unique and vital ecosystem — the flow-on effects will be huge. Cut down the jungle or forests and water quality drops away as the natural filtering process disappears. Erosion sets in. The climate changes. Desertification begins.

If we keep taking from nature in the way we are, be it from the forests or from life in the sea, then the not-so-long-term effects will be catastrophic. The acceleration of global warming, due to loss of carbon sinks (deforestation) combined with the burning of more and more fossil fuels (oil, gas and coal), doesn't bear thinking about.

The latest scientific evidence indicates that the Amazon as we know it could all be gone within 20 years, as a result of global warming; and instead of the Amazon being a crucial carbon sink, it will start releasing all the carbon that it is storing into the atmosphere. Then we will know what global warming really means. In the same time period, the oceans will be stripped of all of the commercial stocks

of fish, which will mean starvation for many. And all because a quick dollar is deemed more important than the longer-term considerations; all because the bottom line of corporate balance sheets is more important than sustainability.

There are those who argue that the predictions of a serious spike in global warming should the Amazon rainforest be cut down, and the forecasts of fish stocks being completely depleted, are scaremongering. They are not. Ask the inhabitants of the Pacific atolls whose islands are already threatened by rising water levels. Ask the cod in the North Atlantic.

One of the greatest tragedies is that sustainable alternatives are available now. Fossil fuels could be replaced very quickly by fuels that do not increase the amount of carbon dioxide and other harmful emissions into the atmosphere. Hydrogen power, solar, wind, water and wave power — all are available right now but await the global commitment that will be required to ensure a sustainable future.

Peter enjoys a dip in the 'deliciously cool' waters of the Rio Arua — a tributary of the Amazon some 50 kilometres from San Carlos.

Right **Downtown Santarem.**
Below **Gap year students
Charlie and Robin.**

The big, wide, brown Amazon River disappears into the haze ahead like an endless liquid conveyor belt. The more time we spend here, the more we appreciate just how enormous this river system is — and we have only just begun our journey.

Part of *Seamaster*'s crew for this expedition are two 18-year-olds — Charlie and Robin — from Emsworth, where I live in England. They are in their 'gap' year before starting university studies. Charlie had just finished his A levels before joining us and will be going on to study geography at varsity when he gets back. We have been receiving a lot of emails from schools around the world asking for more detail on the Amazon and I've asked Charlie to oblige with some facts and figures:

I'm the youngest member of *Seamaster*'s crew so the term 'cabin boy' is often used to attract my attention. It seems such a long time ago that Robin and I joined up with *Seamaster* and her crew in Buenos Aires, Argentina. The past six weeks on board have flown by. In that time we have travelled more than 3500 miles to reach Santarem, which is just a few hundred miles upstream from the mouth of the great Amazon River.

My specialist topic for this journey is 'The River System' and, like everyone else, I can't help but be impressed by the sheer size of the Amazon and its influence on life.

The Amazon is the largest equatorial forest in the world, occupying approximately 42 per cent of the total area of Brazil. The Amazon Basin is the earth's biggest freshwater ecosystem and reservoir, draining an area of more than seven million square km — over half the South American continent and equivalent to three-quarters the size of the continental United States.

It contains 30 per cent of the remaining forest in the world — an area larger than the whole of Western Europe. It comprises one-tenth of our planet's entire plant and animal species and produces one-fifth of the world's oxygen.

From its source, 5168 metres high in the Peruvian Andes and less than 200 km from the Pacific Ocean, the main stream collects water from more than 1100 tributaries as it travels the 6,577 km to the Atlantic. With its tributaries it holds an estimated 20 per cent of the world's liquid fresh water.

At the river's mouth, water flows into the Atlantic Ocean at 160–200,000 cubic metres per second — a flow greater than the world's next eight biggest rivers added together or 10 times that of the Mississippi.

The depth varies dramatically with seasonal flood, its level rising and falling an average of 12 metres across the seasons. The deepest point is supposed to be right near where we are at the moment — more than 80 metres.

For ships, there are more than 3,885 km of navigable inland waterway on the main river — the longest stretch in the world.

We are here in the dry season so the water level is very low. What we see and take pictures of could well be completely submerged in the not-too-distant future.

Location Obidos

We have just wasted an hour by having to backtrack out of a shallow area that was, according to the latest chart, supposed to be very deep. Land that wasn't when the chart was made, now is. Channels that weren't, now are — and very deep as well. It served as a reminder that we must always be on our guard. The river is constantly changing.

We must not forget, either, that this great river carries an enormous quantity of silt suspended in its waters — all the way to the Atlantic Ocean. The late Jacques Cousteau estimated the amount of that silt to be approximately 400 million tonnes per year. That is more than one million tonnes per day! Assuming that a large truck with trailer could carry 30 tonnes in one load, it would take 33,000 truckloads, each day, every day, to move the equivalent amount of material. No wonder the river changes its course, builds new sand bars, washes away old ones — and adheres only to its own rules.

Alistair Moore (24) has been with us since Day One — crossing the Pacific Ocean, rounding Cape Horn, exploring Patagonia and the Antarctic Peninsula, making the delivery up the South American coast, and now a key member of the Amazon expedition. Pretty soon he'll be getting off, temporarily, as a member of the 'Jungle Team' that will make its way through the Casiquaire Channel in Venezuela and then down the Orinoco. These are his thoughts on the Amazon to date:

This place is massive. It appears to go on forever — trees and plants as far as the eyes can see. Even the small towns and villages we pass seem to be under constant threat of being overrun by the trees and vegetation.

The forest seems to drink as much as it can. Water moves from root to leaf and then evaporates. This water, which rises into the atmosphere as vapour, condenses to form clouds that, in only a short time, release the water as rain.

Moisture released from the forest makes up more than 50 per cent of the Amazon rainfall. It can be some of the most violent rainfall in the world, with measurements in some areas exceeding ten metres in a year. It falls on a diverse area and supports a remarkable volume and variety of animal and plant life (i.e. more than 100 different tree species commonly existing in half a hectare).

The largest rainforest in the world, it is home to an outstanding number of different birds, mammals, reptiles and insects. The forest itself works just like a human lung, but in reverse. Each tree and plant absorbs carbon dioxide and gives off oxygen, like a huge filter — one that is 6,500,000 square km in area and that helps keep our planet's atmosphere in balance.

Several centuries ago, most of the world's tropical, subtropical and temperate zones were covered in forest. All these forests helped to filter and clean the world's atmosphere. But those forests have been decimated by man and his grab for timber — to build houses, boats, furniture — and to fuel his fires. The trees were replaced by crops and the land mined for other fuels and minerals.

Brazil is now eyeing the economic value in clearing large parts of the Amazon rainforest and this most wondrous of places is facing the same fate as the rest.

From what I have learned, the world would be a very different place without this awe-inspiring frontier land. There are those who argue that it is unfair for other nations, who have already felled their forests, to condemn Brazil, with its burgeoning population and its economic problems, for wanting to capitalise on its massive natural resource.

That's not good enough. The Amazon rainforest cannot be sacrificed. It is much too important to the world as a whole, far more so than the immediate value of its timber or minerals that lie beneath.

The river rapids at the village of Arua.

18 October 2001

●

I have been reading *Travels on the Amazon and Rio Negro* by Alfred Russel Wallace. Wallace was the co-discoverer, along with Darwin, of the principle of natural selection as the main agent in the evolution of species. He spent four years in the Amazon between 1848 and 1852.

Wallace travelled from Belem to Santarem by canoe — following a similar route to that being taken by *Seamaster*. He recounts:

> Numerous flocks of parrots, and the red and yellow macaws, fly across every morning and evening, uttering their hoarse cries. Many kinds of herons and rails frequent the marshes on its banks, and the large handsome duck is often seen swimming about the bays and inlets. But perhaps the most characteristic birds of the Amazon are the gulls and terns, which are in great abundance. Their cries can be heard all night long over the sand-banks where they deposit their eggs. During the day they constantly attract our attention with their habit of sitting in a row on a floating log, sometimes a dozen or 20 side by side and going for miles down stream as grave and motionless as if they were on some very important business. These birds deposit their eggs in little hollows in the sand. The Indians say that during the heat of the day they carry water in their beaks to moisten the eggs and prevent them being roasted by the glowing rays of the sun. Porpoises are constantly blowing in every direction, and alligators are often seen slowly swimming across the river.

Maybe it's the time of year but, while we have seen many dolphins — both pink and grey, we have seen precious few of the birds that Wallace catalogued, and only one alligator (caiman) to this point. On the other hand, Wallace saw no cattle farming. Tracking his footmarks, we are passing an endless ribbon of farms fronting the river banks. The river in his day was lower. The average level of the Amazon is now much higher — and increasing.

Many of the indigenous people here still exist as they did in Wallace's day — but then there were six to nine million of them. That number has dwindled to no more than 200,000. They have been replaced by 'newcomers'. As land was 'discovered' and 'civilisation' advanced, the indigenous people were massacred, perished from diseases to which they had no immunity, or were absorbed and ended up the poorest of the poor.

While we are finding a different Amazon to that experienced by Wallace, the biodiversity count in the Amazon remains mind-numbing. Life here is almost uncountable — there is so much of it.

The following are all approximate species numbers, because no one knows for sure, and most estimates seem to vary enormously — sometimes by a factor of 10 or more.

Fish	2500
Mammals	300
Birds	2000
Insects	Millions
Trees	Up to 300 different species per hectare
Plants	60,000 to 300,000

What are some of our impressions of the Amazon compared to what we expected?

We thought it would be a wide, brown river where we would be unable to see either bank at times. Not so. While it is huge, we can almost always see the other bank, and the trees, and the houses, and the people.

We thought there would be many biting insects — particularly mosquitoes (carrying malaria and dengue fever). Sure, the insects gather at night, attracted by our lights, but otherwise we have been remarkably insect-free. Particularly interesting was the time spent in the Rio Tapajos and its tributary last week — where there were almost no insects at all. We understand that the Rio Negro is also very good in this respect — due to the acidity of the river water. The bugs don't like it.

We thought there would be at least one heavy shower of rain every day. This is the dry season, with October being the least rainy month. There have been a few showers — some torrential — but nothing at all for the past 11 days.

Completely unexpected has been the constant presence of humanity. There are almost always houses in sight, with small villages and larger towns at regular intervals along the river. Having said that, the river is the main highway and fishing resource, so maybe the people-presence is not so surprising after all.

20 October 2001

●

Location Rio Negro

We have just crossed over from the muddy brown waters of the Amazon into the clear black of the Rio Negro. It was like watching a giant mixer adding thick cream to coffee. The line in the water distinguishing the two great rivers was quite distinct.

It is now 50 days since we left Buenos Aires in Argentina, and the sprawling city of Manaus is off to starboard. The 1000-mile journey upstream, with a few side-trips into tributaries, has taken 18 days.

The Rio Negro, the fourth-largest river in the world, and the second biggest tributary to the Rio Amazonas, will be our 'base' for the next month or so.

We plan to be in port in Manaus for a few days, preparing for what lies ahead, much of which is unknown. This city of more than two million people was founded in 1669 and was originally known as Barra. It grew from a garrison town that was part of the original Portuguese fort. By 1830, there were approximately 3000 inhabitants, mostly trading in the region's products. Renamed Manaus in 1850 and elevated to the status of a provincial capital, it is now a service centre for the region.

The development of a technique to cure the natural latex changed Manaus forever. It became the 'rubber capital' of the world and freighters plied the Amazon waters, taking rubber to Europe and New York and bringing back holds full of the trappings of 'civilisation'. The population of Manaus swelled to more than 50,000, who enjoyed electric trolley transportation, a telephone system, three hospitals, 35 schools and a public library, plus regular trans-Atlantic steamship services.

A most obvious extravagance was the blue-domed opera house, which was home to three theatrical companies (and which has recently been refurbished). This magnificent facility in the very heart of the Amazon could seat 1600 people and attracted world-famous artists including Caruso, Pavlova and Bernhardt.

Between 1908 and 1910, 80 million rubber trees were spread over four million square kilometres surrounding the city. These trees produced 80,000 tons of raw rubber annually. The export duties alone were covering 40 per cent of Brazil's national debt. But the BOOM was soon to go BUST.

Rubber plantations in Malaysia, grown from seeds smuggled out of Brazil 30 years earlier, were in better condition and more productive than their Amazon cousins. Returns dropped sharply until plantation owners started to sell assets at a loss to escape bankruptcy. Whole empires collapsed and the ships returning to Europe were soon full of escaping people.

Manaus went into decline and it wasn't until the middle of the twentieth century that the city slowly started to regain its lost prosperity. High-quality rubber was still produced, albeit in small quantities, and demand for rubber generated by World War II also helped.

In 1967, Manaus became a tax-free haven and refocused on becoming a regional trade centre for all of the products and services that now funnelled through the expanding city.

By 2001, the population of Manaus was close to two million and tourism had become an important part of the city's commerce. The huge floating dock built by the British for the rubber trade is now used by the fleet of riverboats that service the growing number of visitors to the area.

Night-time reflections in the inky black waters of the Rio Negro.

25 October 2001

Location Manaus

I have just returned from a rather quick round trip to Rio de Janeiro — to meet with Dr Klaus Toepfer, the head of the United Nations Environment Programme and attend a UNEP-sponsored meeting of the environment ministers of all the Latin American and Caribbean countries.

The ministers that I spoke to were all very aware of the need to manage the Amazon and its resources with extreme caution, in a very sustainable way. But there are many other pressures being brought to bear and the solutions to saving the Amazon from catastrophic exploitation on a grand scale will not be easily found.

It's a complex problem — one that revolves around what the forest is worth in its present state, to a country that is struggling to cope with an ever-increasing population, massive debt, a ruined economy and high levels of poverty among its people; and what that forest is worth to all mankind, now and away into the future.

I am fast coming to the conclusion that the rest of the world is going to have to act if the Amazon is to be saved. The world as a whole is going to have to invest in preserving this rainforest, which is so essential to the global climate, as a carbon sink, and as a lung that generates one-fifth of the world's oxygen.

Then there's the amazing biodiversity of the region, which is a growing source of yet-to-be-discovered pharmaceutical drugs. And then there are the indigenous peoples and their rights to live as they have always done in their forest.

The fate of the Amazon, then, is a global challenge that will be a severe but crucial test of man's ability to come to terms with the fact that he can, in environmental terms, very definitely influence the future. The big question is whether he will choose to influence for the good or for the bad.

The repair yards along the waterfront of the 'river city' Manaus — now occupied by local ferries.

27 October 2001

●

Seamaster's crew has grown in the last couple of days with the arrival of Dr (medical) Marc Shaw, Dr (scientific) Mark Orams, and our documentary film crew Simon Atkins and James Walsh from Big Wave Productions in the UK.

The two doctors went straight to work. Dr Shaw spent time at a local hospital researching snakes and venoms (he will be a key member of the Jungle Team in the near future). Dr Orams, who is an expert on dolphins, has been looking into the rehabilitation of manatee and the giant otter.

We had hoped to resume our journey yesterday but were held up by local officialdom. It has taken Ollie three days to wade through the process of clearing *Seamaster* to visit points further up the Rio Negro, and extending crew visas and *Seamaster*'s time allowance in Brazilian waters. So we left this morning, complete with two new pilots — one a specialist in the nearby archipelago, the other an expert on the Negro River between Manaus and San Gabriel (which is about as far as we expect to be able to proceed in *Seamaster*).

We are now veering northwest up the Negro, always away from the ocean, towards our next stopping point. Again there are white sandy beaches and sand bars with the dark green of the ever-present forest ribboning both banks. Shallow patches have had us creeping along at minimum speed with the centreboards raised a little. The river banks are far less scoured-out than in the Amazon itself. The flow against us is only a knot or so, much more acceptable than the 3 to 5 knots we have been punching for the last few weeks since Belem.

Miguel talked to the captain of a river ferry this morning. The ferry was on its way downstream to Manaus. The skipper told us that the river Negro ahead was very shallow, far shallower than normal, even for this time of the year.

We were ashore this afternoon, for a visit to some nearby caves. If I had been in the same situation in the bush in New Zealand, I would have felt very comfortable with my surroundings. But here in the Amazon, where there are many of the nastiest creatures to be found, I wasn't so cavalier.

To touch a tree meant being aware of what was on the tree — or what had built its nest in the tree — or what was waiting to land on your shoulders. To step over a log meant being careful to first look what was on the other side, to avoid a possible problem with a snake. But we didn't see any snakes — or anything else particularly unpleasant.

Our guide asked us to be very quiet at one particular point to avoid being attacked by some rather feisty wasps, but apart from these and the usual biting ants, all was disappointingly well.

Left Peter and Alistair in the dinghy and leading *Seamaster* up the Rio Negro.
Below Near Ilha do Capitari in the Rio Negro.

Location Rio Jau

Looking at the depth-sounder plot during this morning, it was like examining a design for an extreme roller-coaster ride. The sandy bottom was in waves driven by the current. And I'm not talking of small waves. These were five to six metre-high sand waves, closely spaced. One extreme wave was 15 metres high — which is like a five-storeyed building.

To port and to starboard is the never-ending green of the forest. There are very few insects. They don't like the acidity of the water — the tannin that makes the water black (hence Rio Negro).

Our destination this evening, and for the next few days, is the Jau River National Park — still 15 miles and probably three hours away, depending on the depths encountered.

This river (the Jau), is approximately 1100 miles from the Atlantic Ocean. We are certainly making some progress into the continent. It should be a good place to start to see some of the real Amazon wildlife — the big caiman and the river otters, both on the endangered list. We also hope to see numerous turtles, but we may need to wait until we near Barcelos, another 100 miles or so further on.

Turtles inhabit much of the Amazon. The tartaruga, one of the largest freshwater turtles in the world, reaching 109 cm and 90 kg, were once abundant in the Amazon River Basin. Since colonisation by Europeans in the 1700s, they have been hunted to near-extinction, millions slaughtered for their meat and fat, and eggs boiled down for oil.

In the upper Amazon, near Tefe, about 48 million eggs were taken annually between 1848 and 1859. Apparently people waited on the beaches for the hatchlings and took them by the thousands. The fat from the turtles and eggs was boiled down to make oil, which was used to light the streetlamps of Manaus. What a familiar tale — almost mirroring what was going on in Antarctica at the same time, but with other species.

As a comparison of what was then and what is now:

The part of the river near Porto Velho was so choked with turtles during the nesting season that it was almost impossible for large ships to pass. Turtles were reported to be eight deep, across the whole width of the river, for four kilometres downstream of the town. Not a single turtle can now be found in the region today.

It has been calculated that hundreds of millions of eggs were taken from the Amazon in the nineteenth century for oil products alone. The same level of destruction was taking place in Venezuela as well.

Humboldt (in 1814) reported that 33 million eggs were taken per year to make oil. This destruction of a species continued until 1961. Despite this ravaging, however, there are still abundant populations of the tartaruga turtle in various parts of Brazil and it may be possible to restore this species to high levels again — if the human predation level can be kept in check.

Turtles have always been a source of food for the people inhabiting this region and that probably wasn't a problem when the human population was around 3.5 million. That population has swollen to 20 million in recent years, and therein lies the problem. What was environmentally sustainable in the past is no longer so.

Left Peter checks his surroundings in the jungle of the Jau River National Park.

Following page The forest reclaims an abandoned village in the Jau River National Park. The inhabitants are said to have been driven away by ants.

Above Tarantula — reckoned the biggest of the Amazon spider species.

Below Petroglyphs on rocks near Ilha do Gaviao — they date back to the early 1500s.

Right Huge boulders litter the Rio Negro near the village of Santa Helena.

Below Leon guides *Seamaster* through the tricky waters near the entrance to the Rio Branco.

The Rio Negro with its almost black water is reflecting the sky and the landscape like a mirror. There is no wind to stir the surface — just the occasional ripples of newly-appearing sand bars, and rocks hiding near the surface, their presence only given away by the tumbling current. It's a silver river today — the blue of the sky and the white puffy clouds imaging out of the water.

We have been zig-zagging upriver since breakfast. Sand bars to port, rocks to starboard, sand bars to starboard, islands to port; narrow channels that are deep, wide passages that turn shallow and more treacherous.

The scenery is the best yet — hidden coves protected by the shimmering white and golden sand, and the flattest surface of any stretch of water imaginable. I have never seen anything like it.

It's hot and humid — with no let-up likely until dusk. The crew manning the dinghy leading the way through the maze of channels are doing a great job, but also getting through the petrol. Whilst *Seamaster* carries considerable diesel reserves, our stocks of petrol for the outboards are limited. We have ordered two more drums for delivery by the regular Manaus to Barcelos ferry, but it apparently left early and passed us a couple of nights ago. No one is sure where the drums have ended up. They might be on a barge just around the next corner or they might have been off-loaded at Barcelos, another 80 miles or so further on. They might even be on their way back to Manaus!

The Rio Branco is a long river that heads off to the north — up to Boa Vista and beyond. Normally, three-metre-draught vessels can ply the river at any time, but not this year. We spoke to the captain of a barge who had just taken four days getting down this river and into the Rio Negro. He suggested that 1.5 metres is now the maximum, the river is that low.

We have had some close calls with the depth in the Rio Negro over the past couple of days. With our rudders up so that they don't protrude below the hull, and the ability to withdraw the centreboards, we have so far managed OK — but there have been sections when we have been sneaking along very slowly, boards completely up, with only a couple of centimetres of water between the hull and the sand. If the river drops another metre, we might end up with a Rio Negro Christmas. I'm not sure how well that would be received.

The Boto
Amazon River Dolphin

Dr Mark Orams, a marine scientist from Massey University in New Zealand, who is an expert on dolphins, has been with us aboard Seamaster for a month. He has written the following very informative piece on the river dolphins:

Dr Mark Orams.

It is unusual for an air-breathing, warm-blooded animal to live its entire life immersed in fresh water. In fact, of the thousands of species of mammals on our planet, the great majority are land-dwellers.

The cetacean group (whales, dolphins and porpoises) are one of the few exceptions to this terrestrial lifestyle (others include the sirenians — the manatees, dugongs and sea otters).

When one looks in more detail at the cetacean group, it is dominated by marine species (that is, those that live in the sea). While there are some that move between salt water and fresh, of the 75-plus species of cetaceans, only five live exclusively in fresh water.

This is the river dolphin family (known by the scientific name of *Platanistidae*). Thus, river dolphins are fascinating from a biological point of view because firstly, they are an unusual mammal that live their entire lives in water and secondly, because they are the only family of cetaceans that live exclusively in fresh water.

I have spent much of the last eight years studying dolphin and whale behaviour in the seas off New Zealand and Australia. So, the opportunity to observe, even for a short time, a species from the river dolphin family has me really excited. As a result, on this Amazon trip as part of blakexpeditions, one of my greatest hopes has been to see the boto (*Inia geoffrensis*) — the river dolphin species found here in the equatorial rivers of South America.

I didn't have to wait long. On the day after I arrived, at the anchorage off Punta Negro outside of Manaus, and barely 40 metres from *Seamaster*, two 'botos' surfaced with a characteristic 'puuuch-ooo' as they exhaled, inhaled and dived back under. I was ecstatic. I wasn't even looking for them and yet here they were barely 10 miles outside of the largest city in the Amazon region. I

waited for the next surfacing of the two botos, but nothing.

Patience, I thought, so I waited, waited and waited some more. Minutes went by and then 'puuuch-ooo' — more than 100 metres away and heading in the opposite direction, then gone again. That was the last I saw of them that day. Wow! I had heard and read that they were difficult to observe due to their quick and erratic surfacing behaviour but this was something else.

No chance to observe them under the water because the Rio Negro is the colour of tea and visibility is extremely limited (it is not dirty, merely stained by the vegetation upstream). I wondered how on earth scientists have been able to study them given what I had just experienced. I am used to cetaceans such as the bottlenose and common dolphins — dolphins that often approach boats and spend considerably more time active at the surface where I am able to observe and record their behaviour.

The following day I had the opportunity to learn more about those challenges when I met Dr Vera da Silva, the foremost scientist studying river dolphins in Brazil, at the Amazon Region National Research Institute (INPA) in Manaus.

INPA has a 'campus' in a park-like setting where many of the most important scientists working on various aspects of the Amazon are based. Dr da Silva is the director of INPA's Aquatic Mammal Laboratory. As I approached her office I was greeted by a strange series of noises — almost like an air-horn. Fascinated, I approached a large caged area about 10 x 20 metres. Inside was a large pool, logs, running water, a sand area, trees and two of the most amazing looking animals I have seen and the source of the noise — giant otters (*Pteonura brasiliensis*).

Almost as tall as I am, they immediately swam up to check me out at close quarters — barking, splashing and jumping. They were loud, obnoxious and playful — and I loved them. There's just something about complex, social, aquatic mammals that gets me going.

Immediately questions came into my mind — how do they reproduce, what is their population status, do they use co-operative hunting techniques, how do their young learn, how do they communicate with one another? Curiosity is the foundation for all good biologists but — as I have discovered — patience and perseverance are other essential attributes. Eventually I dragged myself away for my meeting with Dr da Silva.

Vera da Silva is a dedicated and busy Brazilian scientist so I was grateful for her time. She knows more about the river dolphins of the Amazon than probably any other person. What I learned was that the boto is by far the largest of the world's river dolphins. Males grow to around 2.5 metres (weighing 180 kg) and females to just over two metres (120 kg). Fortunately, and unlike the other river dolphins of the world, the boto seems to be doing quite well (others such as the Ganges River dolphin and the Indus River dolphin are on the verge of extinction).

The boto is widespread throughout the Amazon and its tributaries (the *Seamaster* crew has reported many sightings since they entered the Amazon at Belem) and is also found in the Orinoco River and the Beni River systems. Its appearance (as I have later observed myself) is quite strange and very different to the image most people have of a dolphin.

The boto has a prominent and rounded head with a bulging forehead (melon). Unlike marine dolphins, the boto has a flexible neck and can turn its head sideways and up and down (in much the same way we can). It has an extremely long and narrow rostrum or beak (we don't call it a nose because they don't breath through their mouth but through their blow-hole located on the back of their head). The rostrum is around 18 per cent of the dolphin's body length. Its blow-hole is not located centrally but slightly to the left of centre. It has small eyes

but, in contrast to some reports, it can see quite well.

The boto does not have a pronounced dorsal fin like most dolphins, rather it has a raised dorsal ridge and a slight triangular-shaped hump in the middle of its back. It has large pectoral flippers that often have ragged trailing edges. It quite frequently has a pink coloration, which extends up its flanks from its belly — giving rise to its other common name — the red or pink dolphin.

Dr da Silva has been studying these dolphins for more than 10 years and she confirmed my early impressions regarding the difficulty of studying as reasonably accurate. However, she and her team are fortunate to work in an area where the water is clearer than that of the Rio Negro where I had observed the boto and thus they are able to sometimes observe them under and on the surface.

They also have a long-term monitoring strategy whereby they briefly capture the boto, obtain basic measurements, tag and release them. Through radio tagging, they have been able to learn a great deal about the movements and behaviour of these unusual dolphins. Some of what they have found provides insight into perhaps why this species of river dolphin has remained relatively abundant. They are generalists in terms of their feeding behaviour and have been found to prey on more than 50 different species of fish. Additionally, and most importantly, the fish species they prey on are not targeted by commercial or subsistence fisheries.

The boto takes advantage of the opportunities offered by the huge range of water levels in the river systems of the Amazon Basin. In the dry, it focuses on the confluence areas where rivers join and where, presumably, fish are more abundant. In the wet, it extends its range out into the flood plain, searching amongst the trees on the forest floor where its flexible neck and body are a great advantage.

It is assumed that the boto's echolocation (sonar) abilities are extremely good — the often turbid waters of the river system would seem to require this. Anatomical features such as the boto's small eyes, large melon and elongated rostrum suggest that indeed its echolocation abilities are extreme.

Early in the voyage, further downstream, Ollie was able to record some of the underwater vocalisations of botos with his hydrophone. Listening to these, it was apparent to me that the boto uses a series of scanning clicks (sound impulses), which to my ear resembled rapid-fire 'pops' in bursts of several seconds' duration, then silence for several seconds (presumably to receive the reflected sound waves back) before another scan burst.

A further interesting explanation for the boto's apparent success is not biological at all, but cultural. Apparently botos have many legends associated with them that date back to pre-European times. Many of the indigenous people of Amazonia considered the boto to be souls of drowned people. Other stories tell of an enchanted city under the water where a boto kingdom lies. Another story warns that anybody who looks at a lamp fuelled by boto oil (derived from its blubber) will go blind. Probably the most often repeated story is that the boto can transform into a handsome man who then seduces young women and impregnates them. Thus, unexplained pregnancies amongst young females in the Amazon area were often attributed to the boto. Not so long ago, apparently, the birth register for parts of the Amazon even contained a number of babies with the father registered as the boto!

To this day, to harm a boto is considered to bring bad luck and thus the boto retains a special status amongst the people of the Amazon. As a consequence, it has avoided the hunting pressure that has brought other mammals of the region close to extinction — such as the Amazonia manatee (*Trichechus inunguis*).

Vera da Silva admits that we still have much to learn about this unique dolphin of the rivers. And, while the boto appears to be doing well, there is no reason to be complacent about its future which, inevitably, is directly linked to the future health of the Amazon Basin. Because the boto does not move very far, and because it is restricted entirely to this freshwater habitat, it does not have the opportunity to migrate and find new food sources should those of the Amazon become further depleted. Nor does it have the opportunity to escape pollution.

In recent times, we have learned that dolphins, because they are at the top of the food chain, have a propensity to build up toxins in their tissues. The example of the extremely high levels of toxins found in the beluga that live in the St Lawrence River in North America shows us what can happen to an aquatic animal dependent on a specific ecosystem. Thus, as with all animal life here, erosion of the quality of the Amazonian ecosystem will inevitably mean a decrease in the health and abundance of the boto.

All things are tied together; what we do affects all living things — including ourselves. The decisions we make are important and it is critical that we look beyond our own immediate needs and day-to-day lives when making those decisions — what we purchase, who we vote for, how we act, the causes we support, the harmful actions of others we choose to ignore. All will come back to haunt us if we do not take a broader view of our responsibilities.

This has become more real to me in recent times — not just because I am a marine mammal 'nut' lucky enough to see botos in the Amazon — but because I am now a father. My two-year-old son Daniel and my six-month-old daughter Brianna deserve a world that is healthy and abundant with life. They deserve the wonderful opportunity that I have been given to explore and experience the wonder and beauty of nature, of the living planet of which we are such an important part.

Typical expedition mode — the RIB leads the way for *Seamaster* on the Rio Negro, constantly checking the depths for sand banks and rocks.

Large stone boulders exposed by the low river levels in the Rio Negro near Santa Helena.

6 November 2001

Location Rio Negro, near Ilha Peixe-Boi

After breakfast, some of us went ashore to visit the school in the village of Santa Helena. Don had printed out colour photographs taken when he was with one of the classes yesterday. We went to give them to the teacher, along with a photo of me in Antarctica earlier this year (on my mountain bike next to a seal on the ice, with *Seamaster* in the background). The children thought them quite extraordinary. The school is very short of exercise books, pens and pencils, so we plan to make up a big pack and send it to them before we exit the Amazon.

They went back to their class, and we walked back between the houses to the river and our dinghy. Pigs, ducks, chickens and dogs were everywhere. A green parrot perched on a stick on a window ledge, taking in the scene and muttering to itself. A fisherman was cleaning several large, recently-caught catfish by the water's edge. Youngsters played in the shallows of the river while their mothers scrubbed pots, pans and clothes.

Once back aboard *Seamaster*, we got under way and resumed our journey, threading our way between the boulders and winding our way from one side of the river to the other as we followed the narrow channels.

We slowly began to run out of water and at one stage had to backtrack and find another way through a shallow section, the centreboards fully up and only 20 cm of water under *Seamaster*'s hull. If the river drops more than another 20 cm, we won't get out — well, at least not the way we came today, and that is the main route.

We now have my wife Pippa on board. She arrived yesterday after catching a float plane from Manaus and finding us in the river.

Our resident marine scientist Dr Mark Orams has written the following in response to the many emails we have been receiving from schools asking for more information on the caiman:

There are four species of caimans found in the Amazon basin. During our expedition thus far we have mostly seen the small, spectacled caiman (*Caiman crocodilus*). Other species are the black (*Melanosuchus niger*), smooth-fronted (*Paleosuchus trigonatus*) and musky (*Paleosuchus palpebrosus*) caimans.

The black caiman is the largest of this group, growing to around five metres in length. The spectacled caiman can grow to around 2.6 metres but the great majority we have seen have been under a metre. Caimans grow extremely quickly and reach full maturity in around five years (about half the time of other crocodilian species). They have a wide and varied diet feeding on fish, amphibians (especially frogs), insects, birds, mammals and even crustaceans (like crabs).

Locals here call the caimans 'jacare' and, in some places, they have warned us not to swim because large ones have been sighted. The biggest we have seen has been around 1.5 metres. They are easiest to find at night because they possess a reflective substance in the cornea of their eyes and this shines brightly in the dark when caught in a torchlight.

Unlike my experiences with crocodiles in Africa and Australia, and alligators in Florida, caimans seem very wary of humans and they bolt for the water whenever we approach. What has surprised me is their speed on land. Typically they rest close to the water's edge — sometimes in the undergrowth of the forest nearby — and it is amazing how quickly they can move when they take flight for the water. Their feet are partially webbed and they have sharp claws. When they run they are able to extend their strong legs and lift their body off the ground — they also seem to be able to lift their tail clear and, as a result, they really run, rather than drag their bodies to the water.

There is no way a human could outrun them when they choose to move their way. However, as with most wildlife, they seem more afraid of us than we are of them. It's probably for good reason, as caimans have been widely hunted in the Amazon and millions have been killed for the leather trade (people make belts, boots, shoes and even jackets from their skin). I would ask you to never buy a product made from crocodile, alligator or caiman skin. Do not support the destructive practices that have reduced this interesting family of reptiles to a fraction of its original numbers.

For those of you who are studying biology or zoology and are interested in the taxonomics of caimans, the following simple outline may help.

Kingdom	*Animalia*
Phylum	*Chordata*
Class	*Reptilia*
Order	*Crocodylia*
Family	*Alligatoridae*
Genus and species	*Caiman crocodilus*
	Melanosuchus niger
	Paleosuchus trigonatus
	Paleosuchus palpebrosus

Above Lady Blake arrives at *Seamaster* near the village of Santa Helena. From left Pippa, Robin, Miguel and Peter.

Below Pippa's float plane — smooth landing close to Santa Helena.

Opposite page Santa Helena fisherman mending his nets.

0500hrs: A light mist — like cool smoke — is invading the town and the river, thickening by the minute with tendrils rising from the inky black surface of the water. Orange streetlights have haloes around them and everything looks out of focus. It's cool — down to 24 degrees C. I've just taken over the watch from Charlie and Alistair. Both of them have been wearing their thermal tops. There's not a breath of wind.

A weak and very fuzzy half-moon is managing to penetrate the mist, but the stars are absent. There were some heavy showers of rain soon after we arrived at 12.30 pm yesterday — much-distant lightning forking between the clouds until late evening, and the rumble of thunder a constant reminder that the seasons are soon to change. So the mist this morning is probably part of the same weather system that is still working its way up the Rio Negro.

Looking over to port, the faint river bank only a hundred or so metres away is quite high along the front of the town. To the left are the main market (the fish market that opens at 5.30 am), general stores and houses. Then there's a bridge over a small dry ravine that obviously becomes part of the river as levels rise. To the right is the church — quite imposing, as they all seem to be — backed up by the school and then a hotel that is probably not what most of us are used to. It is like something out of the late 1800s, painted bright pinks and blues internally, with green doors and shutters. Next again is the radio station — Rio Negro — then a university-funded building housing Projecto Piaba, which is to do with the ornamental fish trade.

Many small craft are tied to the river bank, ranging from ferries to the smallest of bongos. Out to starboard of *Seamaster*, with the dawn starting to brighten, the mist turned to fog and the nearby island became an indistinct blur. We haven't had conditions like this before in the Amazon but Paulo says we can expect more as we head further north.

Upriver has been our destination from the beginning. How far we will get we don't yet know, but tomorrow we are heading off again, making for the Rio Itu. *Seamaster* will probably be too big to enter this river but, with a local pilot to help, we will have a try. At worst, we will anchor and carry on in the dinghies.

We want to end up at the small village of Daraqua, where the houses are built on stilts, where they make a living from the aquarium fish trade, and where Dr Richard Vogt, who we met in Manaus and who introduces himself as 'Dick Turtle', teaches and practises turtle conservation.

Up the river — always up the river. Always against the current. This is nothing like an ocean passage. It requires the same constant vigilance, but of a different sort — as Don outlines here:

'Up the lazy river . . . in the noonday sun . . .'

Rodger is on the bow with our Brazilian pilot Bosco. They are discussing which channel we will take, given the three options opening up in front of us. Actually, to refer to the action on the bow as a 'discussion' between Bosco and Rodger is incorrect. Bosco does not speak English and Rodger only a few words of Portuguese — 'thank you' and 'tomorrow' (perhaps the fundamental language of plumbers!).

Most of the discussion is done by hand signals. Bosco describes the course with a sweeping arm movement, followed by another movement that may be translated as 'straight ahead'. It could, however, be 'the fish was this big'.

Then a series of signals akin to conducting an excerpt from Beethoven's Fifth, a couple of traffic signals that you might make with your car window only half open, and finally a quick flick out to port. Was that last one a signal or a pesky fly?

Peter, viewing this from the pilot-house (the pilot being 20 metres away from the bow) is busy translating the signals and wondering if we should undertake the Beethoven's Fifth turn now. Fortunately, Rodger calls through on the VHF and enlightens us: 'Bosco says we should go straight ahead then take the left fork, pass the island to starboard while keeping to the right-hand side of the river bank. Or at least that is what I think he said. I'll get back to you when I know more.'

We refer to the chart — which is more like an extract from *Advanced Medicine* illustrating numerous, very close veins — to see if we can relate all this information to the patient laid out in front of us. However, quite often the chart shows something completely different to that which we see ahead. It is, after all, a river — and a big one at that. It will rise up many metres in the wet season but now it is at its lowest point, we hope.

I'm not sure how you can make a chart for such a changeable highway. Perhaps that is why Bosco does not even refer to the chart. How then does he navigate? I guess that Bosco 'reads the river' and selects the course for *Seamaster* from the appearance of the surface and the flow of the current.

By the time we make our way back out to the Atlantic we will have a good grip on this art form, or we could be celebrating Christmas in the middle of South America.

The river is some 12 kilometres wide in places, full of sand banks and islands with a maze of waterways that present a number of possible options

Following page An aerial view of the Negro showing the amazing contrast of the river bottom with the early morning sun highlighting the sand banks.

on ways to make your way up and down its length. Yesterday we were in a waterway that was only a half a kilometre wide, and the depths varied from 13 metres to 'oops, that was the bottom'.

To avoid spending our day on sand banks — or even worse — we have a dinghy out in front of us, quite often manned by Charlie and Robin. For these two young lads, being from England, it is appropriate for them to 'go out in the midday sun'. With the aid of a depth sounder, they continue to relay back to the pilot-house the depths ahead of Seamaster.

They will quite often spear off at a tangent to our course to investigate depths to port or starboard and report back on a possible route for us to take. If we feel that we are running a bit short on information, Alistair can climb up into the crow's-nest armed with another VHF. Now we can have news and views from the bow, the crow's-nest and the dinghy.

So — life continues, always 'up, up the lazy river'.

Alistair's turn to scout the way ahead for *Seamaster*.

We are midway between the Atlantic and Pacific Oceans — right in the centre of the Amazon Basin. This is as far as *Seamaster* will get up the Rio Negro this year.

We have made it to 1245 miles from the sea against a stiff current, doing so at the 'low-river', experiencing to the maximum the beauty of the scenery, the friendliness of the people and the unknowns that we have had to deal with, whilst fully appreciating the (relative) lack of insects. *Seamaster* has only just scraped through at times — with the bottom of our vessel millimetres from the sand.

Coming upstream has been one thing. Going back down will be something entirely different — the current behind us and giving us a far greater over-the-ground speed but also leaving less reaction time in the difficult sections. We hope we make it back to Manaus without being left high and dry due to a lowering river level, but only time will tell.

Our Jungle Team is getting ready to depart in 36 hours' time. Their lists are long and there is still much to do before we temporarily part company. As

Seamaster turns back down the Amazon to the Atlantic Ocean, the Jungle Team will continue on up the Negro aboard a shallow-draught ferry *Iguana*, to San Gabriel. The river will be extremely low at that point so they will pick up trucks and journey overland to the Venezuelan border — a ride of about six hours of dirt road.

Then, as *Seamaster* heads for the Atlantic swells, the salt air and trade winds once more, and turns left towards the Caribbean, the Jungle Team will be using three bongos (plus one of our inflatable dinghies) to traverse the Casiquaire Channel — the natural reversing waterway that links the Rio Negro with the Rio Orinoco. They will spend time living with a Yanomami Indian tribe and they will be putting up with the privations of river travel at its most basic. The insects will be far more numerous and voracious than anything we have experienced so far.

Iguana, Miguel's 18-metre riverboat, is secured alongside and most of the Jungle Team's gear has now been transferred on board, everything inspected and labelled. The Jungle Team will comprise Marc, Ollie,

The 18-metre river boat *Iguana* alongside *Seamaster* with the float plane from the Rio Negro Lodge.

Janot, Alistair and Dr Marc (alias 'Dr Jab'), along with our photographer Franck and the film crew of Simon and James.

There are many miles yet to cover — on both rivers and on the ocean. The Orinoco lies ahead for both groups — but a long way ahead at the moment.

It is greatly disturbing to find, even as far from civilisation as we now are, that the major environmental issues are the same. Fish are being taken from the sea at a greater rate than they are breeding. It's the same in the Rio Negro. The estimates are that in 25 to 30 years' time, unless action is taken very soon, there will be very little, if any, large-scale commercial fishing left anywhere in the world. Most of the stocks will have been reduced to a fraction of their previous levels or, even worse, will have disappeared altogether.

Here in the Rio Negro, the overfishing has already achieved alarming proportions. There are government guidelines in place to curb or halt overfishing but the commercial fishermen have moved in — en masse — and are taking all the fish. Sound familiar? It goes something like this:

A gill net, up to 750 metres long, is placed right across the mouth of a lagoon. Another is placed right around the edge of the lagoon, while more nets are placed at five-metre intervals right across the lagoon, dividing the water space up into lanes. Nothing escapes. Everything is taken. Everything! The next lagoon follows, then the next, and then the next. The fish are taken to Barcelos for freezing and then on to Manaus for local sale and/or export.

It is estimated that the fish stocks in the upper Rio Negro have halved in the past two years. Leave the commercial fishermen to do as they want for only a short time longer and the whole natural infrastructure here might fail. The fish will be gone and so will many other life forms — including those people who for centuries have lived sustainably within their environment.

This intolerable situation is not the making of the local people, who depend on their small lagoons and stretches of river for their daily food. They, like the fish, are victims as their traditional food supply is decimated. But it appears there is not much they can do. The problem lies in the fact that the government is not backing with action the legislation that it so ably put in place to prevent precisely what is happening. Also, some local authorities might have self-interest at stake.

It is the same with the terrible stripping of the native rainforest. Despite laws to prevent deforestation, it is happening big-time and as much as 80 per cent of the logging taking place is illegal.

I don't really like regulations — I have no doubt, however, that stronger regulations and forced compliance with those regulations are now necessary. Nature can't cope with the results and effects of man's exploding population. The way we are doing things right now is just not sustainable.

Seamaster in the Rio Negro to the west of Barcelos — just about as far upstream as she will reach on this voyage.

16 November 2001

●

The Jungle Team left at 0600hrs, headed further upriver in *Iguana*. They have about six days of daylight travel ahead of them before they reach San Gabriel where trucks will be waiting to take them to the Venezuelan border.

I have just spoken to Ollie on the team's satellite phone. He reports they are making good progress, averaging around 5 knots against the Negro current that will become gradually stronger over the next couple of days.

Don, Leon and I have just been on a flying visit to the Rio Negro Lodge. It was about 20 minutes from here in the four-seater float plane sent by the Lodge's owner Phil Marstellier. Living as they do in the middle of the Amazon Basin, on the banks of the Rio Negro, Phil and his wife have made a commitment to the community quite unlike any other that I have come across in my travels.

The Lodge is a fishing haven. Guests — mostly Americans — come to fish for the famed peacock bass (it's a tag-and-release programme, I am delighted to say). Opposite the entranceway to the thatched main building is a huge fish tank that is full of examples of the riverlife in the surrounding area — turtles, peacock bass, catfish, tambaqui, neon tetras and other small aquarium fishes.

To come here to the Rio Negro to fish, though, is more than just a holiday for some of his customers.

While we were there, Phil had a group of dentists visiting. During their stay at the Lodge, they will roster his dental clinic on certain afternoons of the week and provide free treatment to people of the district.

We also met Clyde, a doctor from Florida. He was manning the Lodge's surgery as part of his 'deal' with Phil and has already provided $50,000 worth of equipment to make this the best-equipped practice around — a practice which offers free care to the locals.

Planned development of the Lodge includes a bigger school — capable of accommodating 120 children — and 20 family houses for the families that work at the Lodge. Phil is also in the final stages of completing a research centre for the University of the Amazon, so that the scientists can have a base from which to undertake research work in this remote part of the region.

The Lodge employs more than 250 people from the surrounding area — some in the tag-and-release programme — but most in the 'not-for-profit' organisation Phil has set up to help the local peoples. All of his carpenters, gardeners, teachers and fishing guides, plus his pilot, are from the surrounding area.

As the son of a missionary pilot, Phil was raised in Brazil and the USA. He has returned to the Amazon 'to give something back'. He is certainly doing that. His ecotourism venture will mean much more to the local economy — on an ongoing basis — than the strip-fishing that will inevitably cease when there are no fish left.

The strip-fishing reminds me of what, I am told, is a saying of the Cree Indian tribe in North America:

> Only when the last tree has died
> the last river been poisoned
> the last fish caught
> will we realise we cannot eat money.

The waterfront in Barcelos with plenty of evidence of low river levels.

17 November 2001

●

D r Mark Orams leaves us today to return to New Zealand. The following are his thoughts on nearly a month aboard *Seamaster* exploring the Rio Negro:

Inevitably, one's perceptions are shaped by one's expectations. I certainly expected a lot when coming here. The Amazon has a mythical status amongst biologists. I understood, therefore, the scale and importance of this ecosystem. The diversity and abundance of life here are unequalled in terrestrial environments.

As a consequence, I expected and hoped to see some wonderful wildlife. In truth, I have seen very little. What I did not understand or appreciate was the important influence people have had on this ecosystem, and it is this, rather than the wildlife, that has made the greatest impression on me.

The people who dwell here in the Amazon Basin live a simple life. Predominantly they are hunter-gatherers, supplementing their existence with some trade and cultivation. There is no doubt, however, that

the river is the most important influence on their lives. It is their base for transport, it provides food, a place for washing, for disposing of rubbish and for ablutions — and this may provide some explanation as to why we have seen so little wildlife on our expedition thus far.

The Amazon and its tributaries provide a home for more than 10 million people. That figure could be as high as 20 million however. Nobody is really sure. Most of these people live like those we have met on our travels — in small villages like Santa Helena and Daraqua on the banks of the river.

The natural environment here is an important source of food, and whether an animal is endangered or not is of little consequence when putting food on the table is a priority. We have seen plenty of evidence of this — numerous turtle carapaces beside cooking fires, along with jaguar and caiman skulls, and dead snakes.

Fish, while still plentiful in some locations in the Amazon, are getting harder and harder to catch and the large-size fish (like the remarkable three to four metre pirarucu) are now extremely scarce. The peixi

Below Santa Helena again — with pots, pans, clothes and kids all getting washed at the same time.

Following page The whole family arrives to trade and buy supplies in Barcelos. The round trip from more remote regions can take long as 10 days.

boi (manatee) continues to be hunted for food even though it is severely endangered as a species and it is illegal to kill one.

The local people also (perhaps understandably) seem to kill anything that could be a threat to their safety. We found a coral snake (or a false coral — I couldn't tell) macheteed, and were told of a large anaconda that the locals had killed near a waterfall we visited. It is sobering to experience this and it influences me to the view that conservation is primarily the cause of the affluent.

When you are worried about providing for your family and keeping them safe, it is of little consequence that an animal or fish is endangered. This is a tragedy. It is a tragedy because the future of the people of Amazonia (and elsewhere) is inextricably linked to the quality of the natural environment in which they live. Yet, it seems to me, the people here are contributing to its degradation. I feel trapped, somehow, by this issue. Here I am, the part-time visitor from an affluent Western country, here for only a matter of weeks but passing judgement on the way of life of a people who are friendly, welcoming and happy, living a simple life.

But I can't ignore the plastic bags and other non-biodegradable rubbish that I have seen all around, every place people live. I can't ignore the tragedy of a jaguar skull while recalling the majestic animal it once was. I can't ignore where I see the future going for the people of Santa Helena, Daraqua and others who depend on the river.

There is no doubt that we, in the so-called developed world, are contributing to this situation. Many of the plastic containers and bags and rubbish that we have seen — the 'packaging' of different peoples and different cultures in different parts of the world — were probably made in developed countries. It is not, however, productive to search for blame. Solutions are what is needed.

The Amazon is vast, beautiful and important — important to the world but of even more direct importance to the people who live here. They are dependent on it and affected by it. So, while my selfish desires to see wonderful wildlife have me feeling a little disappointed with that aspect of our trip, what occupies my thoughts now as I prepare to leave, is a growing realisation that this place may be in serious trouble.

Admittedly, we have not ventured far from the main 'highways' (the Amazon and Rio Negro), but *Seamaster* has now travelled more than 1200 miles inland and we have had fleeting glimpses only of some of the unique and diverse wildlife of this region — wildlife that, after all, should be a reflection of the health and quality of this ecosystem.

So, is the Amazon in trouble? In truth — I don't really know. It certainly is not as it once was and that suggests a downward trend. That is not good news for any of us given the importance of this place to the world environment.

What are the solutions — are there any? I was able to glimpse a potential answer while visiting the small village of Santa Helena two weeks ago. We were welcomed into the village's small school — a tiny, open-air structure with a roof but no walls, some worn old desks and around 15 bright-eyed, smiling young children. We were introduced by the teacher and through our guide and friend Miguel we were able to tell them a little about where we were from. 'In Nove Zealandia', Miguel translated, 'there are no caiman, no jaguars, no snakes or monkeys, no otters, manatees nor river dolphins.' He explained that we were here because we thought the Amazon so special, and the animals that lived here so important. He passed on that these animals are important and valuable alive and told them how special their home was, and how carefully it must be looked after.

As I looked at these beautiful, delightful children I hoped that this seed planted in these growing minds might develop and grow into a sense of pride and caring for their surrounding environment — strong enough to transcend the simple need to survive.

For my part, I continue to think and explore — firstly, about my own decisions and how they impact on the world we all share and secondly, how I can help — what I can do to make a positive difference.

I leave those thoughts with you. I am far from having the answers — but I, and all of us, need to continue to explore and think about how we might contribute to a better future.

That is why blakexpeditions is important. That is why I am proud and privileged to be a part of it and why, I hope, you will join us on our journey, on our quest. ▸

Children of the Amazon.

The school at Santa Helena — the children marvelled at pictures of Peter on the ice of Antarctica with penguins.

18 November 2001

●

From Ollie and the Jungle Team
Location Rio Negro, Cartucho village region

The bow of *Iguana*, our new home, is parked on a beautiful, pure-white sandy beach, on a small, forested granite island midstream in the Rio Negro. Across the river to starboard, drifts of smoke from cooking fires fill the air in the picturesque Indian village of Cartucho (known to the Indians as Uabada). This place, surrounded by large granite islands, a sea of green jungle and mirrored waterways, is stunningly beautiful.

We set off from *Seamaster* on the 15th, heading on upriver through the now familiar jungle landscape, and surprisingly were joined in convoy by a number of large military barges plus two huge ferries loaded with troops on their way to jungle exercises. Without a river pilot, they simply decided to follow us.

The landscape changed dramatically as we then entered the San Tome and Parani do Dara-Ra regions with narrower channels, large granite banks and outcrops, plus stronger, faster-flowing currents. The jungle has also now become a lot denser. Miguel tells us that this is the true jungle. We have left behind the flood plains of the lower Amazonian region.

In no time at all, we reached the strategic river town of Santa Isabel, halfway between Barcelos and San Gabriel and founded by the missionaries approximately 150 years ago. It now has a population of around 4000 people. We fuelled up at the dock while Marc, Janot and the film crew went in search of the 'Monkey Man', a scientist based in these parts in order to study monkeys in their natural environment. We had heard that Monkey Man had recently found a new species in this region.

After an evening enjoying the company of locals, then a sunrise trip around some rapid areas of the river, we left at 8 am today without locating Monkey Man, who apparently was away on an expedition of his own. We then travelled through the most beautiful areas of jungle that we have seen to date to reach this midstream island, passing five small, jungle-covered mountains on the southern side of the river as we approached. Tomorrow morning we are off for a climb to see what's at the top of one of them.

We are planning to arrive in San Gabriel on the afternoon of the 20th. After completing all the required paperwork with the local authorities, we will then head for the Venezuelan border by truck.

Opposite *Iguana* reflections in the black water of the Rio Negro as the Jungle Team sets out for the Casiquiare and the Orinoco.
Below *Iguana* — ashore for the night on the Negro.

22 November 2001

Location Rio Mandu

We are well up an uncharted river — only just afloat in the sandy shallow sections and at less than walking pace, keeping our speed well down even when we have more than a metre of water under *Seamaster*'s keel. The Rio Mandu leads through to the Rio Branco (we think) and is a white river.

But, to backtrack. We left our overnight anchorage before the sun appeared over the many sand banks, motoring in flat calm conditions, zig-zagging between sand bars, slowing down as depths went up and down. At one stage we drifted sideways onto a bank of sand that was only just showing above the surface of the river. The current pushed us on harder. With both dinghies shoving *Seamaster* against the flow, we made little progress until the main engines were given a hard burst and we floated clear. No problem for an ice-breaker but, with the river level dropping again, it could have proved embarrassing.

Before Rio Branco, we turned back north again and into new territory, wanting to visit a small river that we had missed on our way upstream. We haven't been disappointed. As this tributary to the Rio Negro narrows, the depths increase (just as well, as we were nearly stopped by the shallows of the entrance). We are now many miles into it and the scenery only gets better.

Rounding one small island, eight or so giant otters — some of them youngsters — were frolicking in the water. They scrambled hurriedly up the clay bank to disappear amongst the trees. At the same time a number of boto — the pink dolphin — gathered around the bow, along with a few grey dolphin (the tucusi). A toucan flew by, adding to the scene, along with a number of other very large birds that we haven't yet identified. A monkey's loud call broke the silence. The brilliantly coloured kingfishers have shepherded us all the way from the entrance, one taking over from another depending on whose section of river we are in. There are reportedly only 1000 giant otters left in South America, and we have just seen nearly one per cent of them — a very special time indeed.

The trees have thickened up and seem taller the further we have pushed upriver, the banks closing in on us and overhanging trees nearly brushing the rigging as we pass. On some of the tighter turns it has been necessary to keep a close watch on the stern as well as the bow. It sometimes comes very close to the bank when the rudders are hard over. Our crew have manned the dinghy with the echo sounder all day, leading the way, identifying the shallow areas and helping *Seamaster* keep to the deeper sections.

While we have been threading our way up this most beautiful Rio Negro tributary, our Jungle Team are in San Gabriel getting through the exit paperwork and standing by to leave Brazil by truck, headed for the Venezuelan border. They will then head through the Casiquiare Canal that connects the Amazon to the Orinoco River.

It is late afternoon, the fish are rising in the current nearby, the sun is about to hide behind the forest to port, and we won't be sorry to see it go. The comparative cool that usually develops soon after 'big yellow' is in bed will be especially welcome this evening. We are looking forward to the brightest stars imaginable again (there is no such thing as light pollution here).

Our anchorage is quite delightful, the fast flow of the river keeping us away from the high clay river bank only a few metres away to starboard. To port is a golden sand bar with birds nesting in hollows in the middle. Hopefully the mossies will stay away, but there is a fair chance that we'll need insect repellent.

The intense, clear blue sky is unblemished and the pairs of green parrots will soon be squawking their way home across the tops of our masts. It is a time of peace and tranquillity.

Scrabble in the Rio Mandu.

24 November 2001

Location Ilha do Gaviao on the Rio Negro

It's Saturday, and a day to look back at some of the images that stick so well in my mind from the past few days:

- Narrow waterways with trees overhanging
- Steep clay banks with giant otter holes
- Broken trees at the river's edge — a must to avoid
- Shallow patches that demand a lot of concentration and co-ordination with the dinghy team
- Running aground numerous times — but quickly off again
- Sandy beaches and magnificent scenery
- Fast-running water, deep on the bends
- Narrow tributaries with the promise of a lot of life after dark
- *Seamaster* very close to the banks in the tight turns of the river — OK when going up, much more difficult when descending because of our increased speed with the current under us
- A bird leaps off a branch and plunges straight under the water, scared of our presence
- White-throated giant otter families playing at the water's edge
- The count now stands at 15 for the otters (we will keep their actual habitat a secret so that they remain undisturbed)
- Large caiman at night, their bright eyes watching us from the opposite bank
- Larger caiman sunning themselves on a sand bank in late afternoon — unafraid but very wary
- Almost perfect caiman camouflage
- Houses in a row on a high river bank, many with large satellite television dishes
- Boats and bongos of all shapes and sizes
- Long sets of wooden steps from the river to the top of the bank
- A monkey and a parrot — friends
- Children aboard *Seamaster* — cold Coca-Cola and crackers
- Children bringing us bunches of bananas — we now have enough to last a long time
- A thatch-roofed bongo alongside with a catfish for sale (no money wanted — barter for rice, milk powder, tinned corned beef, pasta and cooking oil)
- The catfish is very large and requires the crane to get it on board
- Paulo fillets it — enough for several meals for all the crew
- Playing 'scrabble' in the water — many tiny fish around our feet
- The bow of *Seamaster* ashore on a sand bar, a perfect day — bringing back memories of Antarctica
- A peacock bass cooking on a fire in the forest

- The mirror-like surface of the river reflecting the trees in the day, the stars and moon at night
- The brightest stars imaginable
- Scarlet macaws — hard to believe they aren't painted
- Hoatzins — with claws on the wings of the young, for clambering back up the trees after falling in the river
- A toucan
- Green parrots making an evening racket
- The flash of brightest pink of a boto rising in the morning sunshine
- A turtle's shell, empty and forgotten
- Tendrils of mist off the dawn river
- The nuisance of 'black fly' — tiny insects that leave us bloody in tender places, like many small cuts
- 'Black fly' bites — they really itch the following day. No insect repellent keeps these away. We long to be back on the Rio Negro and into 'black water' once again
- Showers of fireflies, like floating, pulsing ashes in the near night air
- Torrential rain without a poncho
- Phone calls with Ollie and the Jungle Team about to board their truck for the six-hour dust-ride to Venezuela . . .

White heron and toucan.

Baby caiman.

Charlie spent an afternoon with Paulo, talking to some boat people in Barcelos. He wanted to find out more about them so he played roving reporter. This is what he found:

‘As we stroll up the beach, we hear an unexpected sound — The Beatles (the ones from Liverpool) on the radio. To hear such a familiar band in such a remote area of the world comes as a surprise. We are on a sandy beach, below the small town of Barcelos. The beach is packed with riverboats of all shapes and sizes, from two-metre-long, open bongos carrying just a man and his paddle, to 25-metre ferry boats taking more than 50 passengers to Manaus.

Don, Paulo and I first walk over to a bongo with four people on board. This bongo cannot be more than four metres long, and a little more than one metre wide. The people are very friendly and welcoming, inviting us into their 'home'. We feel guilty invading their space with such an intrusive object as our camera.

With the help of Paulo we discover that these people do actually have another home, 20 hours upstream by bongo (it takes them only eight hours coming downstream). They have come to Barcelos for provisions, as they do every month. The father of this family is a fisherman who also makes manioc to sell to the people of Barcelos.

The next boat is bigger, probably eight metres long and two metres wide. Paulo quickly translates, saying the father has been an aquarium fisherman for 14 years and he, too, lives on the boat with his son and his beautiful young granddaughter. He tells us that he

usually fishes with three others and that they make the equivalent of approximately $US3 a day. I wonder how he would feel if he knew how much the tropical fish sell for to the Western world, or that up to 80 per cent of the fish he catches will die before they reach the shops that we would buy them from.

It is time to move on again and we thank him and leave his family some postcards of *Seamaster* and Peter in Antarctica. I love the reaction such small gifts get — the fascination and often incredibly puzzled looks.

The third and final riverboat we look at is another smaller bongo, around four metres long and a little over a metre wide. I am amazed to see seven people on board: five adults, a child and a baby. They have seen me give out the postcards to the previous bongo and I can sense their anticipation. These people are selling manioc, prepared at their home upstream near Santa Isabel, and are also here for provisions. It is a round trip of about 10 days. I don't think I'll ever again complain when my parents ask me to pop down to the local shops to get something that we might need — a 'chore' that takes me maybe 30 minutes or so.

In that comparison, I am lucky and probably take so much for granted in my modern world. But these people are lucky too. They live in a river world, surrounded by nature at her best.’

That's it for today. We are off to the nearby village of Santa Helena shortly. They have invited us to take part in their afternoon football match and Leon in particular can't wait to test his skills with the round ball against the legendary Brazilians.

Following page **Five hours of dusty road on the San Gabriel to Cucui highway.**

Below **Encountered on the river: a local family on their way to market.**

25 November 2001

●

From Ollie and the Jungle Team

Location Rio Negro in Venezuela

We are now aboard our new 'home'. For obvious reasons, she has been christened 'Big Bongo'.

Big Bongo is 15 metres long and is, in fact, a catamaran comprising two bongos, cut from a large tree called the 'cachicamo', and joined together. We are once again on the waters of the Rio Negro but, this time, running down the border between the countries of Venezuela (a few hundred metres away to starboard) and Colombia (off to port). At this point, the border runs right down the middle of the river.

We picked up *Big Bongo* in the border town of Cucui after a 200 km, overland truck trip from San Gabriel that was, to say the least, exhausting. We had intended to set out first thing yesterday but, by the time we had topped up our provisions and visited the federal police for clearance out of Brazil, it was already 11.30 am before we loaded aboard our two rented trucks and were on our way.

The dirt road, surrounded by dense jungle, was extremely bumpy and very, very dusty. For those of us on the back of the flat-bed truck it was a case of hanging on for all we were worth, trying not to breathe in too much of the dust that was everywhere.

The 'Doc', sitting comfortably in the cab and listening to Brazilian music at maximum volume, wondered what all the fuss and commotion were about.

Five hours later, after crossing a spectacularly long but rather inadequate-looking wooden bridge high above the river, we mercifully arrived at the Cucui federal police station to check in. The locals looked at us with surprise as, traditionally, to be covered in such bright red dust (as we were) meant that you had been to a Yanomami party. Alas no, only to hell and back on the dreaded San Gabriel to Cucui main highway.

Unloading the trucks and loading and preparing *Big Bongo* took quite some time, but we completed the task just before dark and took a most welcome and refreshing swim in the river before gobbling down some spaghetti bolognese and literally dropping with exhaustion.

It is now 8 pm on the following evening and we are tied to a sand bank approximately 40 miles further upriver. The crew are all ashore preparing a campsite in the jungle for those who are not sleeping aboard *Big Bongo*. Progress has been slow today due to head currents, low water levels, plus another stop to check in with the Venezuelan military that guard the river.

San Gabriel

Big Bongo in expedition mode with river guide Lucho in his usual position on the bow.

27 November 2001

●

From Ollie and the Jungle Team
Location Rio Casiquiare

Above *Big Bongo* negotiating the rapids on day two in the Casiquiare.

Following page Just inside the Venezuelan border the Casiquiare landscape throws up dramatic rock formations.

We are anchored to a large sand bank, approximately 50 miles up the Rio Casiquiare, and there has not been a dull moment getting here. We left our first-night anchorage in the early hours of yesterday morning and headed for the Venezuelan town of San Carlos, where we had to check in with the military again before proceeding further.

San Carlos, about seven miles south of the entrance to the Casiquiare, is a small military town that faces onto the Rio Negro — and a Colombian village a few hundred metres away on the opposite bank of the river.

The Doc and some of the team took the opportunity to visit the local medical facility where they learned more about the 'nasties' we will have to watch for on the isolated sections of our journey — malaria, typhoid fever, dengue fever, Chagas' disease and travellers' diarrhoea.

We topped up our provisions again — this time at a floating Brazilian supermarket, the top deck of which was loaded with bags of used aluminium cans.

We saw a number of other vessels sporting the same cargo, so recycling is obviously very much a going concern, even this far from so-called civilisation.

Approximately two hours after leaving San Carlos, a turn to starboard took us into the entrance to the Casiquiare, the characteristics of which were noticeably different — narrower, shallower and slower moving. Reaching the Cano Casiquiare, a natural channel that connects the two great river systems of the Amazon and the Orinoco, and one of the most unusual hydrological phenomena in the world, is an important milestone for the expedition.

Professor Mario Christian Meyer, a noted expert on the Amazon, wrote to us to explain that by linking the two river systems, the 220-mile long Casiquiare helps to create the largest hydrographical network in the world. He says that the Casiquiare is the only place on Earth where the river stream changes its course, sometimes going SW from the Rio Orinoco to the Rio Negro, and sometimes — during the rainy season — NE from the Rio Negro to the Rio Orinoco. We have noted, in various publications, references to the Casiquiare sometimes flowing the other way but none of the locals that we have spoken to, including elders, have ever seen this happen.

The Casiquiare was 'discovered' in 1744 by Jesuit missionaries. It was further admired and described in detail by the explorer Alexander von Humboldt during his 1800 Orinoco expedition. It is now classified as a Biosphere Reserve by UNESCO.

The hydrological and ecological importance of the Casiquiare connecting the Amazon and Orinoco is clear. The two river systems share important proportions of their waterlife and the linkage serves as a means for dispersal of plantlife and animals, making the two river basins the same macro-ecosystem. It is equally important, however, for the people of the region, enabling them to readily travel and trade between the two. Apart from some rapids near Puerto Ayacucho, you can pass, as we are doing, from one to the other with comparative ease.

We continued up the Casiquiare throughout the afternoon, passing many small and isolated Indian villages and completing another military check-in, this time at the National Guard post of Solano where they told us that the river level was the lowest in many years, due to minimal rainfall. As a result, the temperature of the river was a lot higher than usual.

Darkness finally forced us to call a halt. We chose for an anchorage a sandy bank surrounded by dense jungle and set up camp. All were sleeping peacefully until around 3 am when bolts of lightning lit up the sky, accompanied by very loud thunder. Not to be caught out as we were by a similar storm the night before, we had our tarps ready and it wasn't long before those sleeping ashore in hammocks were all covered and back to sleep again.

We were due to get an early start this morning but it was still raining heavily and we decided instead to relax a bit and enjoy a leisurely breakfast. Around the next bend ahead, our first set of dangerous rapids was waiting. They required scouting by Lucho, our Captain, who set off with Marc and one of our Yanomami guides while the rest of us secured all the equipment on board for a no-doubt bumpy and wet ride. We also, while they were gone, had time to wash the bin full of the clothing that was smothered in red dust from our infamous road trip.

The rapids proved a tumult of racing water and dangerous rocks. Alistair and Augusto manned the inflatable in case we struck problems. *Big Bongo*, with Lucho at the bow waving directions to Patricio (the driver), started into the torrent, but not for long. Water was pouring in over the sides of her hulls and she was becoming dangerously heavy. The team on board had to bail her out before she could try again.

Second time lucky, and all was going well until the port motor hit a rock and kicked up out of the water. Suddenly, the whole craft was drifting sideways down the river, beam-on to the torrent. The situation was remedied and, with Lucho again waving furiously and the team breathing a collective sigh of relief, the rapids were slowly left behind.

A number of villagers were waving to us from the bank so we pulled over to meet them. They proved to be a group of Yanomami Indians recently relocated to the area. We spent an hour with them, visiting their village nearby, before resuming our travels. As with everywhere we have been so far, they were beautiful people and the encounter left us in good spirits, despite the drama of the rapids.

We are now further upriver and busy setting up 'Hammockville' for another night in the jungle. Hopefully it will not be as wet as the last two — however, clouds which have been lingering above us all day are now darkening. The tarps are ready.

Alistair and Janot — running repairs to *Big Bongo*.

The most effective baler in the world is said to be a bucket in the hands of a desperate man — on this occasion 'Dr Jab' (Marc Shaw).

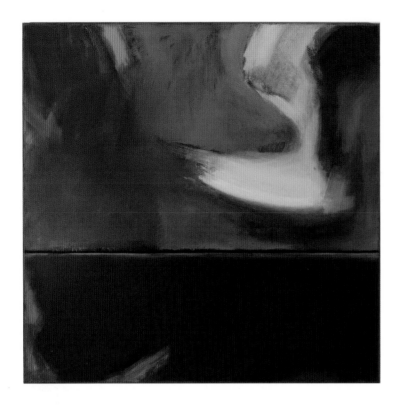

Mandu

Ilha Cuandu II

Barcelos

28 November 2001

●

The sand waves on the recording depth sounder trace large, exaggerated, 'saw's teeth' on the river bed. The bigger the Rio Negro becomes as we head east, with more and more tributaries joining in, the larger these bottom waves become.

We progress downriver to Manaus at almost twice the speed at which we were going the other way and tree-covered islands and sandy inlets seem to fly past, the favourable current adding a couple of knots to our speed.

What a change to the scenery from when we were last here, just a few short weeks ago. Many of the white-sand beaches are now the brightest of green — covered in lush grass that has sprouted during our time away. The dark green of the forest is now a brilliant lighter shade of green giving the land that fronts the river the look of a well-kept park.

The sky is overcast much of the time — for the third day in a row — with welcome cooler temperatures. The rain has mostly stayed away but the lightning and thunder in the huge, towering cumulonimbus clouds flash and rumble on the edge of our consciousness throughout much of the day.

Our aim now is to clear Manaus quickly — in and out before the weekend — to try and arrive at Macapa, on the northern side of the Amazon estuary, before customs and immigration close for the following weekend.

As I write this, we are approximately 40 miles from Manaus, and 1000 miles from Macapa. There is still a long way to go before *Seamaster* feels the swells of the trade winds and we taste the tang of salt in the air.

Pippa has been with us for a month now, but leaves to fly back home to the UK in two days' time. An artist, she has spent much of her time up on the foredeck, painting, or taking photographs of the many places we have visited and sights we have seen. The following is how she has found her Amazon:

It had been a childhood dream to visit South America and the Amazon Basin, a dream fuelled not only by school geography lessons of buttress roots and lianas, but also by the writings of Gabriel Garcia Marquez and Herzog's films *Fitzcarraldo* and *Aguirre: Wrath of God*. So when the opportunity arose to join *Seamaster* I found myself suddenly on a magical journey by flying boat over the canopied flood plains, sand bars and deep orange-brown waters of the Rio Negro. To literally swoop down and skid over the water towards the boat was an arrival not to be forgotten.

I am a painter and the main mission during my four weeks on board was to make as many studies and to take as many photographs as possible to catalyse larger-scale

works when I return to my studio in England. This, of course, combined with learning more about the life of the people living on the river and realising the huge scale of knowledge that the Amazon has to offer.

The Amazonian landscape is daunting, vast and hauntingly beautiful. What has struck me most is the depth of the dark, moody colours in the forests and river waters. Also the mirror-like reflections in the still tributaries — reminding me always of the 'ink-blot' butterfly images one makes as a child by folding paper. The colours are strange and different but always with dashes of brilliance amongst the darkness.

My recent work has been inspired by industrial and urban landscape — oil refineries, docks and factories. So to be enveloped by the chaotic mass of foliage, creepers, trunks and snake-like waters has been challenging — very hard to comprehend and organise onto a rectangular surface.

Initially I could only draw what I knew — the geometric shapes of the varied river craft and simple village buildings. But, as time has gone by, I have tried to put down the more abstract shapes of the jungle itself.

Perhaps the biggest challenge for me has been the intense heat and trying to overcome the languid sullenness and lethargy that creeps up on you every day. But you force yourself, otherwise you would lose.

There is an enigma and mystery about the Amazon that I know has made a deep and lasting impression on me. I now feel very excited about returning home with a stream of images to work from. I am hoping that what I have gained will be with me forever and feel that it has been a profound and humbling experience to have been here. I will be sad to leave.

And, this from Rodger Moore who, in his real life, is a plumber so has much to do with water. Being here aboard *Seamaster* in the Amazon Basin has heightened his awareness of just how precious a resource it is:

It has been calculated that on planet Earth there are 8867 cubic kilometres of water available for human use (approximately 2165 cubic miles) — plenty, you would think, for everyone. Some parts of the world, however, are experiencing severe water shortages, often because the ground water is polluted, because of localised droughts, or because the available water is used wastefully.

On average, Americans use 264 gallons (1238 litres) of water per person per day whereas three-quarters of all of the world's population get by on 13 gallons (58 litres) each per day. In rural Kenya, many people 'make do' with just 1.5 gallons (6.75 litres) each per day.

The world's population now uses nearly five times as much water as it did in 1950.

Above **Pippa — sketching as** *Seamaster* **makes her way back down the Negro.**

Opposite page **Some of the finished work from Pippa's Amazon collection**

Following page **Happy families — Yanomami style.**

Below 'Dr Jab' with new assistant.

Opposite page A Yanomami beauty.

Following page A side-excursion by the base camp Jungle Team members — up a tributary to the Siapa River.

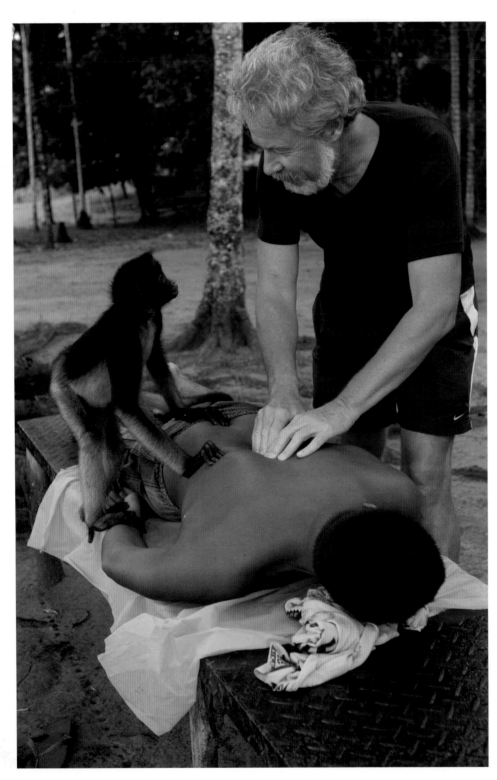

Bees, ants, wasps and flies — all have been with us today. As a consequence, we are fully kitted up tonight, most of us scratching the many bites on our bodies. We are anchored to a small island just west of the entrance to the Siapa River.

Not all the team are together tonight. Marc, Alistair, Janot and our film crew Simon and James left this morning, with Lucho and his two Yanomami crew-members, for a five-day side-trip up the Siapa River. They have taken our inflatable dinghy and two bongos with fast outboard motors attached. The Doc, Franck (our stills photographer) and I are manning *Big Bongo* at our temporary base near the river mouth. We will monitor the communications equipment in case of problems, but we will also be checking out the area around us in the Biosphere Reserve that has been established here to protect the thousands of square miles of virgin rainforest and remote tribes like the Yanomami.

More heavy rain for about five hours yesterday, but once it cleared we pulled into a delightful small village called Porvenir, the first refuelling stop in the Venezuelan part of our journey. We took the opportunity to meet with the chief of the village who also acts as a deputy 'commissaries' (commissioner) for the region. His responsibilities include looking after the health issues of the 37 people in the village and tending to the general day-to-day needs of the whole community (along with those of the surrounding villages). He was an interesting man who was a fund of information on the region's wildlife, indigenous people and unique environment.

As we were walking back to *Big Bongo*, the Doc was asked to have a look at a young man who had fallen and injured his back. In his examination of the unanticipated patient, the Doc had the unexpected help of the village's pet monkey. He was not amused when we suggested that the monkey would make a great assistant for the rest of the journey.

The Siapa River team is headed initially for a large waterfall where they will leave the dinghy and bongos and continue on foot for three days. Their objective is to climb Mount Aracamuni — for a panoramic view of the jungle and rivers below, but also to investigate reports of illegal gold-mining in the protected Biosphere Reserve. They have just checked in, having reached the waterfall and set up camp.

Back at base camp, we have been visited by a steady stream of local people, including the Yanomami chief of the area. They have come to welcome us and extend their hospitality — to complete strangers from lands far away. A very humbling experience.

The Amazon is so large. It is more like a freshwater sea. There are tens of thousands of kilometres of waterways that make up the Amazon Basin — that all eventually flow into the main river. You could spend a lifetime here and see, and experience, only a small part of it. Our being here, even for such a brief time, has had a huge impact on us all. It has made us appreciate how unique an area this is, in itself.

There is extraordinary life, in the water and on the land — in hundreds of thousands of different forms — much of which is yet to be 'discovered'. It has made us appreciate how important this area is to the rest of the world, and how the rest of the world must value the Amazon for what it is, not for what it contains or for what it can produce in cold, hard cash.

In natural terms, it is one of the most valuable assets we have, and it must stay the way it is. As a balance for the world's climate, it is irreplaceable and to destroy it will be to gamble with the future of our children and our children's children. There is also knowledge here that modern man doesn't have, knowledge retained by the Indian peoples — gained over generations — who have lived sustainably within this rainforest for thousands of years, knowledge that could help the rest of the world to a better future.

While I spend the day attending to the daunting amount of paperwork required to clear *Seamaster* and crew for the trip from here to Macapa, on the northern side of the mouth of the Amazon, and then from Brazilian waters for the ocean voyage to the mouth of the Orinoco, I am devoting this log to Leon who provides a special insight to his experience aboard *Seamaster*.

Leon.

❝It took a while for me to get used to waking up in the Amazon. But now I am. There's something 'right' about this place, on so many levels. Sure, it challenges you every day, and I have had to slowly adapt to the pace and ways of Amazonian and tropical life.

Now, however, I am used to rising early to savour the cool and breathtakingly beautiful dawns, to relish the clarity the temperature allows, accepting that later in the day I'll feel vaguely 'vegetative' as the thermometer claws back to its daily 38 degrees C and the afternoon swelter descends (trusting, though, that with the early evening will come blessed reprieve from the fug, and with it will pour the smell of the jungle, the essence of the Amazon).

Like I said, every day is a challenge, but it's also truly beautiful and uniquely Amazon, which is why we came. One of the benefits of a journey such as ours, one that relies upon ocean and river travel, which necessarily require time, is that we get time to read. Sometimes you're in the mood for reading something of specific relevance to the expedition, at other times it's anything but. Recently I sat here in the tropics engrossed in the icy exploits of Stephen Venables, a high-altitude mountaineer and ascender of goliath's — probably in an effort to feel vicariously cool!

To succeed as a high-altitude climber one necessarily needs to become an expert campaigner — or leader of expeditions — and this was the subject of Venables' article. To me, the word 'expedition' conjures up folklorish journeys of old, undertaken when there were oceans to cross and mountains to conquer.

Venables' point is that these days anybody can join or launch an expedition with the swipe of a credit card. Every ocean, jungle, mountain and desert is virtually attainable and conquerable. Even time is no barrier these days. Why take four months when one will do? Which somewhat confuses the term 'expedition' does it not? How do you define what qualifies, or otherwise, to be called an expedition?

For example, back in the 1920s when Mallory and Irvine were lost on Everest's upper slopes, you could be forgiven, as Venables points out, for thinking the drive for that expedition was to fulfil a desperate nationalistic need to be the first to the summit. But the real winner at the end of the day was science — through mapping, botanics and geology, through information with which to progress. Not really the stuff of storybooks.

Venables proceeds with the dictionary definition of an expedition — a 'warlike enterprise' or 'journey, voyage, for definite purpose'. He surmises that 'whilst the military connotations have largely faded, the real essence of what best describes an expedition are the words "for definite purpose"'.

Well, we're on an expedition. The Amazon has such a calming, relaxing effect it sometimes feels like a vacation, but it's not. I've taken time out of my life and career to lend weight where I can and to make my own discoveries. Every day I ask myself, 'What's our definite purpose?', and every day it stares straight back at me. It has taken time for it to sink in, but *being here* is our definite purpose.

We came because we know the Amazon is threatened. We have the information, but we don't seem to be progressing with it. It's taken being here and having time to wander, soak up the sights, the sounds, the smells, the way of life, to slowly realise that the Amazon, in its current form, is a last frontier, still mostly 'right', as it was intended. And this is the big one — just because we, man, can conquer nature, should we?

If you think yes, maybe you should come here too. Experience for yourself what it sounds like as the jungle cacophony descends with the cool evening air, uninterrupted by air traffic overhead; how overpoweringly beautiful nature really smells devoid of man's influence; how intensely bright the stars are; how moving it is to see monkeys and otters and caimans living as they're intended to, as part of the universe, disinterested in our concepts of time and history, but influenced by them nonetheless.

It still is as it was intended, but that will probably change within our lifetimes. To what degree is up to us, which infers a decision. If we want to, we can all play a part in that decision.

My discoveries have been personal. I have developed a profound fear of what the future holds for this place and, consequently, for all of us. I'm not being overdramatic. This is real. We get one shot, so let's face it.

One of Peter's goals for blakexpeditions is to help all of us to fall in love with the planet we live on; to start to regard, rather than disregard; to start to care — not out of fear, but out of awe!

Sure, the issues are big, but so are the consequences.

Peter and Pippa — dwarfed by a giant kapok tree near Velho Airoa. The kapok is the biggest tree in the Amazon rain forest.

1 December 2001

From Ollie and the Jungle Team
Location Casiquiare, near the entrance to the Siapa River

Noticeable by its absence to date in our travels has been the wildlife of the Amazon and Orinoco Basins. We were, then, delighted (and envious) when Peter told us of the wonderful wildlife they have encountered in the Rio Branco.

The sheer size of this natural wilderness might have something to do with the scarcity of wildlife that we are experiencing, but we would have thought that we would have seen animals coming down to the river for a cooling swim or drink. Not so. Which leads us to think that maybe all the communities on the banks of the rivers are having a greater influence on things. Our bongo driver Patricio tells us there are 18 such communities along the Casiquiare, all peopled by hunters and gatherers of many species. They all require food and need to sell or trade in order to buy provisions.

Parked here at this small island in the middle of the Casiquiare highway, we have had the opportunity to witness the process first-hand. Many bongos and aluminium dinghies pull in to say hello and to offer for sale all varieties of freshly-caught animal and fish life. We know that these people have to feed themselves but some of what we have seen is disturbing and we wonder whether the level of hunting that we are witnessing, while probably sustainable in days gone by, is still so when the population of the whole region has exploded.

Yesterday was a particularly sad one for us. A boat called by early in the morning. The several hunters on board showed us three large bags of turtles, some birdlife and, most disturbing of all, a freshly killed and skinned large, male jaguar. The hunters wanted $US300 dollars for the jaguar skin. The head of the once-magnificent beast, with jaw intact was offered separately. A kill purely for profit and, unfortunately, there are still people in the world who will pay a fortune (but not to the hunters) to have such a prize hanging on their wall or laying on the living-room floor.

The jaguar is a beautiful animal with tawny yellow, short and smooth fur covered in black spots. It has a very large head with long, stout canine teeth. It is a very large, heavy cat weighing up to 158 kg. The males are larger than the females. With its short legs and large feet, it is built for power, not speed. Jaguars are to be found in North, Central and South America (Mexico to Argentina). They were once also to be found in the southwest United States and Uruguay but are now extinct in both those countries.

The jaguar is officially listed as an endangered species. The exact numbers remaining are difficult to estimate. While they are still widespread and can be locally common in Amazonia, only a few hundred are thought to remain in Meso-America and they are rare or absent in many other parts of their former range (due to overhunting for the fur trade, loss of habitat by deforestation, persecution by ranchers and probably loss of their prey).

The skin of a freshly-killed jaguar — for sale for a mere $US300, even though the jaguar is an endangered species.

The Doc was in action again today — professionally that is. We were visited by a Yanomami chief accompanied by two male members of his community. I'll let Doc take up the story:

'They had come to help us clear a small area so that we could hang our hammocks in some shade. Guillermo, the chief, is young for his position and was elected to succeed as leader when his father died. He too will be the leader for life. He appears to be a very aware man who speaks Spanish in addition to his own tribal dialects.

After the clearing task was completed, one of the Yanomami men asked me about the spots on his chest and back. I asked him all the usual questions and I looked at them, deciding that they were scabies. This is a condition caused by a mite that burrows under the skin. Once I had completed this assessment, I was approached by the other man who had a cross marked on his forehead. He told me that he had a headache and a fever and that he also had sweats and chills at night-time. I examined him and noted that he was very pale, which usually reflects an anaemia, or low blood count. I also examined his stomach and felt a very large spleen. This is the organ that makes and destroys blood cells. Malaria is the most common condition that presents with all the features that I had noted, so I felt that this was such a case. Malaria is very common in this area, and indeed in all tropical areas of the world. Can you believe that it kills about 200 children every hour of the day?

Malaria can be prevented by taking certain medications and our expedition precautions include taking a very new medication combination called atovaquone and proguanil (Malarone). It is so new that the malaria organisms, called plasmodium, have not become immune to it yet, and therefore it is an extremely effective medicine.

The Yanomami man, however, already had the disease and had come to see me to get examined. It is always very hard to make a decision about treating folk in another community, particularly one as remote as this in Venezuela. As a doctor, I want to do the best for the person that I am treating, but in doing so it is most important that I am aware that I do not meddle in the health concerns of the local communities, or to assume that I have all the answers.

I must also be aware of how this man will be followed up and cared for when we are gone, and that I do seek permission from his community before I manage the man. I say this because each Yanomami community has its own medicine man, called a shaman. His job is to treat any illness in the village community, and he does this by calling in spirits to help him.

Now, I don't believe that this is the best way to treat malaria, but often the community prefers to have this responsibility. If I was practising medicine here for longer, then I would expect to interact with the shaman and assist in helping where I could. But we are not here for long and the potential seriousness of malaria makes me want to give them some of our medication. I ask the chief if I can do this, and he agrees. I was then happy to give him some medicine that treats, rather than prevents, malaria.

As I finished my management of the case, I asked the man about the cross on his head. He explained that it was put there to 'cross out', or get rid of, the headache. I consider this form of medicine very different to my own and, rather than judge it to be right or wrong, I just accept it for what it is — different!'

The Doc.

3 December 2001

●

From Ollie and the Jungle Team
Location Casiquiare, near the entrance to the Siapa River

It is 4 pm and thunder and lightning are all around. The parrots are serenading early as though it is sunset (perhaps a sign of rain to come). At least the clouds and slight wind have dropped the temperature to a comfortable 28 degrees C — an hour ago it was in the forties. Much to our joy, the bugs that seem to consume much of our daytime routine have mostly disappeared.

We have just been speaking by satellite to the Siapa River team and all are safe and well. They are on their way back from the top of Mount Aracamuni but progress is slower than anticipated, so we don't expect them to arrive here for another two days. They did encounter illegal gold-mining but on a small scale and involving migrant miners who appeared to be simply eking out a living in pretty rough circumstances. We will, however, still have to report the situation to the authorities when we are in a position to do so. This is, after all, a completely protected Biosphere Reserve and what the Siapa River team have encountered this time might lead to bigger problems with mining in the future.

Some more local villagers stopped by yesterday and asked if we would like to join them on a fishing excursion in a tributary a few miles further upstream. We jumped at the opportunity and were treated to a day that we will never forget.

Upriver, through several rapid sections, the waters narrowed considerably as we wove our way through large boulders and jungle until we arrived at a very small cut in the bank. Through the gap we went — and it looked as though our trip would end there. The way forward was blocked by trees. Not a problem, however. The Yanomamis chopped and hacked a way through with machetes and once again we were on our way. This process was repeated many times in the next half hour or so.

One of our guides pointed out a small otter running from the water. There was a strong smell of fish all around us. This, we were told, was common in areas populated by otters — and also when anacondas were present. All eyes were wide open.

A small distance further in, the water changed amazingly in colour, clarity and coolness. It was a bright red (but we could still see the bottom a few metres below) and its temperature was several degrees cooler than the Casiquiare — clear signs that this water was running from the surrounding mountains of the Siapa region. Not quite a mountain stream but a most welcome change all the same.

The small tributary widened and we were suddenly in paradise — a scenic waterway that resembled a giant landscaped Japanese garden. A flock of white herons cruised above as we glided past boulders, balsa trees and low grassy marshland areas. The water-grass looked like a perfect home for manatee but our Yanomami hosts told us that none were around.

We cruised on upstream for an hour then pulled the bongo into a bank so that the three young boys from 'our' village could go fishing. They were quickly and enthusiastically into the water with mask and small slingshot spears. The first fish was soon on board. Several small turtles were caught and brought to the surface for us to look at before being released. Not to be outdone, Franck was next over the side (with still camera) followed by the Doc (with mask) and Ollie (with video camera). Bongo following behind, we all drifted slowly downstream with the current.

To our surprise (and excitement), the river bed sparkled up at us. Alas, it wasn't gold that had set our pulses racing — nothing more than the mineral pyrite (more commonly known as fool's gold). We glided downstream for nearly two hours in this cool and tranquil water land, Franck and Ollie photographing and filming the many varieties of fish, until the youngsters had speared enough for the evening meal. Two hours in paradise had raced by.

The Amazon, and now the Casiquiare, truly are places to behold, and seeing them makes it easier to understand how scientists and explorers, even after centuries of looking, are still finding new species of flora and fauna throughout the region.

Opposite page **Giant boulders litter the shores of the Amazon and the Rio Negro.**

4 December 2001

●

Location Nearing Macapa

Dusk has turned the surface of the river into a greasy grey — the sky quickly darkening after the sun's orange and golds have gone. We always hope for a clear night, and tonight the moon will be up soon after 9 pm — two and a half hours of real blackness before then.

There are flashes of lightning up ahead and the radar is showing a band of rain stretching out either side of our course. There are lights of ships, barge traffic, ferries and small towns — and the flaming floating pots marking the extremities of the fishing nets that have to be avoided. A cool breeze blows out of the lightning cloud and the as-yet unfelt rain.

The moon is up but soon disappears behind the arriving ragged cloud. A few cold drops are felt but that passes, leaving us in clearing conditions, the only breeze provided by our forward speed. The rain has fallen before reaching our position and we are left with air full of the smells of damp earth and warm vegetation.

The river tonight is flat calm, then briefly choppy in puffs of wind from the clouds, then calm once more. At times the swirls and small waves are caused by the current flowing over the very uneven river bed — 40 metres at times with sheer cliffs to 20 metres, then deep again. Sand waves up to 12 metres high beneath us show on the depth sounder — as regular as a geometric design — the sand marching slowly to the Atlantic on a journey that began thousands of miles away, driven onward by this vast amount of moving fresh water.

There is a crew-member on lookout duty on the bow of *Seamaster*. The main obstacles to our progress are large logs, patches of floating weed, or fishing boats without lights. He has the big searchlight with which to check from time to time. It can be quite cold up front and thermal clothing is occasionally needed. How strange to be in the Amazon with polar-fleece jacket and trousers on.

The lookout is in continuous communication with the pilot-house — the crew there monitoring engine gauges, making hourly checks of the engine room, pumping fuel, marking our progress on the chart, and keeping an eye on the radar and depth sounder — our two most useful instruments for river travel. Hardly more than a few minutes goes by without a change of course to keep in the deepest section, or avoid a sand bar, or pass an island. There is not much time to relax.

Tonight there are bands of smoke — thick smoke — pouring out of some of the inlets and out of the forest, making walls right across the river. The smell of the burning forest fills the air and also our cabins. Strong wafts of the aroma of piles of Brazil nuts add to the tang of the smoke.

But we have the river flowing with us, and so are making great progress — covering in one day what it took three days to do on the way up.

The dawn is always welcome although, with the seasons now rapidly changing, the clear, fine days are becoming less frequent — clouds and high haze foretelling the not-too-distant arrival of the wet season.

We have been passing the high land around Almeirim, over to port. The green frame of the Amazon rainforest is ever present, contrasting with the red-earth scars on the higher ground and the yellow clay by the water's edge.

Peter in reflective mood in Macapa — thinking back to the Amazon and Negro and planning the way ahead for blakexpeditions.

We haven't hoisted sails for more than two months now, but this will soon be corrected when we turn left out of the mouth of the river and enter the Atlantic trade winds early next week — fingers crossed!

Again I raise the question — why are we here? What has been the point of leaving Antarctica in March, refitting in Buenos Aires over the southern winter, then undertaking the long haul north to spend some time in the Amazon? Why is part of our team off in the jungles of Venezuela?

We want to restart people caring for the environment as it must be cared for, and we want to do this through adventure, through participation, through education and through enjoyment.

Technology gives us the ability to bring our experiences into homes, offices and classrooms around the world on an almost immediate basis, through the Internet and our website: www.blakexpeditions.com.

We are reporting on what we find — not glamorised — just how it is. The photos that we send out each day — either from *Seamaster* or the Jungle Team — are generally only a few hours old. They capture the river, the wildlife, the plants, the trees, the scenery, the people. If we are hot, then you know we are hot now — not last week or last year. If we are concerned, or have a problem, it is now.

Our aim, using all this technology, is to have as many 'crew' as possible travel with us and share our experiences. Those people may then gain a better appreciation of the reasonably remote parts of the world that we visit. And, even more importantly, begin to understand the reasons why we must all start appreciating what we have before it is too late.

We could have come here by commercial plane, stayed a few weeks and left. But that wouldn't have given us the essence of the Amazon. To travel by *Seamaster* means we appreciate the immensity of this water region and, in turn, have a real feeling for it.

Exploring isn't about 'getting there' as fast as possible. It is about the logistics, the planning, the research, the operation of our vessel, the crew, the meals, our equipment, the bureaucracy surrounding taking all of us and *Seamaster* where yachts rarely venture.

When we meet people, they also have a different appreciation of what we are and why we are here. The environmental messages that we are passionate about apply all over the planet — not just the Amazon. The quality of water and the quality of life in all its infinite forms are critical parts of the overall, ongoing health of this planet of ours — not just here in the Amazon, but everywhere. With nearly 50 per cent of all the peoples of the world now living in towns or cities, we want to begin the process of bringing back the appreciation of nature that may be missing from many daily lives.

The two one-hour television documentaries about our three months in Antarctica are now finished and about to be shown in many countries. Right now, our film crew is with other members of blakexpeditions, descending from a mountain climb in the Venezuelan jungle. That will be part of our next series of television documentaries that will focus on our Amazon journey — part adventure, part educational, part environmental, but also fun.

We work closely with the United Nations Environment Programme. UNEP's messages are our messages, but translated and transmitted in our own way. We have support from many companies and individuals. The top of the environmental awareness mountain that we are endeavouring to climb may be out of sight through the clouds right now. But to win, you first have to believe you can do it. You have to be passionate about it. You have to really 'want' the result — even if this means years of work.

The hardest part of any big project is to begin.

We have begun. We are under way. We have a passion.

We want to make a difference.

We hope that you and as many of your friends as possible will join us.

All the best from the blakexpeditions team onboard *Seamaster* and in Venezuela.

Kind regards

Peter

NB: This was Sir Peter's final log from Seamaster. The following night, while anchored off Macapa, ready to leave the Amazon at dawn, Seamaster was boarded by river pirates, and Sir Peter was fatally shot while defending his boat and crew.

As soon as formalities were completed, Sir Peter's body was flown back to Britain, accompanied by Don Robertson, Charlie Dymock and Robin Allen, for burial near his southern England home in Emsworth.

Seamaster sailed to Grenada, in the Caribbean, and then, after a brief return to the Amazon, on to Newport, Rhode Island, in the United States, to await the future.

The Jungle Team completed its journey down the Orinoco River and rejoined Seamaster in Grenada. They felt that is what Sir Peter would have wanted.

Postscript

6 December 2001
●

Location Emsworth, England

A man who cast a very large shadow and who will be sorely missed.

Sir Peter Blake, KBE, was shot and killed by armed intruders who boarded the 'blakexpeditions' vessel *Seamaster* at the mouth of the River Amazon early this morning (UK time).

Sir Peter apparently died instantly despite desperate resuscitation efforts by members of the *Seamaster* crew.

He is survived by his wife, Lady Pippa Blake, and their two children, Sarah-Jane and James.

Seamaster was anchored off Macapa, waiting to depart Brazilian waters, after a two-month expedition exploring the Amazon and the Rio Negro as part of the 'blakexpeditions' programme to monitor the effects of global warming and pollution on the most environmentally sensitive regions of the world.

She was due to depart tomorrow for the Orinoco River, in Venezuela, to meet and pick up the 'blakexpeditions' jungle team, which has continued the exploration work, crossing from the Rio Negro into the head waters of the Orinoco and down to its mouth in the Caribbean.

The group of seven or eight armed and hooded intruders boarded *Seamaster* at approximately 10.15 pm local time. Sir Peter was fatally shot and two other members of *Seamaster*'s crew were injured, one with a gunshot wound across his back, the other with a blow to the face. Both injured men are back aboard *Seamaster* after receiving hospital treatment. The other seven *Seamaster* crew were badly shaken but unharmed. Brazilian police are investigating.

The 'blakexpeditions' organisation is deeply shocked and devastated by this senseless killing.

'Sir Peter was a very special person to many people around the world, highly regarded because of the man he was, because of everything he had achieved and because of everything he represented,' said spokesman Alan Sefton.

'He had left behind his many major achievements in sport to dedicate himself to creating greater awareness of the need to take better care of the world in which we live. And, typical of the man, he was giving it his heart and soul along with all those other virtues with which he had become synonymous — total passion, charisma, commitment, leadership and integrity.

'We are struggling to come to terms with his loss and our hearts go out to his immediate family here — Lady Pippa, Sarah-Jane and James — and to his mother Joyce and family back in New Zealand.'

blakexpeditions news release

9 December 2001

●

From Marc and the Jungle Team

Location Orinoco River, heading downstream to Puerto Ayacucho

It is now three days since we received the terrible news from Macapa. We don't have the words to sum up how deeply we feel the loss. We are simply shattered — personally and as part of the blakexpeditions team.

What could we do to help the others in the team on *Seamaster*? We were so far away in one of the remotest parts of the planet and we couldn't just leave everything. It was agreed that Ollie and Ali would leave immediately for Macapa, while the remainder of the group would complete the expedition objective of reaching Puerto Ayacucho down the Orinoco. This, we felt, was what Peter would have wanted.

We still had with us some water from the Antarctic. This would be poured into the river at the junction of the Casiquiare and the Orinoco — a small tribute to a remarkable man who had come to recognise that everything in nature is interrelated, and our way of symbolising one of his most important messages — 'water is life'.

Ollie, Alistair and Franck set off in a fast chartered fishing boat, to make a flight connection from San Esmeralda to Caracas. A few hours later, they were back, with a broken outboard motor. Fortunately, we had a spare on board *Big Bongo* and they were soon on their way again. They just managed to make San Esmeralda before darkness closed the landing strip.

We have since completed the journey down the Casiquiare and are now travelling down the Orinoco River. We stopped to salute Sir Peter as we had determined — where the Casiquiare joins the Orinoco — and clambered ashore to mark the spot with a simple but elegant cross fashioned by Janot. The Doc summed up our feelings with the words:

> Sir Peter was a man who loved the natural world. He was intrigued by it and he was happiest when he was in it. He wanted others to see that natural world, to appreciate the beauty all around us, and to treat it well so that, in the world of the future, zoos and gardens would not be the only places where animals and plants could be found.

At the going down of (the Amazon) sun.

10 December 2001

●

Location Nairobi

Klaus Toepfer, Executive Director of the United Nations Environment Programme (UNEP), spoke today of his sadness and shock on learning of the death of Sir Peter Blake, the round-the-world yachtsman and environmental champion.

Mr Toepfer said Sir Peter, who was appointed a Special Envoy to UNEP in July 2001, was a remarkable person, sportsman and environmentalist.

'In a career littered with achievements, he reached the pinnacle of his chosen sport in 1995 and 2000 when he won and successfully defended the America's Cup,' he said.

'Sir Peter brought the same determination, leadership, creativity and care to his activities with respect to the environment and we are all diminished by his loss. One of Sir Peter's special skills was to make the beauty of this planet, and the environmental threats to it, accessible to the scientist, the politician, business leaders and the "men and women" on the street. This is a great and singular talent and one greatly admired by myself and the staff at UNEP who knew him personally and through his pioneering voyages.

'We are deeply saddened and shocked that the life of a person of so much ability, generosity and influence has been taken in this way. Our sympathy goes to his family and friends, and to the people of New Zealand. I sincerely hope that Sir Peter's friends and colleagues can carry on his great work.'

UNEP supported Sir Peter's latest 'blakexpeditions' project through provision of information and advice on environmental issues around the world.

In February, Sir Peter spoke to environment ministers gathered in Nairobi for UNEP's Governing Council from his expedition yacht *Seamaster* in Antarctica. He had sailed further south along the Antarctic Peninsula than anyone had been before, due to the lack of sea ice and collapsing ice shelves, caused by changing climate conditions.

Last month, within hours of arriving at Manaus, the major Amazon port in central Brazil, he flew to Rio de Janeiro to meet Mr Toepfer and Latin American environment ministers, to become involved in discussions about environmental protection and preparations for next year's World Summit on Sustainable Development taking place in Johannesburg.

'In a lively and thought-provoking speech to the ministers, he talked about the great beauty he had seen on the Amazon and urged them to reflect on the importance and the need to protect these wonderful ecosystems,' said Mr Toepfer.

'Sir Peter's vision, determination and actions were a great complement to the work of the United Nations. I hope that his message about the need to protect the world's oceans and wild places will become an enduring legacy of this remarkable man.'

UNEP New Release

Calling Nairobi — Peter at 70 degrees South in the Antarctic talking by satellite phone to environmental ministers meeting at UNEP headquarters.

21 January 2002

It is now a very sad part of history that Sir Peter Blake, KBE, the head of blakexpeditions, was tragically shot and killed on 6 December 2001, in Macapa at the mouth of the Amazon River.

Sir Peter was buried in the St Thomas a Beckett Church, near his home in Emsworth on the south coast of England, on 14 December 2001. More than 1000 people, including representatives of the British royal family, of the United Nations Environment Programme, and of the New Zealand and British governments, attended the service.

On 23 December 2001, in his native New Zealand, a memorial service to Sir Peter was held in the Auckland Domain overlooking the city and the harbour where, and upon which, Sir Peter grew up. More than 30,000 people gathered to celebrate Sir Peter's life and to hear tributes from such as New Zealand's Governor-General, Her Excellency The Honourable Dame Silvia Cartwright, New Zealand's Prime Minister, the Right Honourable Helen Clark, the Kaumatua of the Ngati Whatua tribe, Sir Hugh Kawharu, and the National Secretary of Sports, Mr Lars Grael, representing His Excellency, President Fernando Henrique Cardoso of the Federative Republic of Brazil.

The service was broadcast live on nationwide television and, later in the day, an estimated 8000 boats took part in a moving sail-past on Auckland Harbour as New Zealand's 'yachties' bid a final farewell to their favourite son.

Throughout this period, and since, thousands upon thousands of tributes and messages of condolence to Sir Peter's family have been pouring in from all around the world, by letter, telephone, email and facsimile.

At blakexpeditions, we had to double the size of our server in order to cope with those messages that were communicated through our website. The overwhelming majority of the messages have urged strongly that the work of Sir Peter must be carried on, in his name and in his memory.

In the short and enormously sad period since, while we have been striving to come to terms with Sir Peter's loss, we have also begun taking the first steps towards ensuring that his work will continue, under the blakexpeditions banner.

This is the wish of Sir Peter's family, Lady Pippa Blake, Sarah-Jane and James.

It is also the determined intent of myself, of my colleague Scott Chapman, and of the rest of the blakexpeditions 'crew'.

Alan Sefton
blakexpeditions

Auckland Domain, New Zealand. Some of the more than 30,000 crowd that turned out to celebrate Sir Peter Blake's life.

Addendum

Seamaster and her crew returned to the Amazon in March 2002, to complete filming for a Sir Peter Blake tribute documentary made by the BBC. This documentary went to air in February 2003. The BBC production crew spent only a short time aboard the vessel but investigative journalist and presenter Donal MacIntyre had this to say:

'*Seamaster* has magic to it. Even in the aftermath of Sir Peter's untimely death, the boat resonates hope and enthusiasm — and a determination to make a difference.

The torch was handed down by Peter and is carried by everyone on board. It captivates everyone who comes on board. The boat is a family and crew-members are visibly a 'band of brothers' with a shared vision for life and the environment.

Seamaster is Peter's boat and the vehicle for his environmental ambitions. Everyone on board back-references everything they do by what they feel their friend and leader would have wanted. There is a sense that, although Peter has left this world, he has not left this boat.

Extraordinary is an overused word but, in its true sense, that's what Peter was — simply extraordinary. He had intended to return to the Amazon to finish some of his environmental work but now his boat and his crew returns without him. His spirit pervades. His team and his family are determined that his work should continue.

For me personally, I was charmed and mesmerised by Peter's commitment to the environment. When talking with him by satellite telephone a week or two before he was killed, he persuaded me that the biggest journalistic story today is the protection of the environment. I was won over.

Peter's story is a remarkable one and it has been a great honour to be a guest of *Seamaster* and to be able to play a small part in the telling of it. I know everyone on the BBC team feels privileged to be here.'

Investigative journalist Donal MacIntyre astride a raft of confiscated, illegally-logged Amazon mahogany near Altamira in the Rio Xingu. This particular raft was 20 logs wide (the logs metres in diameter) and snaked for nearly 22 kilometres (12 miles) along the bank of the Xingu — the tip of the deforestation iceberg threatening the Amazon rain forest.

The Life of Sir Peter Blake

Sir Peter Blake KBE
1948–2001

ir Peter was the outstanding yachtsman/ adventurer of his time, an international sporting celebrity who in his native New Zealand achieved status and esteem to rival that accorded the country's other favourite adventurer son, Sir Edmund Hillary.

Born and raised in the Bayswater suburb of Auckland's North Shore, he grew up in boats, in a sailing family and in a sailing environment.

His first yacht, at age five, was a Frostply dinghy. At the age of eight he graduated to the 7-foot P-Class dinghy, the home-grown Kiwi trainer class that continues to spawn so many of New Zealand's astonishing production line of world-class sailing talent.

At age 14 he moved up into the two-man Z-Class and, when aged 16, did his first blue water race — the Pacific Islands in a 50-footer called *Red Feather*. By the time he was 18 he had built his first keel yacht — a 23-foot Van der Stadt design called *Bandit* in which he won the New Zealand JOG (Junior Offshore Group) championship.

Then followed a steady progression through the various sailing classes and events until he reached the very pinnacle of his sport and became the most highly regarded figure in the long-distance racing that he had come to love the most. The climb wasn't always easy. There were set-backs, misfortunes and inevitable losses. But the 6-foot 4-inch, blond-haired and Viking-like young Kiwi took it all in his considerable stride, learning from every experience to emerge a sailing campaigner almost without equal.

His many major achievements included:

- Line honours and the course record in Britain's Fastnet Classic (*Condor*, 1979)

- Line and handicap honours in Australia's famed Sydney–Hobart Race (*Ceramco New Zealand*, 1980)

- Line honours in the inaugural Two-Man Round Australia Race (*Steinlager 1*, 1988)

- Line and handicap honours (in all six legs and overall) in the Whitbread Round the World Race (*Steinlager 2*, 1989–90)

- The record non-stop circumnavigation of the world under sail — 74 days, 22 hours, 17 minutes, 22 seconds (in the giant catamaran *ENZA*, in the 1994 Trophée Jules Verne attempt)

But in blue water racing folklore Peter Blake is also remembered for the seamanship and determination that he and the crew of *Ceramco New Zealand* displayed when their 68-foot Bruce Farr design lost her mast

when 120 miles north of Ascension Island on the first leg of the 1981–82 Whitbread Round the World race. Cape Town was still 2500 miles away, upwind to the southeast. For many sailors, that would have been the end — race over.

But Peter and his crew were made of sterner stuff. They fashioned a jury rig from the parts of the broken spar and rejoined the race. They then had to sail nearly 1500 miles further than the rhumb-line course, arcing around the western then southern

fringes of the South Atlantic High in order to find favourable reaching conditions (*Ceramco* could not sail remotely close to the wind with her junk-like jury rig). They still reached Cape Town 18th in the 26-boat fleet and were on the start line, complete with new rig, for the second leg, through the Southern Ocean to New Zealand. They went on to finish third in fleet in terms of elapsed time around the world and won two of the remaining three legs on corrected time. *Ceramco*'s jury rig recovery is still regarded as one of the great feats in modern sailing.

In more than 650,000 ocean miles, including six voyages through the fabled Southern Ocean and around Cape Horn, the Blake name became synonymous with excellence, commitment and success.

The Whitbread remained unfinished business until the 1989–90 race, when Peter skippered the 84-foot Farr design *Steinlager 2* to line and handicap victory — in all six legs and overall — in the now re-shaped circumnavigation.

The Blake family celebrates
Steinlager 2's victorious arrival in
Auckland in the 1989–90 Whitbread
Round the World race. From left:
James, Peter, Sarah-Jane and Pippa.

By this time he was already involved in discussions with other ocean-racing luminaries (notably French) about a new challenge — to see how fast a non-stop circumnavigation of the world under sail could be achieved. The stage was being set for another epic Blake voyage — this one a high-speed dash around the world on the giant catamaran *ENZA*.

The group settled on a minimum of rules. There would be no restrictions on size or design of vessel. The start and finish would be between the Isle de Ouessant (Ushant) and Lizard Point in the English Channel, leaving the Cape of Good Hope (South Africa), Cape Leeuwin (Australia) and Cape Horn (South America) to port and Antarctica to starboard. Record attempts would be officially monitored by appointed representatives of the international sailing authority.

It was to be a modern version of 'Round the World in 80 days' so, appropriately, the event would be called the Trophée Jules Verne. Peter was voted president of the Jules Verne Federation.

Racing through the Southern Ocean can only be realistically contemplated in the summer months of the Southern Hemisphere, so this in turn dictated a December or January start from the English Channel. The speed machines of the day were big catamarans and trimarans, but nobody knew whether these craft, with completely different stresses and strains and a reputation for irrecoverable capsizes, would survive in the notoriously rugged conditions of the deep south.

Three vessels were prepared for the first attempt on the Trophée — *ENZA*, then an 85–foot catamaran, *Commodore*, an 85–foot catamaran, skippered by Frenchman Bruno Peyron, and the 94–foot trimaran *Charal* skippered by another Frenchman, Olivier de Kersauson.

All three made quick time down the Atlantic and into the Southern Ocean, but *ENZA* and *Charal* were holed — *ENZA* by what was thought to be a shipping container floating just beneath the surface about 1000 miles south and east of the Cape of

Good Hope, *Charal* by ice well to the south of *ENZA*'s position. Only *Commodore* remained to complete the journey. This she did in just under the 80-day target, proving that multihulls, in the right hands, most definitely could make it through the Southern Ocean. For Peter Blake, this created more unfinished business.

ENZA was shipped to New Zealand from Cape Town, lengthened to 92–feet, strengthened, and then shipped back to England for a second attempt on the Trophée. De Kersauson was back too, his big trimaran now named *La Lyonnaise des Eau Dumez*, so there was a rival to beat as well as a record to lower.

The pair got a sling-shot start from Ushant and, with *ENZA* in the lead, roared down the North Atlantic at breakneck speed. Record after record tumbled to *ENZA*'s remorseless rush and when de Kersauson fell off the pace he abandoned his pursuit and turned left for Cape Town too early — smack into the grip of the South Atlantic High.

To the Frenchman's eternal credit, he did not give up and came back strongly when *ENZA* got pinned down by adverse weather systems at around 62 degrees South in the Southern Ocean between New Zealand and Cape Horn. This was way lower than planned and *ENZA* got a real hammering as she clawed her way into full-gale northeasterly headwinds in Drake Passage — the legendary passage of water between the southern tip of South America and the Antarctic Peninsula.

As the two rivals crossed the equator again, this time from south to north, they were neck and neck in terms of distance to run, if hundreds of miles apart on the water.

Peter and his co-skipper Robin Knox-Johnston went for one last roll of the dice when confronted by two very severe weather systems blocking *ENZA*'s path through the Bay of Biscay to the Channel finish. They identified a course that promised a way between the two systems and went for it.

In huge, confused seas in the Western Approaches, *ENZA* came close to disaster when she careened off the front of one huge wave and ploughed into the back of the wave ahead, burying herself back to the mast in turbulent water and on the point of pitch-poling end over end. She was going too fast, even though she was down to storm sails only, and had to be slowed down before she destroyed herself and probably her crew.

ENZA finishing the 1994 Trophée Jules Verne dash under storm jib only. The big Kiwi cat slashed 4 days 7 hours 58 minutes 34 seconds off the existing record for sailing non-stop around the world.

The America's Cup win in 1995 was greeted in New Zealand by ticker tape parades, the likes of which had been rivalled only by the return of New Zealand's troops from two world wars. Team New Zealand and its formation, management and deeds became the subject of a study paper at the Harvard Business School and a key chapter in the book *Peak Performance*, which catalogued business lessons from the world's top sports organisations, including including FC Bayern Munich, the Williams Formula One race car team, the All Blacks rugby team, the Chicago Bulls, the San Francisco 49ers and the Atlanta Braves.

Yet even while being feted nationally and internationally, Sir Peter was planning to turn his back on it all.

In his years of racing through the major oceans of the world, he had become alarmed by the changes he was seeing. Pollution of the seas was evident in even the remotest corners of the globe, and wildlife such as the glorious wandering albatross was disappearing. The very life source of planet Earth was under major threat and something had to be done. Typically, Peter took up the challenge. With Team New Zealand colleagues Alan Sefton and Scott Chapman, he established 'blakexpeditions' with the objective of helping to protect the waters of the world and life in, on and around those waters.

In the polar exploration yacht *Seamaster* he set out on a series of expeditions to those parts of the world that are key to the world's ecosystem, using innovative television documentaries and exciting web site activities to educate people and inspire them to take better care of Planet Earth.

As this book describes, the first expedition was to the Antarctic Peninsula to help record and assess the affects of global warming on a part of the world that plays a crucial role in the earth's well-being. *Seamaster* reached 70 degrees south latitude in George VI Sound, further than any vessel had been before.

Then it was north to Brazil, where *Seamaster* plied more than 1400 miles of Amazon and Negro river waters as Sir Peter and his crew, including film-makers and scientists, looked into the impact of global warming, deforestation, mining and the exploitation of rare and endangered species.

Tragically, Sir Peter was shot and killed while defending his vessel and crew against river pirates as *Seamaster* prepared to leave the Amazon for the Caribbean and the mouth of the Orinoco River.

He was just 53 years of age, at the peak of his powers and beginning to succeed in his mission to make a difference to the way humankind regards and cares for the environment.

Sir Peter is survived by Pippa, Lady Blake, and their two children, Sarah-Jane and James.

Peter ordered every piece of chain and rope on the boat to be plaited into a giant bridle that was attached to *ENZA*'s twin transoms to trail astern of the yacht in a big loop. It was a precarious operation that tested the considerable seamanship, experience and fortitude of everyone on board. But it worked. The bridle slowed *ENZA* enough to curb her wild charge. She crossed the finish line under storm jib only, still trailing the bridle, to complete her dash around the world in a remarkable 74 days 22 hours 17 minutes 22 seconds. By this time, the English Channel had been closed to passenger ferries and the French navy had hastily shelved plans to send a destroyer out to meet *ENZA*, replacing it with a considerably larger pocket-cruiser — so big and boisterous were the seas that were driving in from a very angry North Atlantic.

With no more Whitbread or Jules Verne mountains to climb, Peter switched his attentions to the America's Cup, the 'Holy Grail' of sailing and the oldest competition in sport.

In more than 140 years of high-profile, often controversial defences and challenges, the cup had only once been lifted from America. The contests had involved some of the world's most successful and powerful individuals, including the Rockefellers, the Vanderbilts, Sir Thomas Lipton, T.O.M. Sopwith, Ted Turner and Alan Bond.

Peter first won the cup in 1995 with Team New Zealand and then successfully defended it in 2000, the first non-American to do so. He earned himself a knighthood from Queen Elizabeth and a bigger chapter in sporting history.

Sir Peter Blake, KBE

Born 1 October 1948, in Auckland, New Zealand

Died 6 December 2001, at the mouth of the Amazon river

Education Takapuna Grammar School
Auckland Institute of Technology (1966–1969)

Profession Engineer/Yachtsman/Adventurer

Wife Pippa, Lady Blake

Children Sarah-Jane, James

HONOURS

1983	MBE, for services to yachting
1991	OBE, for services to yachting
1995	KBE (Knight Commander of the Civil Division of the Most Excellent Order of the British Empire), for services to yachting
1995	Made a life member of the Royal New Zealand Yacht Squadron
1995	Made an honorary member of the Royal Yacht Squadron
1995	Inducted into the America's Cup Hall of Fame
1996	Made a Fellow of the Royal Geographic Society
1999	D Com, Massey University
2000	Honorary doctorate, Auckland University
2001	Appointed a Special Envoy for the United Nations Environment Programme (UNEP)
2002	Awarded the Olympic Order (from the International Olympic Committee) 'to pay tribute to Sir Peter Blake's outstanding sailing career and to his genuine passion for sport and adventure'

POSITIONS HELD

President of the Jules Verne Association
Patron of Devonport Yacht Club (New Zealand)
Patron of Gulf Harbour Yacht Club (New Zealand)
Patron of Essex Yacht Club (England)
Vice-president of Royal Port Nicholson Yacht Club (New Zealand)
Trustee of New Zealand International Yachting Trust
Life member of West Mersea Yacht Club (England)
Honorary member of Royal Southern Yacht Club (England)
Honorary member of Royal Southampton Yacht Club (England)
Member of the Emsworth Sailing Club (England)
Member of the Ocean Cruising Club (England)
Member of the Association of Cape Horners

AWARDS

1982	New Zealand Yachtsman of the Year
1989	New Zealand Sports Personality of the Year
1989–90	Communicator of the Whitbread Round the World Race
1989–90	New Zealand Yachtsman of the Year (with Steinlager 2 crew)
1990	New Zealand Sporting Team of the Year
1990	New Zealand Sporting Team of the Year (with Steinlager 2 crew)
1990	ABC 'Wide World of Sport' Athlete of the Week (May)
1990	Public Relations Institute of New Zealand's Communicator of the Year
1990	Yachting Magazine's (USA) Yachtsman of the Year
1994	International Yacht Racing Union's World Sailor of the Year (with Robin Knox-Johnston)
1994	Hobson Medal for excellence in New Zealand Maritime Endeavours
1995	New Zealand Sportsman of the Year (with Team New Zealand)
1995	New Zealand's Sports Team of the Year Award (with Team New Zealand)
1995	New Zealand's Outstanding Management and Marketing Achievement Award
1995	Royal Yacht Squadron's Sir Francis Chichester Trophy (with Robin Knox-Johnston)
1995	British Yachtsman of the Year (for 1994) (with Robin Knox-Johnston)
2002	International SeaKeepers Society's SeaKeeper Award for 'extraordinary dedication and leadership in the cause of marine conservation'
2002	Ocean Stewardship Award from UNEP (at the World Summit on Sustainable Development in Johannesburg)

YACHT RACING MILESTONES

1967–68 Won New Zealand Junior Offshore Group
(JOG) Championship (in *Bandit*)

1971 Line honours in the inaugural Cape Town to
Rio de Janeiro race (watch leader on
Ocean Spirit)

1973–74 Contested the inaugural Whitbread
Round the World race (watch leader on
Burton Cutter)

1974 First monohull in Round Britain Two-Man race
(on *Burton Cutter* with Robin
Knox-Johnston))

1977 Line honours in inaugural Round the North
Island (of New Zealand) Two-Man race
(on *Gerontius* with Graeme Eder)

1977–78 Contested the second Whitbread Round the
World race (watch leader on *Condor*)

1979 Line honours in Miami to Montego Bay race
(skipper of *Condor*)

Line honours and race record in Antigua to
Bermuda race (skipper of *Condor*)

Line honours and race record in Fastnet Race
(skipper of *Condor*)

1980 Line and handicap double in Sydney to Hobart
race (skipper of *Ceramco New Zealand*)

1981–82 Handicap wins in legs two and four of the third
Whitbread Round the World race
(skipper/navigator of *Ceramco
New Zealand*)

Roaring Forties Trophy for best corrected time
performance in legs two and three (the
Southern Ocean legs) of the Whitbread
Round the World race (skipper/navigator of
Ceramco New Zealand)

1983 Team captain, New Zealand's Admiral's Cup
challenge and skipper of *Lady B*

1984 Line honours in Sydney–Hobart race
(skipper/navigator of *Lion New Zealand*)

1985–86 Contested fourth Whitbread Round the World
race (skipper/navigator of *Lion New Zealand*)

1988 Line hours in inaugural Round Australia
Two-Man Race (on the trimaran *Steinlager 1*
with Mike Quilter)

1989–90 Line honours in the English Channel Race
(skipper of *Steinlager 2*)

Line honours in Fastnet Race
(skipper of *Steinlager 2*)

Line and handicap honours in all six legs of the
Whitbread Round the World Race (skipper
of *Steinlager 2*)

Overall line and handicap honours in
Whitbread Round the World Race (skipper
of *Steinlager 2*)

Roaring Forties Trophy for best corrected time
performance in legs two, three and four (the
Southern Ocean legs) of the Whitbread
Round the World race (skipper
of *Steinlager 2*)

1991–92 Manager of New Zealand's America's Cup
challenge in San Diego (New Zealand lost
to Italy in the challenger final)

1993 Contested the inaugural Trophée Jules Verne
(non-stop around the world) attempt
(skipper of the catamaran *ENZA*)

1994 Won Trophée Jules Verne with a record 74 days
22 hours 17 minutes 22 seconds
circumnavigation (skipper of the
catamaran *ENZA*)

1992–95 Founded (with Alan Sefton) and was syndicate
head of Team New Zealand

1995 Won the America's Cup (syndicate head of
Team New Zealand and crew on the Match
winner *NZL 32* 'Black Magic')

1995–2000 Syndicate head of Team New Zealand

2000 Successfully defended the America's Cup — the
first non-American to do so (syndicate head
of Team New Zealand) Founded (with Alan
Sefton and Scott Chapman) and was head
of blakexpeditions to focus greater
attention on the need to take better care
of the environment, particularly the
world's oceans

2001 Undertook inaugural blakexpeditions voyage of
exploration — to the Antarctic Peninsula
(reaching 70 degrees South in
George VI Sound)

Undertook second blakexpeditions voyage of
exploration —1400 miles up the Amazon
and Negro rivers in Brazil

Acknowledgements

This celebration of the life and achievements of Sir Peter Blake KBE would not have been possible without the immediate cooperation of the photographers who journeyed with blakexpeditions aboard *Seamaster* and who shared our objective to help make a difference.

Don Robertson was a key member of *Seamaster's* crew and, with Peter, shouldered the onerous responsibility of producing the more than 200 daily logs that recorded, on the blakexpeditions.com website, *Seamaster's* journeys to the Antarctic and up the Amazon and Negro rivers.

Ivor Wilkins is a highly respected journalist/photographer who freelances out of Auckland. An experienced blue water sailor, he jumped at the chance to join *Seamaster* for the first half of the expedition to the Antarctic Peninsula.

Frank Socha is a freelance French photographer who specialises in high-profile sailing events. He joined *Seamaster* for the Amazon and Negro rivers expedition because he believed in what Peter and blakexpeditions were seeking to achieve.

The author would also like to thank *Seamaster* crew members Alistair and Rodger Moore, Ollie Olphert and Leon Sefton for being there and for their help in selecting and identifying the images contained in this work.

The team at Penguin Books in Auckland (in particular Geoff Walker and Rebecca Lal) were marvellous in their response to producing this book on extremely tight deadlines and in their enthusiasm for the project, while the support of my blakexpeditions colleague Scott Chapman was, as usual, instant and unstinting.

I sincerely hope that our collective efforts have done justice to the vision and ambition of a great human being who was taken from us far too early.

Alan Sefton

Picture Credits

Alexander Turnbull Library — pp. 61(T O H Lees Collection PAColl-2094-67), 59 (T O H Lees Collection PAColl-2094-25), 58 (F-116771-1/2)

Bob Fisher — pp. 200–1, 201

Dave Gunson — pp. 81, 83

New Zealand Herald — p. 195

Richard Krall — p. 205

Ollie Olphert — pp.92 (right), 79 (left)

Mark Pepper — p. 35

Barry Pickthall — pp. 20–1

Pickthall Picture Library — pp. 198–9, 202, 203, 204, 206–7

Leonide Principe — p. 145

Don Robertson — pp. 21, 22, 33, 34, 36, 37, 42, 43, 44, 45, 46, 47, 48, 49, 62, 69, 77, 78, 79, 80, 82, 84, 85, 86, 87, 88, 89, 90, 92 (above), 93, 94, 95, 100, 101, 102, 103, 106, 114, 115, 116, 117, 118, 119 (below), 120, 132 (right), 133, 138, 139, 144, 151 (above), 152, 154–5, 157, 163, 167 (above), 185, 190, 192, 194

Neil Rutherford — introduction

Seamaster crew — pp. 32, 48 (above), 98, 99, 166

Leon Sefton — pp. 125, 196

Franck Socha — contents, From Pippa, foreword, pp. 112–3, 119 (above), 121, 123, 124, 126, 127, 128, 129, 130–1, 132 (below), 135, 136–7, 140–1, 142, 143, 147, 148–9, 150, 151 (below), 153, 156, 158–9, 160, 12–3, 164, 165, 166 (above), 167 (below), 168, 169, 170–1, 172, 173, 174–5, 176, 177, 178–9, 180, 181, 182–3, 184, 186, 187, 188, 193

Patrick Wallet — pp. 20, 26

Kim Westerskov — p. 25

Ivor Wilkins — title page, pp. 30–1, 38–9, 41, 50–1, 52, 54, 55, 56–7, 63, 64–5, 66, 67, 68, 70–1, 72–3, 74–5, 76, 91, 96–7, 105, 107, 109, 110–11

Maps by Terralink

Index